MW01485619

WHAT'S WRONG WITH THE FIRST AMENDMENT?

What's Wrong with the First Amendment? argues that the US love affair with the First Amendment has mutated into free speech idolatry. Free speech has been placed on so high a pedestal that it is almost automatically privileged over privacy, fair trials, equality, and public health, even protecting depictions of animal cruelty and violent video games sold to children. At the same time, dissent is unduly stifled and religious minorities are unduly burdened. The First Amendment benefits the powerful at the expense of the vulnerable. By contrast, other Western democracies provide more reasonable accommodations between free speech and other values though their protections of dissent and religious minorities are inadequate. Professor Steven H. Shiffrin argues that US free speech extremism is not the product of broad cultural factors, but rather of political ideologies developed after the 1950s. He shows that conservatives and liberals have arrived at similar conclusions for different political reasons.

Steven H. Shiffrin is Charles Frank Reavis, Sr, Professor of Law Emeritus at Cornell University. He is the author of *The Religious Left and Church-State Relations* (2009), *Dissent, Injustice, and the Meanings of America* (1999), and *The First Amendment, Democracy, and Romance* (1990), as well as the winner of the Thomas J. Wilson Award. He is also a coauthor of *Constitutional Law*, 12th edition (2015), and *The First Amendment*, 6th edition (2015). His writings have appeared in many publications, including the *Cornell Law Review*, *Harvard Law Review*, *Michigan Law Review*, *Northwestern Law Review*, *UCLA Law Review*, *Virginia Law Review*, *Commonweal*, the *New York Times Book Review*, and the *Washington Monthly*.

What's Wrong with the First Amendment?

Steven H. Shiffrin

CAMBRIDGE
UNIVERSITY PRESS

University Printing House, Cambridge CB2 8BS, United Kingdom

Cambridge University Press is part of the University of Cambridge.

It furthers the University's mission by disseminating knowledge in the pursuit of education, learning, and research at the highest international levels of excellence.

www.cambridge.org
Information on this title: www.cambridge.org/9781107160965

First published 2016

Printed in the United States of America by Sheridan Books, Inc.

A catalogue record for this publication is available from the British Library.

Library of Congress Cataloging-in-Publication Data
Names: Shiffrin, Steven H., 1941– author.
Title: What's Wrong with the First Amendment? / Steven H. Shiffrin.
Description: New York: Cambridge University Press, 2016. |
Includes bibliographical references and index.
Identifiers: LCCN 2016024220| ISBN 9781107160965 (hardback) |
ISBN 9781316613771 (pbk.)
Subjects: LCSH: United States. Constitution. 1st Amendment. |
Freedom of speech – United States.
Classification: LCC KF4770.S555 2016 | DDC 342.7308/53–dc23
LC record available at https://lccn.loc.gov/2016024220

ISBN 978-1-107-16096-5 Hardback
ISBN 978-1-316-61377-1 Paperback

For Neesa Levine, Seana, Benjamin, and Jacob Shiffrin

CONTENTS

Acknowledgments   *page* ix

Introduction 1

PART I

1   Privacy 13

2   Justice 25

3   Race 35

4   Sex 47

5   Violence 62

6   Commerce 79

7   Democracy 95

PART II

8   Dissent 115

9   Religion 133

PART III

10 How Did We Get Here? .159

11 What Next? 184

Notes   193
Index   224

ACKNOWLEDGMENTS

This book has emerged from a long journey with many people to thank. I first opposed absolute First Amendment protection with an article in 1978. My belief was that absolutism did not account for the views that "absolutists" actually held. But, with some exceptions, I had no particular brief for the view that free speech was significantly overvalued. In fact, for twenty-five years I have insisted that dissenting speech is undervalued.

Indeed, I have regarded myself as a strong proponent of free speech. But I have never thought that free speech should be absolutely protected, and since the dawn of the twenty-first century, the Court has pushed me over the edge. It never occurred to me that tobacco advertising would garner First Amendment protection. And the cases in the Roberts Court involving intentional infliction of emotional distress at funerals, depictions of animal cruelty, gruesomely violent video games sold to children, and campaign finance struck me as wrong-headed, even outrageous. I knew it was time to write a book.

I no longer think that the "nuanced" absolutists and I merely disagree about method. We strongly disagree about substance, and among First Amendment scholars, my perspective is distinctly in the minority. I am grateful that my wonderful acquisitions editor John Berger found two readers who endorsed the book and offered valuable suggestions and criticisms. One of those readers profoundly disagreed with my views, and my other readers for the most part disagree as well. They are in no way responsible for my excesses and mistakes. The book is far better than it would have been were it not for their criticisms and constructive suggestions.

Nelson Tebbe's comments on the manuscript were characteristically insightful, and his comments on the religion chapter were indispensable. Aziz Rana shared his vast knowledge of the political literature, pointed me to what I needed to read, and emphasized important themes that were undeveloped in the chapters on dissent and the chapter on how liberals and conservatives came to a relatively shared position. Wendy Brown brilliantly discussed the latter chapter with me, and her comments led me to develop important themes outside that chapter as well. Thanks to her, I realized that far greater attention to the role of business in the development of conservative views on free speech was needed (discussed in Chapter 10), and that I needed to criticize conservative commitments to the marketplace argument (see the Introduction). But she also gave me insightful comments on pornography and on the ways in which the positions taken by liberals and conservatives affect power relations in the society. Mike Dorf gave me comments on parts of the manuscript on at least three occasions. Mike's smart and wise comments influenced the framing of the manuscript, parts of the organization, and a variety of substantive issues, in particular, aspects of the liberals' approach to free speech. Seana Shiffrin gave a close, prudent, and dazzling read to the entire manuscript. Every chapter has been altered in response to her comments.

I also received supportive and valuable comments at a Cleveland-Marshall faculty workshop and at the Nimmer lecture at UCLA, which resulted in an article presenting an early incarnation of some of the themes in this book: "The Dark Side of the First Amendment," 61 *UCLA L. Rev.* 1480 (2014). I did my best to defend the contents of that article in a debate with Robert Corn-Revere in the First Amendment Salon. The primary audience in the Salon were media lawyers in New York and Washington in the law offices of Levine, Sullivan, Koch, and Schulz. I am grateful to Bob for his skilled participation and for the audience for their sharp questioning and civility. I am also grateful to Ron Collins and Lee Levine for giving me the opportunity and to Vince Blasi for attending and especially for asking a supportive question when I was under siege. It was a stimulating evening. I also benefited from the support and comments of my colleagues at the Cornell Law School, in particular, at a faculty retreat where I was permitted to present several chapters.

The views I have shared in this book were also presented over a period of years in my First Amendment classes. I was fortunate to have the opportunity to teach bright students whose commitments to free speech typically were greater than my own in a variety of contexts. It was fun and rewarding for me (and I trust for them) to engage in daily discussions and debates about the First Amendment. And the Cornell staff has always been a pleasure to work with. In particular, I appreciate the cheer and excellent work of Christina Price in preparing the manuscript and associated tasks.

Finally, I would like to thank Neesa Levine, my free-spirited companion and wife of thirty-six years, who regularly reminds me that there is a world outside the First Amendment.

INTRODUCTION

I have been teaching classes in the First Amendment for nearly forty years. Students love the First Amendment. Like the overwhelming majority of their fellow citizens, they celebrate not only its protection of a basic human right, but also its role as a part of their identity as Americans.

There was a time when those celebrations were justified, but I believe we have come to a point when it is *thinkable* that the First Amendment does more harm than good. Don't get me wrong. The First Amendment does a lot of good. At its best, freedom of speech promotes many values including liberty, freedom, equality, tolerance, respect, dignity, self-government, truth, justice, and associational values, along with cultural and communitarian values. Perhaps most important, it protects dissent, speech that criticizes existing customs, habits, traditions, institutions, and authorities. Indeed, it protects criticism of public officials and public figures to a greater extent than other countries in the world. It even protects advocacy of illegal action so long as it is not directed to incite and likely to incite and produce imminent lawless action. It could do more to protect dissent than it does and it should. I will argue in Part II of this book that the First Amendment fails to protect dissenting speech as much as it should and that its failure to protect religious minorities is even more pronounced than its failures in protecting dissent.

The main problem with the First Amendment, however, is that it overprotects speech. We take pride in protecting the speech we hate and in tolerating speech that offends. But no one justifies regulating speech on the ground that we should hate it, and regulating speech merely on the ground that it offends is a nonstarter. But speech that causes significant harm (or unreasonably risks such harm) ordinarily should be regulated to avoid the harm, and that kind of speech should not be exempted from regulation because it is also hateful or offensive.

Free speech doctrine downplays the harm that speech can cause. Indeed, its most problematic assumption is that free speech is considered to be so valuable that it almost always outweighs other values with which it comes into conflict. Of course, free speech is ordinarily valuable, but there is no good reason to assume that it invariably should outweigh other values. Nor is that assumption harmless. Because of it:

- The First Amendment rides roughshod over human dignity protecting privacy-invading speech such as that which provides a voyeuristic public with the names of rape victims and protecting demonstrations intended to inflict emotional distress even at funerals.
- The First Amendment protects pretrial publicity that feeds public curiosity while jeopardizing the rights of the accused to a fair trial.
- The First Amendment protects racist speech despite its undermining of racial equality.
- The First Amendment protects pornography despite its encouragement of violence and discrimination against women.
- The First Amendment protects a market for depictions of animal cruelty that harms animals and promotes sadism or masochism.
- The First Amendment protects the marketing of violent video games to children despite the conclusions of respected medical associations that these games desensitize our children to violence and promote a needlessly violent culture.
- The First Amendment protects commercial advertising that encourages a materialistic and hedonistic culture substituting consumer pleasure for human flourishing. It even protects tobacco advertising that promotes the needless death and suffering of hundreds of thousands of people each year who have become addicted to the tobacco habit.
- And the First Amendment undermines American democracy by permitting corporations and wealthy individuals to dominate American political campaigns at local, state, and federal levels. Simply put, a democracy cannot function when its representatives look to moneyed interests before they look at the will of the people and the common good.

Some might say that all this is the price we pay for free speech. Some argue that the legitimacy of government depends upon respect for the autonomy of the individual and that respect demands that free speech be absolute, at least in the absence of coercion or manipulation of another.[1] We can agree that government must respect each of its citizens; nonetheless, it can disrespect the speech choices that individuals make precisely because the speech causes harm outweighing the speech's value whether or not that harm flows from coercion or manipulation. So, too, some argue that the legitimacy of democratic government depends upon protection for the right of citizens to participate in democratic dialogue or public discourse defined to include the building of the culture or the formation of public opinion.[2] But public dialogue or discourse can trigger substantial harm, and the privileging of free speech over that harm is difficult to defend in terms of democratic legitimacy. For example, if pornography and some forms of racist speech create unjust conditions for women and people of color, it is odd to be told that the legitimacy of government depends on protecting speech that undermines equality.[3]

Examples such as these show the lack of wisdom in supposing that under our Constitution there is no such thing as a false idea. Of course, there are false ideas. State governments could not propagate racist slogans without violating constitutional principles of equality. So the notion is not really the mindless suggestion that there is no such thing as a false idea. The suggestion is that government should be agnostic about the value of an idea or the value of speech (whether it presents an idea or not) in enforcing the First Amendment. To be sure, there is risk in government sanctioning speech and taking its value into account in doing so. History is littered with governmental bad judgments particularly in its censorship of dissent.[4] But First Amendment doctrine is already permeated with judgments about the value of speech.[5] It assumes, for example, that most forms of political speech are more valuable than commercial advertising, credit reports, obscene speech, or nearly obscene speech. There are strong arguments for the view that speech should not be sanctioned in the absence of harm, but when harm is created, there are good reasons to evaluate the extent to which the values of free speech are or are not implicated by the speech at issue. As the examples detailed plainly show, the assumption that speech is uniformly valuable would lead to unacceptable results.

A commitment to freedom of speech need not commit us to this unwholesome path. Other Western countries, for example, have not taken this course despite their own commitments to the free speech principle. Some might say so much the worse for those countries, but if you were born and raised in Toronto, Berlin, Paris, or London, it is likely you would believe that the Canadians and Europeans are right and the Americans are afflicted with a form of First Amendment idolatry. Moreover, through most of our history, the United States and other Western countries were quite close on free speech issues. Indeed, the historic judicial approach to freedom of speech has been to respect the alternative interests involved. When, however, the First Amendment protects violent video games sold to children, intentional infliction of emotional distress at funerals, depictions of animal cruelty, and tobacco advertising, it seems clear to me that a good thing has been stretched far beyond reasonable bounds.

This leads to the question of how the US judges – whether liberal or conservative – (there are exceptions on some issues) have turned free speech into a fetish. The answer is not simple, but it is fascinating; it is different for conservatives than it is for liberals; and neither conservatives nor liberals are all alike.

Of course, liberals and conservatives are influenced by centuries of thought on freedom of speech, but so are Canadians and Europeans. On the other hand, many have pointed to the American distrust of government, individualism, and antihierarchical views as significant explanations for the different approaches to freedom of speech. The difficulty with these cultural explanations is that the strong free speech tradition was rather late in coming. If the standard cultural factors were so important, the free speech tradition would have emerged much sooner.[6]

In the United States, an important, but, as we shall see, not exclusive influence for liberals was the dispute over free speech for communists in the 1950s. Conservatives argued that communists should not be afforded free speech rights because the interest in national security outweighed the interest in free speech. Instead of emphasizing that this claim wrongly inflated the national security interest, Justice Hugo

Black and prominent commentators associated with the American
Civil Liberties Union (ACLU) developed the argument that balancing
First Amendment freedoms was inappropriate. The Constitution had
done all the balancing that needed to be done. As we will see, this position requires a lot of backing and filling, but it set the stage for liberals
to ignore other interests when free speech claims were rightly present. Liberals also were attracted to the view that the First Amendment
embraced a "profound national commitment to the principle that
debate on public issues should be uninhibited, robust, and wide-open."[7]
This perspective led to the position that the libel laws should not easily suppress criticism of powerful figures in American government and
civil society. But it also led to the conclusion that the right to demonstrate about public issues at a funeral was privileged over respect for
the privacy and dignity of a grieving family. Although the liberals work
within this tradition, they are hardly homogeneous. As we will see, for
example, Justice Breyer has a distinctive approach and Justice Kagan
may be moving toward his methodology – at least in part.

On the conservative side, after the fears of communists fell below
paranoid levels and after Senator Joseph McCarthy resigned in dis-
grace when his relentless campaign of guilt by association became no
longer politically sustainable, a number of factors led the Republicans
toward a stronger commitment to freedom of speech. And, we will
see, those factors played out in different ways with the conservative
Justices on the Court. What moves Chief Justice Roberts, for example,
is different from what has moved Justices Scalia and Thomas, which in
turn is different from what moves Justice Kennedy. Looking more generally, however, one factor inclining Republicans toward free speech
is that they perceived themselves as the victims of subtle censorship
through the imposition of political correctness. If the liberals saw the
First Amendment as protecting political (from communists to civil
rights demonstrators) and cultural dissent (from sexually oriented
novels to the hippies), the conservatives ultimately came to see themselves as being silenced in the liberal universities and denigrated by the
liberal media.

More important, the idea of balancing interests against each other
was regarded by many conservatives as appropriate for legislatures, but
not for judges. Confining the exceptions to free speech to historically

based categories appealed to these conservatives because it imposed judicial constraints by substituting history, albeit a fictional history, for subjective judicial judgment. In the case of these conservatives, the jurisprudential tail wags the First Amendment dog – except, as the Court well knows, virtually all of the reigning categories of unprotected speech are now markedly different from what they had been in the past.

Finally, conservatives recognized the importance from their perspective of affording strong free speech rights to business interests. Accordingly, they gradually began to be comfortable with the view that if the free market made sense in the economic sphere, it made sense in the intellectual sphere. Indeed, despite potent criticism of the view that truth emerges in the economic marketplace or the intellectual marketplace,[8] both liberals and conservatives agreed that intervention by government through speech regulation to suppress facts or ideas in the intellectual marketplace was generally inferior to letting the market work. Any such suppression, censorship, or regulation could be justified if, but only if, the government could show that the action was necessary to achieve a compelling state interest.

Requiring a showing that a government regulation of speech is necessary to achieve a compelling state interest relies on a lot of faith in the marketplace. What emerges in the marketplace may be true or just, of course, but it also may be that the cozy arrangements of the status quo have settled on something substantially less than the true or the just, and that the marketplace tolerates quite harmful speech. In fact, it may be that the marketplace reflects the disproportionate communicative resources of the powerful rather than a shiny version of truth and justice, and it may be that the outcome unfairly serves the powerful at the expense of the vulnerable.

As a practical matter, different cultures produce different accounts of the true and the just. This is not surprising. Different cultures involve differing power constituencies and accommodate different clashes of values. Whatever the configurations may be, culture plays a substantial role in the formation of our own views. As Charles Taylor remarks, culture "shapes our private experience and constitutes our public experience, which in turn interacts profoundly with the private. So it is no extravagant proposition to say that we are who we are"[9] because of our participation or immersion in the larger life of our society.

When we realize that quite different beliefs about freedom of speech have emerged in the European and US market, and when we realize that the citizens who adopted our Constitution had a quite different view of the truth about race, slavery, and male/female relations than we do, it is hard to embrace the sunny view that truth and justice are routinely reflected in what emerges in "the" market or in our markets or in markets different from our own. Even when the truth of what emerges in the market is unassailable, it may be that other interests are more important, as we will see in our discussions of privacy, fair trial, and depictions of animal cruelty.

The answer is definitely not that that government should be free from suspicion when it intervenes. It is that neither the marketplace nor the government can be trusted. So when speech clashes with other substantial interests, there is no reason automatically to privilege the speech interest over the other interests without affording proper respect for each. In the end, it should be clear that speech interacts with too many other values in too many other concrete contexts to hope or expect that a theory privileging it could reliably lead to sensible results.

Human life is all about choices, and we cannot have it all. When important values come into conflict, the sensible approach is not to resolve ahead of time to pick one over the other. Instead, as Isaiah Berlin observed, the sensible approach is to recognize a need for humility,[10] a recognition that it is folly to ignore relevant factors,[11] and to appreciate that "the collisions, even if they cannot be avoided can be softened. Claims can be balanced, compromises can be reached."[12] The conflict of values, he continued, can "be minimized by promoting and preserving an uneasy equilibrium, which is constantly threatened and in constant need of repair – that alone [is] the precondition for decent societies and morally acceptable behavior, otherwise we are bound to lose our way."[13]

In these pages, I propose to examine the bitter and the sweet, but I will concentrate on the damage caused by important forms of protected speech and shine a light on the alternative approaches to free speech employed in Europe and Canada. I will ruminate about why other countries are not infected with free speech idolatry, and I will critique the theories used to justify that idolatry. But I must introduce a few caveats.

First, as I will argue in Chapter 8, in the hands of the conservative majority, the idolatry stops in contexts where most of the liberals would rightly insist on First Amendment rights. In Part I of the book, comprising the majority of the chapters, I deal with what most would consider the core of the First Amendment: cases in which the government outlaws a category of speech across the board because it believes that the harm done by the speech outweighs its value. But there are other kinds of free speech cases that impinge on the rights of dissenters where the conservative majority has assembled a shoddy record by underprotecting speech. In institutional environments such as schools and workplaces, for example, government acts to smother dissent, and the conservatives support the government. The same is generally true when dissenters seek access to government property in order to conduct demonstrations. The Supreme Court, over liberal objections, gives relatively free reign to government when it imposes unnecessarily restrictive time, place, and manner regulations. In both of these lines of cases, the Court values bureaucratic authority over free speech values. In these and other cases, the Supreme Court is insufficiently sensitive to the values of dissent. I regret to report that Canada and Europe do no better in protecting what should be the rights of dissenters.

Second, I recognize my thesis is controversial and provocative. I aim to provoke second thoughts about First Amendment worship. But I have deliberately refrained from the sober and lawyerly on-the-one-hand and on-the-other-hand rhetoric of the standard academic monograph. The latter is well worn and obvious and the rejoinders well plotted. To go down the avenue of give and take would double or triple the size of the book with little gain. So consider this an opening argument for the view that the Court is valuing speech more heavily than it should. In making that argument, I attempt to take representative cases and give them flesh and blood to make them interesting. I also try to do the same with cases from Europe or Canada to show that alternative approaches are available.

Third, in using examples from Canada and Europe, I do not mean to suggest that their jurisprudence is more interesting than that of

Israel, South Africa, or many other countries around the world. I use the examples I use because they are the ones I know. Moreover, I do not mean to suggest that Europe is homogeneous unless I otherwise specify, but I would contend without fear of contradiction that the free speech sensibilities in Europe and Canada are vastly different from those in the United States. The point of the examples is to suggest that other democratic countries can and do arrive at different conclusions regarding how to adjudicate clashes between speech and other values.

Finally, some might wonder why I am complaining about the First Amendment and not simply the Court's interpretation of the First Amendment. After all, Charles Evans Hughes once said, "We are under the Constitution, but the Constitution is what the Court says it is."[14] Of course, I am complaining about how the Court interprets the First Amendment. And, in Part III of the book, I will explore how various justices have come to their conclusions and the different paths they have taken to get there. I will also explore what decisions could be changed with small modifications in the Court. But I will argue that the broad sweep of the conclusions discussed in Part I are here to stay. They were brought about by Court decisions, but they are now firmly embedded in the culture, or, at least, the legal culture. They are now the First Amendment – not merely what the Court says the First Amendment is.

In pursuing my argument, Part I, maintains in seven chapters that the First Amendment overvalues privacy-invading speech, pretrial publicity, racist speech, pornography, depictions of violence, commercial advertising, and political speech by the wealthy, including corporations. In all but one of these chapters (commercial advertising burdens many values), I first discuss the value burdened by speech to show that it is counterintuitive to suppose that the value should always be subordinate to free speech. I then turn to the most important US case or cases that argue free speech should be privileged over such values. I argue that the justifications they advance on behalf of the First Amendment regime are strikingly inadequate. In doing so, I try to put as much flesh and blood as I can on those cases to give life to my thesis. After criticizing those cases, I look at cases from Europe or Canada to show that reasonable alternatives are possible.

Part II explores the extent of the First Amendment insensitivity to those who swim against the current. Chapter 8 argues that the First Amendment undervalues dissent. Chapter 9 argues that the First Amendment insufficiently protects the religious freedom of religious minorities. Although this book is predominantly about freedom of speech, I think that the Court's handling of religion under the First Amendment offers a basis for interesting comparisons and contrasts. Just as the Court is not sufficiently sensitive to the importance of protecting those who use speech to dissent, the Court is insensitive to those whose religions mark them out as different from others. Moreover, it is often overlooked that government speech about religion is itself a part of the system of freedom of expression and a controversial part at that. In addition, the handling of religion when combined with the cases in Section I serves to support the view that the First Amendment is generally interpreted to serve the needs of the powerful. Finally, it also shows that a majority of the Court is willing to promote sectarian religious values without regard for the views of others. This willingness to promote values is in tension with some of the rhetoric employed in the free speech cases.

Part III of the book discusses how we got to this unsatisfactory place and where we might go from here. Chapter 10 rejects many of the standard cultural explanations of American free speech exceptionalism. It argues that liberals and conservatives separately arrived at this unsatisfactory state for quite different ideological reasons down different historical paths. Chapter 11 discusses what a First Amendment that was responsive to our social needs and responsibilities would look like. It would be a First Amendment that afforded stronger, but not absolute, protection for dissent and religious minorities. It would recognize that nondissenting speech typically has significant value, but it would abandon free speech idolatry and reach results closer to those of other Western countries. That chapter also explores the extent to which this ideal is within the realm of the possible. It concludes that much of this ideal can be achieved, but much of it is not within the realm of the possible for the foreseeable future. Free speech idolatry is so deeply entrenched in the American culture that it is hard to see how it might be shaken. And that lies at the core of what's wrong with the First Amendment.

PART I

1   PRIVACY

Privacy is a much treasured right in the American Constitution even though the word does not appear in the written document. In addition, privacy is protected in various statutory and common law contexts wholly apart from the constitutional reach of privacy protection. At its most general level, privacy refers the right to be left alone. It seems to protect a sphere of private autonomy. Thus, we refer to the "private" market, which many conservatives feel should not be regulated.

More centrally, however, privacy refers to a zone of intimacy in which human beings can live flourishing lives without the intrusion and scrutiny of others. That zone can include the right to determine whether or not to bear a child, including the right to use contraceptives or to have an abortion, the right to engage in sexual relations including same-sex relations, and the right to be free from unreasonable searches. Privacy protects communications between spouses, lawyer and client, doctor (or psychotherapist) and patient, priest and penitent. In some states, it provides that data about a human being cannot be collected or disseminated. It might promote government efficiency in combating crime and it would surely advance the cause of the social sciences, but we would not tolerate cameras and recording devices in our homes, let alone our bedrooms. Human beings require a private life in which they are not on a public stage. Friendships and intimate relations are rooted in the disclosure of our "private" selves. Our public face ordinarily wears a mask of formality, which to various degrees we shed in private. We may never be a wholly open book, but we are more open to some than others.[1] In addition, privacy enables us to develop our own independent personality, our sense of creativity, and our critical

sensibilities and substance. Without privacy, the evidence suggests that
we tend to conform, to do what is expected of us, and to succumb to
social construction, inhibiting play, innovation, and independence.[2] In
this respect, to protect privacy is to encourage values supported by the
First Amendment.[3]

If government, another institution, or a person invades our privacy,
we believe that our human dignity has been compromised.[4] Freedom
of speech itself is partly based on a commitment to the dignity of
human beings and their right to make autonomous decisions as to how
their lives should be lived. We are free to choose what books to read,
what movies to see, and what persons we choose as friends and associ-
ates. On this understanding, freedom of speech is not based (or not
exclusively based) on the power of truth to emerge in the marketplace
of ideas, but on human liberty as well as other values.

Since a respect for human dignity can implicate multiple rights, it
can and does implicate rights (whether developed in the Constitution
or in other sources of law) that can come into conflict.[5] Clearly, free
speech can conflict with privacy. If I reveal intimate aspects of your
private life, I am using free speech to violate your privacy. Even if
I do not reveal intimate aspects of your life, I can speak in ways that
interfere with your privacy. My contention in this chapter is that free
speech has been unduly privileged in the clash between speech and
privacy. The Court has not been sufficiently sensitive to the place of
privacy in the human condition.

The case of *Snyder v. Phelps*[6] is an important example. Albert
Snyder's son, Matthew Snyder, a Lance Corporal in the US Marines,
was killed in the line of duty in Iraq on March 3, 2006. His father
Albert arranged a funeral a week later at St. John's Catholic Church
in Westminister, Maryland, the town in which Matthew had lived and
gone to high school.

The funeral was picketed by members of the Westboro Baptist
Church of Topeka Kansas including its pastor of fifty-two years, Fred
W. Phelps. Phelps's church had sixty to seventy members, fifty of
whom were children, grandchildren, or in-laws of the pastor. Phelps
preached a "fire and brimstone" fundamentalism. According to his
brand of fundamentalism, God hates homosexuality and hates and
punishes America for its tolerance of homosexuality. God's wrath

on this account is specially inflicted on American soldiers whether or not they are gay (Matthew Snyder was not gay) and this wrath is also accountable for the tragedy of 9/11, which Phelps regarded as a blessing.

Phelps and his followers decided to gain the attention of the press and spread his message by demonstrating at military funerals. Neither he nor any of the demonstrators had met Matthew Snyder or any member of his family, but they alerted police that they planned to demonstrate at his funeral as they had at many others before. Presumably, because they knew their message would be offensive, they asked for and received police protection. The concern about violence led law enforcement to deploy five sheriffs and a SWAT team. The fire department and ambulances were in the area on standby. Other equipment and personnel were drawn in to provide government protection for Phelps and his followers. The school across the street from St. John's was placed in lockdown mode to protect the children.

Not surprisingly, Phelps and his followers complied with police directions and ordinances that they maintain a certain distance from the church. There they displayed signs that said, "You're Going to Hell," "God Hates You," "Semper Fi Fags," "Fag Troops," "Fags Doom Nations," "Thank God for 9/11," "Thank God for Dead Soldiers," "Thank God for IED's," "God Hates the USA," "Don't Pray for the USA," "America Is Doomed," "Pope in Hell," "Not Blessed Just Cursed," and "Priests Rape Boys."[7]

Albert Snyder was fully aware of the demonstration. The Phelps demonstration made it impossible to use normal access to the church campus and transformed the entire atmosphere of the service for Snyder. As Snyder's lawyers put it, Phelps's presence created "a negative and circus-like atmosphere during a solemn and religious occasion."[8] Although Snyder saw the tops of the signs on the way to the funeral, he did not see their specific messages. He learned of their content later that day when he saw a television program with footage of the Phelps family and their signs. After the Phelps family returned to Kansas, the church stated on its website that Albert Snyder and his former wife "taught Matthew to defy his creator," "raised him for the devil," and taught him that "God was a liar."[9] When Albert Snyder saw these assertions, he vomited and cried for three or four hours.

Snyder testified that every time he thinks of his son, he sees the signs employed in the demonstration. He testified that he knew he would think about the sign "Thank God for Dead Soldiers" every day of his life. He said that he is often tearful and angry and becomes so sick to his stomach that he physically vomits. Expert testimony disclosed that Snyder's depression and diabetes were exacerbated because of the church's conduct and that he suffered severe emotional distress because of it.

Snyder sued Phelps and other members of the church for their conduct. Most significantly, he sued Phelps for the intentional infliction of emotional distress and for the invasion of privacy. Although the tort of intentional infliction of emotional distress has been recognized for less than forty years in the State of Maryland, it has been a tort in the United States for some eighty years. In Maryland, the plaintiff must show that the defendant intentionally or recklessly engaged in extreme and outrageous conduct that caused the plaintiff to suffer extreme emotional distress. The defendants primarily argued that the First Amendment protected their speech. The trial judge rejected this defense, and the jury found Phelps, two members of his family, and the church liable for $10.9 million, an award that the trial judge reduced to $5 million.

On appeal, the Phelps defendants (I will refer to them as Phelps) conceded that their conduct met the requirements for the intentional infliction of emotional distress cause of action, but invoked the First Amendment in their defense. The defendants prevailed in the court of appeals and the US Supreme Court agreed with the court of appeals.

The Court's essential argument was simple. The country has a "profound national commitment to the principle that debate on public issues should be uninhibited, robust, and wide-open."[10] Displaying a rich capacity for euphemism, the Court stated that the signs "may fall short of refined social or political commentary"[11] and that some of the signs seemed to be addressed to the Snyder family in particular (how else does one interpret signs like "God Hates You" or "You're Going to Hell"). Moreover, the Court disposed of the website messages by resort to a technicality that excluded them for consideration by the Court. This opened the way for the Court to conclude that the signs at the funeral were *primarily* addressed to public issues, such as "the political and moral conduct of the United States and its citizens, the fate of our Nation, homosexuality in the military, and scandals involving the Catholic clergy."[12] It was downhill from there. The Court concluded that because the "speech was at a public place on a matter of public concern,"[13] it was "entitled to 'special protection' under the First Amendment."[14]

The district court had argued that the interest in freedom of speech needed to be balanced against the burdens placed upon Snyder and his family. Yet the Supreme Court's opinion reads as if nothing can outweigh the free speech interest. Although the Court at one point acknowledged the severity of the injury to Snyder (while minimizing it in other parts of the opinion), it never sought to balance Snyder's interest against that of Phelps. The speech interest was automatically privileged.

This conclusion that freedom of speech embraced the intentional infliction of emotional distress of private persons was unprecedented. The Court had previously held that a joke in a magazine about a public figure could not give rise to an action for intentional infliction of emotional distress,[15] but it had not afforded similar speech protection to cases involving private persons in any context, let alone in the context of a funeral. Chief Justice Roberts, who wrote for the Court, did not acknowledge the lack of precedent for the decision, but he did initiate a frontal assault on the tort of intentional infliction of emotional distress. He stated that the finding of outrageousness by the court below was based on a subjective standard.

Of course, this is partially true. "Outrageous" conduct is not self-identifying; there is no objective measure for it. But a judgment that it has occurred is not the product of arbitrary, individual decision making either. It is determined in large part by the customs, habits, and traditions of the society. To be sure, free speech is all about the challenging of those customs, habits, and traditions, but it should not be ignored that this particular challenge was embedded in the intentional or reckless infliction of severe emotional distress. Indeed, it is feckless to indict the outrageous standard for being subjective in a context in which the defendants *did not question* that their conduct was outrageous within the meaning of the law.

Moreover, the Court acknowledged that the outrageous standard can be used when the speech does not relate to a public issue, but is private in character. It is plausible to maintain that the harms of subjectivity are less damaging when the speech being considered is less valuable than the speech on public issues. But this assumes that there is much of value in the speech at a funeral involving public issues that intentionally inflicts emotional distress. The Chief Justice attributes value to this speech by deemphasizing the negative parts of the context and concentrating on those facts that are positive. So the Chief Justice argues that Phelps primarily spoke about public issues on public streets (obeying police orders about where to stand), and did not yell, use profanity, or engage in acts of violence.

But his characterization abstracts away from a lot of the context. It blinks at the intentional infliction of emotional distress; it ignores the insults permeating Snyder's discourse; and it looks away from the circus-like atmosphere created by the need to protect Phelps because of the offensive character of his speech, and the severe effects on Snyder. More important, it assumes that speech on public issues at funerals is comparable to public speech in other contexts. As Justice Alito argued in dissent, Phelps could have displayed his signs connected to public issues virtually anywhere else across the State of Maryland and across the United States.

Indeed, the Court suggested that Maryland could outlaw demonstrations near funerals so long as there was no discrimination on the basis of content. States and localities across the country passed such rules. Of course, the reason they passed these regulations was to prevent Phelps and his followers from demonstrating at funerals. But the result is that the carrying of a sign saying "We loved you Matthew" would be treated the same as the ugly attacks of Phelps. There is nothing inappropriate about signs near funerals designed to express admiration for the deceased. It is utterly inappropriate to launch verbal assaults at a funeral – knowingly victimizing mourners at an especially vulnerable moment in order to gain publicity for a message.

The Court's mechanical application of the First Amendment rode roughshod over the dignity of Albert Snyder without any showing that anything of genuine value was being protected. In short, it is one thing to say that the nation has a profound national commitment to the principle that debate on public issues should be uninhibited, robust, and wide-open. It is quite another to assume that demonstrations at funerals calculated to inflict severe emotional distress make a valuable contribution to public debate. Democracy can flourish quite nicely without permitting calculated exploitation of such sensitive occasions.

Albert Snyder, a private person, suffered severe mental distress because of the vicious speech of Phelps and his followers. Minimal decency counsels that he should have recovered. Indeed, in my view, demonstrations at funerals designed to criticize the dead or their families deserve no constitutional protection even if they are directed at public figures[16] and even if the recipients are so thick skinned that they suffer no mental distress. Respect for the privacy of mourners demands no less.

I wish that the *Phelps* case was an isolated example in which our First Amendment law permits persons to disrespect the right to maintain a private life in the name of free speech. Regrettably, it is not the case. Most conspicuously, American free speech law promotes a voyeuristic culture in which the intimate details of private lives are revealed for no better purpose than to satisfy the public's grasping curiosity and to allow the press to make a buck. In other words, the dignity of human beings is sacrificed for the commercial purposes of tabloids, not to mention the more respectable press, and to satisfy the public's yearning for gossip. This tawdry cultural practice is not only permitted; it is elevated into a constitutional right.

Tabloids and the mainstream press (sometimes it is difficult to tell the difference) are free to report on the intimate private lives of public and private individuals. For example, in two cases the Supreme Court has ruled that a press publication of the name of a rape victim is protected under the First Amendment. In *Cox Broadcasting Corporation v. Cohn*,[17] the Court ruled that the fact that the name was contained in the indictment charging the accused with a crime opened the door to publicizing a rape victim's name to millions. In *B.J.F. v. Florida Star*,[18] the name of the victim was present in a police report and inadvertently made available to the press. This mistake also was seized upon to support mass publication. Yet, it is hard to understand why the inclusion of the name in the indictment or the inadvertent disclosure of the police report should have authorized the press to violate state statutes prohibiting the publication of a rape victim's name.

The Court postulated that information in a public document was public information. But an indictment is designed to communicate to an accused the nature of the crime he or she is alleged to have committed. The accused is entitled to have fair notice of the specifics of the alleged crime. That the name is included in an indictment does not warrant disclosure to everyone in the world even if any member of the public is entitled to see that record. Similarly, the name of an alleged victim naturally will appear in a police report. That a police report is inadvertently made available to the press does not overturn a statute enacted by the legislature forbidding publication particularly when the statute is designed to protect the privacy of someone outside of government.

Of course, in rare cases, the publication of the name of the victim might cause additional evidence to be discovered. But there was no call for the Court to remind us that a democracy could not well function without the information provided by a free press. So, too, it is not helpful to maintain that the public citizenry plays a role in overseeing the administration of justice. For one thing, the role of the citizenry in overseeing the administration of justice is hardly central to the democratic process. In fact, the administration of justice is significantly designed to assure that public opinion does not sway the outcome of cases. It is the function of reviewing courts, not the public at large, to determine whether justice is done in an individual case. Even assuming a citizen's participation in a democracy could be affected by their view concerning the fairness of the criminal justice system; it would be the rare citizen whose democratic participation would be affected by the outcome of cases involving rape victims. Any suggestion that the democratic process has a significant stake in revealing the names of rape victims seems excessive.

And that is crucial because the real issue in these cases is how important for a functioning democracy is the publication of the names of rape victims and whether that importance (such as it may be) outweighs the privacy damage that inevitably follows publication. For example, in *B.J.F. v. Florida Star*, the victim testified that she had suffered emotional distress, that fellow workers and acquaintances called the article to her attention, and that she received several threatening calls from someone who said he would rape her again. She changed phone numbers and addresses. She sought police protection and mental health counseling.

Revealing the name of a rape victim breaches a fundamental aspect of privacy: the ability to choose who will know intimate details about her private life.[19] The revelation of her victim status to the public at large automatically transformed her relationship to anyone who had even a passing acquaintance with her. It is one thing for a close friend to know of her tragic situation; it is quite another for her to know or wonder whether the waitress in the coffee shop or a coworker in the building now sees her as a rape victim rather than a mere customer or fellow employee.

Only an abstract commitment to speech of "public interest" permitted the Court to override the privacy interests of B.J.F. It is ironic that the Court used the victim's initials instead of her full name in order to protect her privacy. Of course, this was too little, too late. But it also shines light on the thinness of the Court's belief that the public disclosure of the names of rape victims is important to the democratic process. In the highest court of the land, the identity of the rape victim was concealed while the Court simultaneously argued that the publication of her identity was important to the functioning of the democratic process.

ALTERNATIVE APPROACHES

There is another way, and the European Convention on Human Rights is an exemplar. The Convention protects freedoms of speech and press, but it also protects the right of privacy. When the two rights conflict, the courts decide which right is more important – not in the abstract – but in the specific context of the case. Consider the British case of *Campbell v. MGN* LTD.[20] Naomi Campbell, an internationally famous model, brought suit complaining that a newspaper had reported that she attended Narcotics Anonymous together with the details of her treatment (e.g., how often she went), and that the newspaper had published a photograph of her leaving the meeting. She won in the lower court, lost in the appellate court, but was ultimately vindicated in the House of Lords (then the highest appellate body on most domestic matters in the United Kingdom).

Although the Lords upheld Campbell's right to privacy with respect to several aspects of the publication, they did not question the right of the press to report that Campbell was addicted to drugs and that she was receiving treatment for the addiction. At the same time, the Lords did not maintain that the press could report on the drug habits of public figures in general. Campbell was a special case because she had previously denied she used drugs and had said she was not like other models in this respect. In so doing the Lords believed that she had opened this issue up to public scrutiny. Uncovering these public lies was, therefore, thought to be a matter of legitimate public comment.

On the contrary, publicizing the details of her treatment constituted an invasion of privacy. Narcotics Anonymous, argued the Lords, is successful because it is anonymous. Covert photography of her leaving the building where the meetings took place jeopardized her anonymity in seeking treatment (not to mention the anonymity of others). In short, the Lords recognized the right of freedom of press and the right to a private life. Neither was privileged over the other. The outcome was determined not by abstract slogans about the importance of each right, but by close examination of the force of each claim in the specific context.

England is a latecomer to privacy protection. It has been markedly influenced by continental protections that stretch back for centuries. Those protections have evolved from the protection of the honor of royalty to the protection of everyone.[21] Central to the German Constitution, for example, is the explicit protection of human dignity. That protection extends to consumers, to workers, to prisoners, and to those whose privacy is compromised by the mass media. In the case of the mass media, France also has generous privacy protections. For example, a gay man marched in a gay parade in Paris. His photograph was published in a national newspaper. The French court held that his public marching did not justify singling him out for an individual photograph, let alone a photograph published in a national newspaper.

Contrast the law in the United States. If Naomi Campbell had sued in the United States under similar circumstances, the courts would have said that she was a public figure and her life story was open to the public. The courts would do this without the slightest attention to nuance. They would ignore the observation of Baroness Hale of Richmond in *Campbell* that "The political and social life of the community, and the intellectual, artistic or personal development of individuals, are not obviously assisted by pouring over the intimate details of a fashion model's private life."[22] As Anita Allen remarks, "It could be best to let celebrities have their privacy since ... the 'moral ecology' of our society may suffer if the populace grows coarsely inquisitive and celebrities are egregiously abused."[23] Instead, the courts in the United States would posit that a public figure's desire for publicity for some purposes would be opening it up for all purposes. Similarly, marching in a public parade would open one up to be the subject of a photograph and for subsequent publication.

Indeed, Oliver Sipple, a gay man in San Francisco, interfered with an attempted assassination of President Gerald Ford. His act of interference was celebrated nationally. The press reported that Sipple was gay. That was well known in San Francisco, but not known to his family in the Midwest. Sipple sued. Of course, he lost.[24] Later he committed suicide.

I do not mean to suggest that privacy always loses to freedom of press in the United States. For example, when Kobe Bryant, a famous basketball star, was accused of rape in Colorado, he wanted to introduce evidence of prior and subsequent sexual activity by the alleged victim. Under a rape shield law, Colorado law prohibited the introduction of such evidence except in narrowly defined circumstances. A private hearing was held to determine what portions of the victim's sex life could be introduced into evidence. Inadvertently, a clerk sent the transcript of this hearing to those members of the press who had asked to receive the transcripts of public hearings. The Colorado Supreme Court upheld a court order restraining the press from publishing this private information.[25] But this kind of decision is rare.

In the United States, protections for privacy are largely rooted in protecting the liberty of a person against government tyranny, rather than against violations of human dignity by the media or the market.

So, as I have mentioned, persons have a constitutional right to use contraceptives, to have an abortion, to send their children to private schools, to form associations and to determine who will be or not be members of the group, and to practice their religion. In addition, there are protections against unreasonable searches and seizures particularly in the home. Finally, there are protections (some constitutional, some not) for the privacy of conversations with lawyers, doctors, priests, and spouses.

Nonetheless, what has been exposed to third parties is fair game. Under the Fourth Amendment as interpreted, police may rummage through your garbage, collect the return addresses of all incoming mail (even e-mail) and the addresses of those written to by snail or electronic mail, as well as the telephone numbers of those whom you have spoken with on a land line, and your banking and credit card records without providing you with any notice and without any showing of probable cause. If the invasions of privacy tolerated by police reflect concessions to law enforcement and fear of criminals, they also reflect a shriveled sense of human dignity.[26]

In some senses though, the failure to protect mourners at funerals, rape victims, and public figures, however remote their connection to democratic politics might be, is even worse. Permitting tyrannical police practices out of fear is inexcusable, but understandable. Permitting gross violations of human dignity in order to protect astonishingly slight contributions to public discourse is nearly inexplicable.

2   JUSTICE

One of the hallmarks of a civilized political system is respect for the right of a fair trial. In the United States, the right to a trial by jury in criminal cases is regarded as "fundamental to the American scheme of justice."[1] If defendants are to receive a fair trial, assessments of their guilt or innocence should be decided in the confines of a controlled courtroom by an impartial jury, uncontaminated by the frenzy of a sensationalistic press barrage. The fair trial requirement is important not only for individual defendants, but also it is in the public interest in a democratic society that defendants are acquitted or convicted through trials that both are fair and appear to be fair.

Although our system of criminal justice has many significant deficiencies, the overwhelming majority of criminal defendants who go to trial are tried by a jury that has not been contaminated by pretrial publicity. Their stories are not sufficiently newsworthy to garner press attention. But some defendants are not so lucky. In their circumstances, the press is eager to publish all the evidence they can find without regard to the effects on prospective jurors. I wish I could say that our system places limits on the press in an effort to safeguard our system of criminal justice and the individuals involved. But our system does no such thing. Our system caters to the press desire for profits and the insatiable appetite of the public for gossip – at the expense of justice. This, of course, is the effect of our system and not its motive. The protection of the press is thought to be justified on a much higher plane, and there is no admission of a compromise with justice. But I find the claim that justice is not compromised to be a reckless gamble, and, as I indicated in Chapter 1, the claim that the press serves a valuable democratic function in these circumstances is feeble. Indeed, there is a strong argument that the values underlying the freedom of the press are disserved by permitting the publication of materials that threaten the fairness of individual trials. Such publications do not respect the dignity of the accused individuals, circumvent the very basis for rules of evidence at trials, and mock the rule of law, which is central to any theory of democracy.[2] Equally important, there is simply no reason to assume that freedom of press should be given constitutional priority over fair trials.

The leading case, *Nebraska Press Association v. Stuart*,[3] involved the shotgun killings of six members of the Kellie family in the small town of Sutherland, Nebraska – including three children ages ten, seven, and five. Florence, a ten-year-old, was sexually molested before death, and her body was sexually molested after death too. The body of Marie, the guardian of Florence, was also sexually molested after death. Her husband Henry had been killed shortly before she entered the house. Subsequently, Henry and Marie's older son David entered the house with his two young children, Deanne and Daniel. The two youngsters witnessed the murder of their father, and seven-year-old Deanne was killed followed by five-year-old Daniel.

Edwin Charles Simants was charged with the murders. Central to our discussion is the fact that he confessed to the commission of these murders to his parents and to the police and the fact that Federal District Judge Hugh Stewart ordered the press not to reveal that Simants had previously confessed until a jury was impanelled. The basis for Judge Stewart's order should be obvious: it would be extremely difficult to find an impartial jury if the press reported the existence of these confessions. Indeed, the institutional press had previously agreed not to publish confessions in voluntary press guidelines. Nonetheless, the press fought this order all the way to the Supreme Court where it won a victory for free press and a defeat for our commitment to fair trials.

The case produced five opinions, but the two most important were a concurring opinion written by Justice Brennan, joined by Justices Stewart and Marshall, and a majority opinion written by Chief Justice Burger. Chief Justice Burger suggested that he would uphold restrictions on the press in some circumstances, but the showing he would require to uphold a restriction was impossibly high.[4] Justice Brennan made it clear he would never uphold restrictions on the press in order to protect a fair trial. In the end, there is no significant practical difference between the two opinions. Both stand for the proposition that protecting the press and providing a fair trial are not incompatible. Brennan's opinion was simply more forthright.

Justice Brennan cast his argument as opposed to "prior restraints" against the press. In context, this means that he was opposed without qualification to judicial orders telling the press not to publish news or opinions – whatever they may be – about a crime or an upcoming criminal case. But the arguments he made would also apply to legislation, preventing the press from publishing confessions prior to the commencement of a trial.[5] For Brennan, it is doubtful whether anything really turned on the form of the governmental regulation. His conclusion was that the press is to be left alone to publish as it sees fit.

From Brennan's perspective, a free press in this area is valuable because it "does not simply publish information about trials but guards against the miscarriage of justice by subjecting the police, prosecutors, and judicial processes to extensive public scrutiny and criticism."[6] Secrecy, he argues, leads to ignorance and distrust. Even if one accepted this characterization of press reporting regarding sensational crimes, however, these generalized assertions do not explain why there was a constitutionally sanctioned rush for the public to get the information before a jury was impanelled. No one was arguing that the police, prosecutors, and judicial processes should be immune from extensive public scrutiny and criticism. The question was not *whether* the scrutiny would be permitted to take place, but *when* such scrutiny would be appropriate. To be sure, if one is devoted to the autonomy of the press as an end in itself, a pretrial order forbidding it to publish about confessions infringes upon that autonomy, but then one would have to explain why such devotion would be appropriate in the face of a threat to a fair trial.

But this leads us to the heart of the matter. Justice Brennan denies that massive press coverage poses a realistic threat to a fair trial, and this assertion is really quite dubious. First and foremost, the social science evidence discloses that pretrial publicity predisposes potential jurors toward believing in the guilt of the defendant, a disposition obviously incompatible with a system committed to the presumption of innocence.[7] Brennan argues that there are "adequate devices for screening from jury duty those individuals who have in fact been exposed to prejudicial pretrial publicity."[8] Foremost among these devices is the questioning of prospective jurors. Questioning, of course, can be helpful if the prospective juror remembers being exposed to the pretrial publicity and discloses it. Some jurors, however, do not remember being exposed to pretrial publicity during the questioning, but then recall having read about a confession or other evidence during the proceedings. It would be the rare juror who would report his or her recollection at that point. And I suspect it would be the rare juror who would ignore the existence of a confession or the seizure of material evidence even if the evidence had been illegally procured. The effectiveness of questioning to combat prejudicial pretrial publicity is undercut even more significantly by the fact that potential jurors are not always forthcoming.

I was once called for jury duty in downtown Los Angeles. Of course, as a law professor, I was thrown off many juries. Against all odds, I was actually impaneled on one (alas the case ended in a mistrial). After being thrown off the other cases, I would return to an assembly room with others who had been thrown off, and I was surprised (how naïve I was) at how many people made statements clearly revealing they had lied during the questioning. When asked if they leaned one way or another, they claimed they were neutral during the questioning; when they returned to the assembly room, they revealed a strong pro-prosecution or pro-defense orientation (in the criminal context) or pro-plaintiff or pro-defendant orientation (in the civil context). Potential jurors lied to get on juries or to avoid being on juries. Questioning cannot protect defendants against prejudicial pretrial publicity when potential jurors do not reveal that they have been exposed to the publicity.

Brennan also argued that defendants can be protected without restrictions on the press because restrictions can be placed on prosecutors and criminal defense attorneys who are officers of the court, witnesses, and even the criminal defendant.[9] Missing from this list are police officers who often give the information to the press (sometimes on a confidential basis).[10] If Brennan were right that restrictions on lawyers and witnesses effectively protect the defendant, we would not have prejudicial publicity because the press would not have the information. But we do have such publicity, and we have it because the press often gets the information.

Apart from the effectiveness of the restrictions Brennan would have permitted, there is the puzzle of *why* Brennan would permit these restrictions. If the reason why restrictions on the press are inappropriate is that the public needs the information to evaluate the quality of the administration of justice, why is it appropriate to take steps designed to prevent the press from getting the information the public allegedly needs? If the restrictions are to be defended, it must be on the ground that it is inappropriate to try a case in the mass media. But, if that is so, restrictions on the press must be countenanced in order to protect a fair trial.

Now it may be that judicial orders are an imperfect way to protect a fair trial. Judges can restrict parties only within their jurisdiction. In nationally prominent cases, they could have an impact only on the quantity of pretrial publicity. On the other hand, a federal statute prohibiting the publication of information about confessions or about material seized in searches (which might later be deemed to be illegal searches) prior to trial or resolution of the case (perhaps by a plea bargain) could solve the jurisdictional issue. Clearly, however, the Court would strike such legislation down as a violation of the First Amendment. But it is doubtful whether the Court has persuasively made the case that our democracy requires the dissemination of this information prior to the trial or resolution of the case without a trial. I conclude that the Court privileges the right of a free press over the right of a fair trial in ways that are quite difficult to justify.

I do not contend that direct restrictions on the press need be a frequent phenomenon in this area. If prosecutors were effectively sanctioned for revealing incriminating evidence to the press, and if police were similarly sanctioned,[11] the press would be indirectly limited. If, however, incriminating information comes to the press from whatever source, considerations of fair trial justify the limitations on publication.

ALTERNATIVE APPROACHES

It is worth discussing the different approach taken in England to this issue.[12] Indeed, it is arguable that England goes too far the other way. *Attorney General v. British Broadcasting Corporation*[13] presents a good example. On a very popular quiz show, celebrities were asked to identify pensioners who had allegedly been defrauded by Ian and Kevin Maxwell and their father who had since died. After the celebrities had tried to identify the pensioners, the program host Angus Duffy said, "The BBC are in fact cracking down on references to Ian and Kevin Maxwell just in case programme-makers appear biased in their treatment of these two heartless scheming bastards."[14]

The broadcast of these remarks was run on Friday, April 29, and rebroadcast the following day. It was heard by an estimated audience of 6,140,000 people. The Attorney General brought an action for the contempt of court against the BBC and the show's production company, Hat Trick Productions Limited. The charge was that the show created a substantial risk of prejudice in the pending criminal trial.

The court recognized that the remarks were made six months before the trial, that the time between the trial and the making of the remarks made it more likely that memories would fade, that the public has a short memory, that a jury could be expected to follow a judge's directions, and that a long trial itself could focus a juror on the evidence rather than on a six-month-old joke, albeit told by someone who was respected and perhaps might be thought to have inside knowledge. Nonetheless, the court ruled that the statements went directly to the matter to be tried and that they created a "risk that one or more jurors would not begin and continue their jury duty with an open mind, and thus that there was a substantial risk that the course of justice in the trial would be seriously prejudiced."[15]

From the perspective of the American courts, the outcome is outrageous. From the tone of the British court, it appears to be a close case. Although it is not discussed, it appears that the British court does not see much free speech value in public pretrial discussion of the guilt or innocence of criminal defendants.[16] Given that judgment, any risk of prejudice might seem unwarranted. If that is the court's view of jokes on a quiz show, how much greater would be the concern be if alleged confessions were openly discussed in the mass media? The gulf between the British and US perspectives is wide indeed.

On the continent the contrast with the United States is also stark.[17] In addition to protecting the presumption of innocence, the continental focus is on the right to a private life and the right to a reputation. The Committee of Ministers of the Council of Europe has observed that "The mere indication of the name of the accused or convicted may constitute a sanction which is more severe than the penal sanction delivered by the criminal court. It furthermore may prejudice the reintegration into society of the person concerned."[18] It, therefore, suggests that the identity of a suspect or an accused not be published. The same applies to witnesses and to victims in some situations, for example, where the publicity would unduly affect the victim's "private life or dignity."[19] Of course, if a public figure is accused of a crime or the crime is of general public concern, exceptions are made, but the committee cautions that the presumption of innocence should not be prejudiced "through opinions and information relating to pending criminal proceedings disseminated by the media."[20]

Although the recommendations of the committee are not legally binding, they are considered persuasive on the continent and they are indicative of how far removed the continent's perspective is from the devil-may-care thinking of the United States. For example, the German Press Code cites the committee's recommendations and provides that when reporting on accidents, crimes investigations, or trials, the press usually shall not identify victims or perpetrators: "The need for sensation alone never can justify the public's right to be informed."[21] Again exceptions are made when prominent people are involved, but the code provides that the presumption of innocence applies not only to the government, but also to the press. Accordingly, the German Press Code recites that, "Reports on investigations, criminal court proceedings, and other formal procedures must be free from prejudice."[22] So too the European Court of Human Rights has cautioned that journalists must respect the presumption of innocence.[23]

A striking case of the latter principle is to be found in *Worm v. Austria*.[24] There the European Court of Human Rights upheld the conviction of a journalist for his reporting on a criminal trial of a former vice chancellor and minister of finance in Austria. The former

public official, Hannes Androsch, was accused of tax evasion, and
Alfred Worm, reporting on the trial, expressed the view in no uncertain terms that Mr. Androsch was clearly guilty of the charges filed.
Worm was convicted for violating Section 23 of the Austrian Media
Act, which forbids discussion of the probable outcome of the proceedings or the value of the evidence in a way "capable of influencing the
outcome of the proceedings."[25]

Worm argued that leeway should be afforded to journalists to comment on public proceedings and that leeway should be particularly
generous when public officials or former public officials have been
accused of criminal activity. The Court agreed, and it found no evidence that Worm's biting commentary had influenced the proceedings or even that any of the judges in the Androsch case had read his
writing. Nonetheless, the Court upheld the view that Worm sought
to influence the proceedings and that his commentary was capable
of influencing the outcome of the trial. It noted that Worm had written many articles about Androsch and might well be regarded as an
expert. It expressed particular concern about the possibility that the
lay judges involved in the trial could be influenced. Accordingly, the
Court concluded that Worm's trial commentary was not protected
under the European Convention's free press protection.

The *Worm* case strongly shows the continental commitment to protecting the authority of the judiciary in their attempts to safeguard
the presumption of innocence and a fair trial. But protections on the
continent go even beyond protections for the accused. I have already
mentioned that the identity of a convicted person is ordinarily not to
be revealed, but even in jurisdictions where revealing the identity of an
accused is permitted, protections for the accused from some publicity
may be afforded.

Norwegian law, for example, prohibits the taking or publication of
photographs of an accused or convicted person on his or her way to
or from a court hearing. Similar restrictions exist in England, Wales,
Cyprus, Austria, and Denmark. In *Hanseld v. Norway*,[26] "B" (a woman
whose identity was well known to the public), was convicted of participating in a brutal triple murder and was sentenced to twenty-one
years in jail. She left the courthouse in tears and three photographs of

her were published in two major newspapers. The editors of the newspapers were convicted of violating the Norwegian law. They argued
that the law violated the freedom of press protection of the European
Convention on Human Rights.

Both the Norwegian courts and the European Court of Human
Rights disagreed. B was shown "in tears and great distress, was emo-
tionally shaken and at her most vulnerable psychologically."[27] This state
of "reduced control … lay at the core of the protection the relevant
statutory provision was intended to provide."[28] The courts ruled that B
was to be treated with respect for her privacy and dignity. Indeed, the
Norwegian Supreme Court regarded the statutory provision as essential to the due process of law. Due process of law should inspire trust
in those brought before the courts and requires treating the parties
with consideration. This consideration is not shown when a defendant
is burdened by the need to force her way "between photographers and
television teams." Although the European Court was more impressed
by the privacy argument than the due process argument, it regarded
both considerations taken together to be sufficiently strong interests to
outweigh the interest in the freedom of press.

I do not suggest that the European cases exhibit perfection in free
press analysis. The conclusion that a six-month-old joke created a substantial risk of prejudice to the fairness of a trial seems unlikely. On
the other hand, a rule generally permitting the press to report upon
or laugh about the guilt of the accused risks the creation of a circus
atmosphere that is far from conducive to a fair trial. The Austrian case
does not seem to take seriously enough the distinction between pretrial
publicity and critical commentary about an ongoing trial. It would be
appropriate to require that judges not read commentary upon cases
in which they are participating. Nonetheless, in a media-saturated
society, there is risk that they will do what they should not do. I would,
however, take the press side in the Austrian case. On the other hand,
I think the Norwegian case is rightly decided. I think a democratic
society can function in an informed way without gaining access to the
tears of a convicted woman leaving a courthouse.

Whatever imperfections might lie in some of the European cases,
they do not indulge the fiction that fair trials take place regardless of

the amount and nature of pretrial publicity, and they do not indulge a free press fetish. They may go too far the other way on occasion. But they recognize that there is a clash between free press and considerations of justice, and that sometimes the press must be limited to preserve justice.

3   RACE

The election of Barack Obama to the presidency was a milestone in American history that many of us thought we would never see. But, an end to racism it did not mark. The facts on the ground remain disturbing. Three times as many black children live in poverty as opposed to white children.[1] Black unemployment rates are substantially higher than those of whites.[2] Black men are more than six times as likely as white men to be imprisoned.[3] Efforts to exclude blacks from the polls have been upheld by the Supreme Court on specious grounds.[4] Facts such as these are not uniformly appreciated.[5] Although racial attitudes have improved over time, any claim that we have moved to a post racial environment is exaggerated.[6] Indeed, after reviewing substantial data and the evidence of racial polarization, David McAdam and Karina Kloos conclude: "Far from the imagined post-racial society Obama's election was supposed to herald, we find ourselves living through the period of greatest racial tensions and conflict since the 1960's and early 1970's."[7]

Nonetheless, publicly blatant racist speech has long been socially unacceptable. Unacceptable, as it may be, it is constitutionally protected. That protection has long been identified as a constitutional marker separating the United States from other civilized countries. Many Americans are proud that our Constitution protects not just "free thought for those who agree with us but freedom for the thought that we hate."[8] On the other hand, some speech we hate can cause significant harm and does not deserve to be protected. The legal toleration of racist speech is incompatible with the nation's commitment to equal citizenship. It tolerates the denigration of vulnerable citizens on the basis of their skin color or ethnic background, factors that should be irrelevant to their relationship to the state or society. This toleration is inconsistent with the kind of public culture a just society needs to foster.[9] To be sure, I can see the attraction of a free-wheeling society where anyone can say anything, of maintaining a tolerant posture, and some find attraction in the stereotypically masculine emotionless posture that irrational words cannot hurt me. But the ACLU liberals who take these positions are not for the most part the potential victims of racist speech. The public culture they endorse, constitutionally protects verbal assaults, which, taken as a whole, cause or unreasonably risk subordination in the daily lives of those who are attacked. This should not be surprising. If defamation of a particular individual can cause harm to that individual, group defamation can cause damage to the reputation of each and every individual in the defamed group. Finally, racist speech can sometimes threaten public order.[10]

Despite the harm caused by racist speech, the courts have held it is entitled to full First Amendment protection. The issues were fully canvassed in a series of cases dealing with the plan of the National Socialist Party of America, a group that identified with the Nazis, to march in the Village of Skokie, Illinois, a stronghold of Jews and survivors of the Holocaust. From the perspective of the Nazis, Jews are a race. For example, I had an ethnically, but not religious, Jewish father and an Anglo-Catholic mother. From the perspective of Israel, I am not Jewish. Regardless of my religion, however, Hitler would have condemned me as a Jew quite fit for the concentration camps.

Frank Collin, the leader of the Nazis, believed that Jews and blacks were biologically inferior, that Jews should be stripped of their citizenship, and that blacks should be sent to Africa. Although he identified with Hitler, on occasion he denied that he wished to kill the Jews. Nonetheless, with reference to the survivors in Skokie, he said: "I hope they're terrified. I hope they're shocked. Because we're coming to get them again, I don't care if someone's mother or father or brother died in the gas chambers. The unfortunate thing is not that there were six million Jews who died. The unfortunate thing is that there were so many Jewish survivors."[11]

Initially, Collin and his group had no intention of marching in Skokie. Their base was Marquette Park in the City of Chicago, and they wanted to march there as they had on previous occasions. Marquette Park was an ethnically white neighborhood animated by a desire to keep blacks out, but surrounded by black neighborhoods. When the Martin Luther King Jr. coalition confronted the Nazi demonstrations, violence erupted. In response, the Chicago Park District attempted to stop the demonstrations by imposing a requirement that the demonstrators carry $250,000 in liability coverage. Collin's group of 10–25 members could not meet this demand, and with the help of the ACLU brought suit to challenge it.

Collin was advised that the litigation would likely take a year, and he would not march in Marquette Park in the interim for fear that he would go to jail. Instead, he struck upon the idea of carrying his demonstrations to the northern suburbs of Chicago where there were substantial concentrations of Jews. Accordingly, he sent out leaflets to approximately seven of the suburbs north of Chicago. The leaflets were headlined "WE ARE COMING" and had a swastika reaching out to batter a Jew. The leaflet said that where one finds Jews, one finds Jew haters. He sent letters to the park districts in the northern suburbs asking for permits to conduct rallies.

Skokie, of course, was one of the northern suburbs. It is a few miles north of Chicago and west of Lake Michigan. Its seventy thousand person population included approximately thirty thousand Jews including eight hundred to one thousand survivors, the largest group outside of New York City. Initially, the leaders of Skokie were inclined to let the Nazis march without fanfare. This was the recommendation of the Anti-Defamation League and of the major Jewish organizations since World War II. The strategy was to ignore them and deprive them of the publicity they sought. When word of this strategy went out to the ten synagogues in Skokie, the survivors, already a well-organized force in Skokie politics, were profoundly hostile to the proposed policy, and turned the leaders around rather quickly.

The survivors threatened violence; they said they would be out there with baseball bats. To have the Nazis march with swastikas on their home turf would be to relive the horror. Moreover, many of the survivors felt guilty that they had not done enough before. Although few would fault their past conduct, from their perspective, they would not stand idly by – this time. The leaders of Skokie became concerned about the prospects of violence and realized that they had underestimated the profound emotional impact that a march would have on the survivor population. Accordingly, they decided to stop the march. Alone among the northern suburbs, they responded to the Nazi request to march. They said no permit would be issued unless the Nazis put up a $350,000 insurance bond. But no insurance company would issue such a bond, and the Nazis did not have the money to purchase a bond even if one were available.

Collin was outraged. He decided to march in Skokie. Formally, his march was in protest of the violation of his First Amendment rights. But his overall political message was clear. He planned for the demonstrators to wear the uniforms of Nazi storm troopers and to carry signs saying "White Free Speech," "Free Speech for White Americans," and "Free Speech for the White Man."[12] A flurry of litigation ensued. Skokie sued for an injunction to stop the march, and the Nazis secured the help of the ACLU in their defense. Skokie won in the Illinois courts, but the Supreme Court of the United States reversed and sent it back down for reconsideration.[13] The Illinois court of appeals lifted the injunction against the march except for a provision prohibiting the wearing of a swastika during the march.[14] Subsequently, the Illinois Supreme Court ruled that an injunction prohibiting the swastika violated the First Amendment.[15]

Meanwhile, in addition to asking for an injunction, Skokie passed a set of ordinances designed to stop the Nazis. For our purposes, the most important of these outlawed racial slurs included the display of swastikas and Nazi uniforms. In response, the ACLU on behalf of Collin and the Nazis filed suit in federal court maintaining that the ordinances, including the racial slur ordinance, were unconstitutional. The Nazis prevailed on all counts in *Collin v. Smith*.[16]

Two arguments against the demonstration were the center of attention in the state and federal litigations. The first government interest was the prevention of violence. Skokie produced testimony that twelve thousand to fifteen thousand people were expected to participate in a counter-demonstration and that bloodshed would occur if the Nazis marched. Indeed, the mayor of Skokie testified that the situation would be uncontrollably violent. The lower court concluded that there was a virtual certainty that thousands of irate Jewish citizens would physically attack the Nazi demonstrators. In response, the Illinois appellate court ruled that the First Amendment foreclosed considering the threat of a hostile audience and the foreseeable violence flowing from that audience in determining whether an injunction should issue. In short, concerns about an uncontrollably violent audience were inadmissible.

There is much to be said for this perspective. Speculation about possible violence is easy to manufacture. Jurisdictions should strongly be encouraged to protect the speaker from a hostile audience. If it was appropriate to call out the National Guard to safeguard the equal protection interests of black children in integrating the schools, it may be appropriate to demand similar protection on behalf of First Amendment rights. On the other hand, some situations are so explosive that demanding protection may trade on an excessively sunny view of the abilities of law enforcement to prevent violence. Moreover, if substantial law enforcement resources must be committed to protect a speaker, those same resources will not be available to combat other crimes of concern in the jurisdiction. More on the violence issue after we have considered the second governmental interest.

Skokie argued that it had a right to prevent the infliction of psychic trauma on resident Holocaust survivors. The response of the federal appellate court on this issue was representative of those courts that considered the issue. It did not deny the trauma. It did not deny the intent of the Nazis to inflict the trauma. Consider the fanfare: "I hope they're terrified" and six hundred thousand "WE ARE COMING" leaflets with a swastika reaching out to batter a Jew.[17] The court suggested that these facts were beside the First Amendment point. The First Amendment point was that any shock effect "must be attributed to the content of the ideas expressed. [P]ublic expression of ideas may not be prohibited merely because the ideas are themselves offensive to some of their hearers."[18] Of course, the expression of ideas should not be prohibited merely because the ideas are themselves offensive to some hearers. The expression rolls trippingly off the tongue. It is a nice slogan and a worthy principle. But it also downplays the cruelty of the facts in Skokie. It fails to distinguish between "offense" and mental shock and suffering. It is one thing to say there should be a right to speak in ways that offend; it is far less obvious that there should be a right deliberately to inflict psychic trauma on resident Holocaust survivors just as it was not obvious that the parishioners of the Westboro Baptist should have had a right to intentionally inflict emotional distress on a father grieving the loss of a son. As Wendy Brown has observed in a different context, "when suffering as such is reduced to a problem of personal feeling, political redress of inequality is more important than calling on the victims to turn the other cheek and be tolerant. The victims do not need sensitivity training to abide harsh rhetoric. The victims deserve justice."[19]

The courts abstracted away (1) from the dangers of violence in Skokie by clinging to the principle that they would not be pushed around by a captive audience; (2) from the infliction of psychic trauma by supposing that speech inflicting trauma was an example of merely offending hearers; and (3) from the morally and constitutionally obnoxious character of the speech by characterizing it as merely the expression of ideas.[20]

Faced with this parade of abstractions, Skokie had no chance of victory. I have said enough to challenge the second abstraction, but I want to question the third abstraction and suggest in addition that if the value of the speech is low, the absolute character of the first abstraction is problematic.

To what extent does Nazi speech of this character carry First Amendment value? Is it sufficient to compensate for the infliction of trauma it was designed to achieve? One might argue that the Nazis are a political party arguing for political change and that its speech, therefore, contributes to political dialogue. Yet the Nazi objective was to create an all-white America, an America where only persons of the white race (as the Nazis defined it) could be citizens. The Nazis maintain that persons of color and Jews should not be treated with equal concern and respect. If our legal system has any claim to be legitimate, however, it must be founded on the premise that all of our citizens must be treated with equal concern and respect and that citizenship cannot be denied on racial grounds. If successful, the Nazis would create an illegitimate government. To put this another way: the best test of truth in this limited context is the system's foundational premise of equality, not whether racist speech can emerge in the marketplace of ideas.

This is not to deny that there is limited marketplace value to Nazi speech of this character. False speech, as John Stuart Mill insisted, can create a livelier impression of truth, and it can stimulate responses that contribute to the democratic dialogue. Finally, Nazi speech undeniably makes it clear that some Nazis are in our presence. But I find it hard to conclude that this limited marketplace value justifies the imposition of trauma on the survivors.

Alternatively, the Nazis could argue that preventing them from marching infringes on their liberty, self-realization, or autonomy. It is not clear why a system based on a principle of equal concern or respect would regard it as important to protect the liberty of attempting to deny the right of equal concern or respect. Moreover, it could be argued that the Nazis are estopped from making the argument. Even if the speaker would be inconsistent in demanding a right flowing from a premise the speaker otherwise denies, the system would not be inconsistent in respecting it. The system could regard it important that individuals have the autonomous right to choose the right or the wrong. But any such autonomy cannot be absolute. For example, there is no autonomous right to defame another in many circumstances. Once it is recognized that rights of liberty or autonomy cannot be absolute, the claim of liberty or autonomy cannot of itself show when it should be privileged over harms caused by its exercise. Here again, the exercise of liberty or autonomy in this circumstance can be privileged only by valuing racist speech designed to terrify and to inflict emotional distress over the special needs of the survivors.

Finally, there is a question of American identity at stake. We are told that we live in a land committed to free speech and that commitment includes protection for the speech we hate. To deny the Nazis the right to march betrays that commitment and compromises the American identity. Of course, the reason to deny the Nazi speech is not because we hate it, but because it threatens serious harm. Moreover, there is a substantial attraction to the idea of committing to free speech. But that commitment has already been compromised in many ways including defamation, obscenity, copyright, fraud, perjury, and some forms of indecent speech. If free speech can be compromised in a clash with reputation or morality, it is not clear why it should be privileged when it clashes with racial equality, order, and the avoidance of deliberately induced trauma. Moreover, if it is attractive to maintain an American identity placing emphasis on free speech, it is also attractive to foster an American identity of racial equality and an antiracist public morality. In any event, it seems indefensible to justify the tolerating of real harm in the name of symbolism.

I conclude that the racist speech in Skokie carried little First Amendment value. Some would argue, however, that the difficulties in defining racist speech are so pronounced that regulating it would imperil too much speech that is valuable. University of Hawaii Law Professor Mari Matsuda once argued in a justly famous article that racist speech should not be protected and that that speech should be defined as "speech with a message of racial inferiority, that is directed against a historically oppressed group, and that is persecutorial, hateful and degrading."[21] It seems to me that speech coming close to this danger zone is unlikely to be valuable.[22] But, on Matsuda's definition, serious writings, however flawed, arguing for racial superiority would be protected even though they might cause harm. This is not a contradiction. It is a conclusion rooted in an attempt to balance the free speech interests against the interests on the other side.

On this analysis, face-to-face racial insults directed to a member of a historically oppressed group would be unprotected as would a Ku Klux Klan rally. The proposed march in Skokie seems to me to fit into Matsuda's definition though there are arguments on the other side. On the one hand, marching as Nazi storm troopers with swastikas sends a message of racial inferiority that is persecutorial, hateful, and degrading. It might be argued, however, that Jews were once historically oppressed, but are not *oppressed* now (though elements of discrimination persist) and are pillars of the community establishment in Skokie. What tips the balance for me is the harm to the survivors and explosiveness of the violent context. If it is accepted that Nazi speech has but slight First Amendment value, then the absolute commitment to ignoring the possibility of violence created by a hostile audience strikes me as excessively precious.

Indeed, the court's refusal to consider the likelihood of violence smacks of a river boat gamble. If the Nazis had marched in Skokie, there would have been major bloodshed. Moreover, if the courts were betting that Collin would not dare to march, they were looking into a crystal ball. Collin was not the most stable of men. It turned out that his father was not only Jewish, but also a survivor of Dachau. For a child of a survivor to become a Nazi speaks volumes about his family history. Collin was ultimately convicted of child abuse and left the Nazi party. Fortunately, however, he had a lively sense of self-protection. After he won the cases and was permitted to march in Skokie, he was advised that there would be tens of thousands of counter demonstrators. Moreover, he was concerned about the possibility of snipers. Concerned about this explosive situation, the Justice Department intervened in the hopes of creating a deal to stop the march. Collin agreed that if the way were cleared for his group to march in the safer environs of Marquette Park, he would march there instead of in Skokie. The way was cleared; he declared victory and marched in Marquette Park.

I will come back to this issue in Chapter 5, but my conviction is that First Amendment law unreasonably parades in abstractions when it deals with a number of categories of speech that at least in part deserve to be unprotected. Racist speech is one of those categories. This does not mean that racist speech is always protected in the United States. If racist speech is part of an unprotected category of speech, it is not protected. Racist threats, for example, will not be protected merely because they are racist. Similarly, racist "fighting words" will not be immunized merely because they are racist. But if a municipal ordinance outlaws racist fighting words instead of outlawing fighting words altogether, the Supreme Court has declared the ordinance unconstitutional.[23] There are some complexities to the law of racist speech, but the overall approach is simple: a legislature cannot outlaw racist speech or hate speech of any kind. In this regard, the United States is the Lone Ranger. It is out of step with the rest of the world. Indeed, its opinions arrogantly do not take into account the arguments made in other jurisdictions. Nonetheless, as I have argued in previous chapters, I believe we can profit by examining the approach taken in other jurisdictions.

ALTERNATIVE APPROACHES

The United States is unique in its protection of racist speech. Its approach is rejected throughout Europe and Canada. Perhaps the best exposition for prohibiting racist speech is contained in an opinion by the Canadian Supreme Court. Canadian law prohibits the "wilful promotion of hatred, other than in private conversation, towards any section of the public distinguished by colour, race, religion, or ethnic origin."[24] *Regina v. Keegstra*[25] involved a particularly vicious case of anti-Semitism. Jews were described by him to his high school students as "treacherous," "subversive," "sadistic," "money loving," "power hungry," and "child killers."[26] According to Keegstra, the Jews created the Holocaust to gain sympathy. They were "inherently evil."[27] Keegstra expected his students to repeat these teachings in class and on exams.

In fairness, a public high school teacher in the United States could be fired for such statements. In class statements of public teachers are subject to greater regulation than statements of the ordinary citizen. But Keegstra was being prosecuted under a Canadian law applicable to the citizens at large. In the United States, the prosecution would be unconstitutional. Writing for the *Keegstra* Court, the Chief Justice of Canada, Robert George Brian Dickson, upheld the statute against a constitutional attack.

Dickson argued that the speech targeted by the statute was not merely offensive. A response of humiliation and degradation from an individual targeted by hate propaganda could reasonably be expected. In addition, the lessons drawn from advertising appeals and Hitler's emotionalism undermine any confidence that rationality invariably prevails and set the foundation for the concern that serious discord between cultural groups could be triggered or that beliefs in racial inferiority might be fostered even if not consciously accepted. These effects, he suggested, could not be lightly brushed off in a society dedicated – as Canada is – to equality and multiculturalism: "Hate propaganda seriously threatens both the enthusiasm with which the value of equality is accepted and acted upon by society and the connection of target group members to their community. ... When the prohibition of expressive activity that promotes hatred of groups identifiable on the basis of colour, race, religion, or ethnic origin is considered in light of [the Charter's direction to interpret it in a way that would strengthen and preserve Canada's multicultural heritage], the legitimacy and substantiality of the government objective is therefore considerably strengthened."[28]

Of course, these interests might be outweighed by the importance of free speech values. Here again, the Canadian Court did not settle for abstractions. It considered the arguments that hate speech could advance truth, is important for self-expression and autonomy, and is an important part of democracy. Dickson conceded that the state should not be the sole arbiter of truth, but neither should one overplay the capacity of the market rationally to evaluate false or mendacious statements. He maintained that there was very little chance that hate speech would lead to truth or a better society. "To portray such statements as crucial to truth and the betterment of the political and social milieu is therefore misguided."[29]

Dickson also conceded that the restriction limited the self-expression and autonomy of the Keegstras of the world. But the value of this exercise of expression and autonomy, he argued, must be "tempered insofar as it advocates with inordinate vitriol an intolerance and prejudice which view as execrable the process and self-development and human flourishing among all members of society."[30]

Finally, Dickson denied that the speech in question could be defended by its political relevance. The importance of political speech, Dickson argued, lies in its connection to democracy. Political speech is important not merely because it leads to better policy, but because it ensures that political participation is open to all persons who are to be afforded equal respect and dignity. So understood, hate propaganda threatens democracy and cannot be defended by resort to democratic values.

Dickson does not deny the presence of some free speech value in hate propaganda. The statute does muzzle the participation of some individuals in the political process, but he does not regard the degree of the limitation to be substantial and he denies that the speech advances truth, democracy, or self-expression and autonomy overall. Indeed, the Court maintains that the statute is itself an expression of commitment to the public values of equality and multiculturalism and the role that free speech plays in the constellation of Charter values.

Finally, Dickson acknowledges that the Canadian approach differs from the US approach. He carefully parses the US cases and concludes that the interpretation of the First Amendment is primarily driven by a purported opposition to government discriminating against speech on the basis of its content. He observes, however, that the aversion to content discrimination is not invariable. He suggests, for example, that the category of obscenity is a strong example indicating that the aversion to content discrimination is not absolute. Finally, he submits that the commitments to multiculturalism, equality, and democracy may play a stronger role in the Canadian context. Indeed, all three values appear in the Charter text, and the free speech values are required to be tested against the demands of a democratic society.

It seems clear to me that the United States could have joined Canada and other countries in condemning hate speech through law. Indeed, in 1952, the US Supreme Court declared that an Illinois statute prohibiting racist speech was constitutional.[31] That decision has been undermined by subsequent precedents, but it need not have been that way. Although the United States does not constitutionalize the value of multiculturalism, the Civil War produced the Fourteenth Amendment's commitment to equality, and one can appropriately weave a national narrative in which the country moves toward the goals of equality and democratic inclusion by repudiating slavery, obliterating Jim Crow, granting voting rights to women, and otherwise affording greater equality rights to women and to those whose sexual orientation stretches beyond the heterosexual. The country has far to go, but we do not have to achieve perfect equality before we recognize that stigmatized groups deserve protection from many forms of hateful speech.

4   SEX

Like racist speech, pornography is incompatible with the nation's commitment to equal citizenship. In addition to attacking persons on the basis of an irrelevant characteristic, pornography makes the subordinate status of women sexually attractive. Indeed, it erotizes the domination of women including violence against women. In short, the First Amendment protects a billion dollar industry glorifying and sexualizing the subordination of women. This protection is inconsistent with the kind of public culture a just society needs to foster if it is to maintain a semblance of legitimacy. Here too, it should not be surprising that pornography causes violence and discrimination against women. When pornography becomes a significant form of sex education and sexual pleasure for men, it follows that many men will regard women primarily as sex objects and seek to enjoy their pornographic fantasies in actual encounters with women. The courts have yet to provide an adequate explanation as to why this harmful speech should be tolerated, let alone constitutionally protected.[1]

A particularly important pornography case concerns an Indianapolis antipornography ordinance that was drafted by Andrea Dworkin and Catharine MacKinnon. The Indianapolis ordinance defined pornography to include the "graphic sexually explicit subordination of women through pictures and/or words that also includes" one or more types of depictions thought to be particularly problematic such as women being "presented as sexual objects who enjoy pain or humiliation" or "experience sexual pleasure in being raped"; women presented as "sexual objects tied up or cut up or mutilated or bruised or physically hurt, or as dismembered or truncated or fragmented or severed into body parts"; "presented in scenarios of degradation, injury, abasement, torture, shown as filthy or inferior, bleeding, bruised or hurt in a context that makes these conditions sexual."[2] The ordinance included other examples (some too far reaching in my view), but the common theme of the examples was that it sought to prevent the eroticization of sexual domination particularly, but not exclusively, when that domination took a violent form.

A similar ordinance had been proposed and debated in Minneapolis. In support of the ordinance, as Paul Brest and Ann Vandenberg report, many women testified that they had been forced by men to submit to degrading and painful scenarios taken from pornographic films and magazines.[3] For example, one woman testified that she was seen walking in the woods by three deer hunters who were reading pornographic magazines. One of them said, "There's a live one";[4] they took turns raping her and forced her to have oral intercourse with them. Another woman testified that the man she was living with would bring pornographic books and magazines into the bedroom and tell her that if she did not perform the sexual acts described or shown there, he would beat her and kill her. If she told anyone or tried to leave, he threatened to mutilate her. Experiences such as these were reported by many women.

Although some of the legislators had no prior conception of events such as these, they were well known to therapists. One psychotherapist testified that "It feels crazy to many of us working in therapy with offenders and victims that society is so silent on what looks to us like a clear link between written and visual images of victimization and acts of victimization."[5] Another therapist who worked with imprisoned sex offenders said that offenders "get very specific ideas in reading pornography of exactly what they will do in their crimes."[6] And Edward Donnerstein, a psychologist at the University of Wisconsin, testified that 60 percent of male college students exposed to aggressive pornography in which women were assaulted and raped reported some likelihood that they would commit rape if they could get away with it and that long-term exposure to such materials leads to even more callous attitudes toward women.[7]

The position of Dworkin and MacKinnon is that the graphic eroticization of male dominance and submission leads to the view of women as sex objects ready to be taken and used. To be sure, social science methodology is limited in its ability to show causation. Still, its findings particularly with respect to violent pornography are more than strongly suggestive.[8] But MacKinnon and Dworkin would argue that we need not wait for science to demonstrate the obvious effects that women testify to and psychotherapists discuss every day. The failure of social science to be able to demonstrate the links may say more about social science than it does about human behavior. Of course, some men do not act on their beliefs. But it is counterintuitive to suppose that many men do not act on their aggressive desires. The therapists who have dealt with imprisoned sex offenders are not speaking purely out of their imagination when they conclude that pornography has played a role in the journey these men have taken.

Even more important are the implications to be drawn from the widespread availability of pornography on the Internet.[9] It is deeply troubling that pornography has become a primary form of sex education for millions of males and females.[10] By eroticizing male domination and female subordination, the ingestion of pornography causes the internalizing of gender roles that are deeply at odds with the forms of human connection any self-respecting form of education would honor. Certainly, no public school system in America would turn to pornography as a part of its sex education program.

Equally important, it is counterintuitive to suppose that men who think of women primarily as sex objects treat women as full equals. Their contribution to intellectual discussions is unlikely to be taken seriously. Sex discrimination by many of those who are male pornography consumers might well be expected. Similarly, those female consumers who internalize this model of sexuality are torn between what it means to be "sexy" and what it means to be an equal in a democratic society. College coeds who feel compelled to wear short skirts and high heels in applying for sororities in the Ithaca winter while attending a school preparing them to be serious professionals are juggling gender roles and images that are hard to fit together either by men or women. It is hard to believe that a multibillion dollar industry contributing to this distortion of gender roles not by arguments but by erotic manipulation deserves constitutional protection.

Psychotherapist Wendy Maltz specifically argues that pornography is bad for its consumers. Maltz decades ago used to recommend pornography to her clients. She now, together with many other analysts, has concluded that pornography distorts human relationships in very serious ways. It is a major cause of divorce and relationship difficulties. Maltz describes it as a cousin to sexual abuse. She says:

> Added to my pile of concerns about porn, the realization that porn could be used as weapon against vulnerable children and women was the last straw. The clearer I became about conditions necessary for experiencing healthy sexuality – consent, equality, respect, trust, safety – the more doubt I had about advocating pornography as a sexual-enhancement product. *How can I support something that portrays sex as a commodity, people as objects, and violence, humiliation, and recklessness as exciting? What am I doing encouraging people to condition their arousal to self-centered, sensually blunted, loveless sex? Do I really want to be advocating a product that's associated with causing sexual harm and relationship problems?*
>
> My primary concern about porn wasn't that it was sexually graphic, explicit, or hot: it was that porn conveyed harmful ideas about sex and could lead to hurtful and ultimately unrewarding sexual behaviors.[11]

Pornography leads to sexual addiction and unhealthy obsessions. According to Maltz, pornography has grown from a side issue to a central issue in sexual counselling. I suppose this is not surprising. Pornography, according to Malz, is a $13 billion dollar industry in the United States and $100 billion worldwide. It accounts for one-third of all downloads. It is not surprising that psychotherapists see a rise in sexual dysfunction.

Nonetheless, many feminists argue that pornography serves a useful function. They indict the antipornography perspective as puritanical and antisex. They do this for the most part by focusing on parts of MacKinnon's proposal that could be interpreted as covering sexually explicit depictions of the missionary position, and they couple their critique with MacKinnon's well known claim that most sexual relations between men and women take place under conditions of inequality. MacKinnon might be right about that, but it is not at all clear she intends the legislation to extend to depictions of the missionary position, and, if she does, the proposal is unwarranted. Equally unwarranted, however, is the claim by pro-pornography feminists that eroticizing the combination of sex and violence (or sex that subjects women to treatment that is degrading or dehumanizing) is a form of speech that ought to be protected. Many women may have rape fantasies, but this hardly means they want to be raped. Many women may enjoy depictions of sado-masochistic sex, but this pleasure does not outweigh the harm to women generally. And it does not warrant the conclusion that pornography is harmless.

Indeed, when the Seventh Circuit Court of Appeals assessed the constitutionality of the Indianapolis ordinance in *American Booksellers Association v. Hudnut*,[12] Judge Easterbrook accepted the premises of the legislation. He concluded that "Depictions of subordination tend to perpetuate subordination. The subordinate status of women in turn leads to affront and lower pay at work, insult and injury at home, battery and rape in the streets."[13] Easterbrook did maintain that it would be possible to make a film with a pornographic scene or scenes where the film nonetheless had serious literary, artistic, political, or scientific value. But nowhere did Easterbrook contend that any sizeable fraction of pornographic films or books have *any* significant value. He might, therefore, have concluded that the statute was constitutional except for those films with serious literary, artistic, political, or scientific value. Moreover, in the absence of a woman being forced to participate in a pornographic film, supporters of the ordinance might have regarded such a ruling as a major victory since the percentage of pornographic material possessing serious value is vanishingly small – contributing little to the overall harm.

But led by Easterbrook, the court struck down the statute despite the admitted lack of value in pornographic material. Easterbrook spied a direct path from outlawing pornography to government "control of all of the institutions of culture, the great censor and director of which thoughts are good for us."[14] At another point he worried that a contrary opinion would lead to the "end of freedom of speech."[15] He suggested that the ordinance is a form of thought control that unfairly favors one point of view about sexuality over another. And he worried that the ordinance is totalitarian in that it interferes with the "absolute right to propagate opinions that the government finds wrong or hateful."[16]

Why you may wonder would approval of the ordinance lead to the control of all of the institutions of culture? Easterbrook argued that the harms associated with pornography depend on mental intermediation and that it is effective speech. The same he suggested is true of racial bigotry, anti-Semitism, violence on television, communism, religion, and reporters' biased communications.

This is the familiar stopping place argument. It supposes that if a court permits pornography to be banned, it will have opened the floodgates for the total control of the institutions of culture. The argument assumes that the judiciary is incapable of making distinctions. If the court limits valueless pornography on the ground that it creates severe harm, it would hardly be required or permitted to uphold a ban on other forms of speech without a similar showing. If a communist advocated illegal action in a manner that was directed to inciting or producing imminent lawless action and likely to produce such action even despite the presence of some value, he or she could be punished, but a ruling one way or the other on pornography would not come close to justifying a ban on communism or religion or communications resulting from reporters' biases. Canada's prohibition of pornography has hardly led it down the path to totalitarianism. Why not? Easterbrook's reaction of hysteria was specious from the start.

The same applies to his wild assertion that a contrary ruling threatens the end of freedom of speech. Easterbrook observed that much cultural stimuli provokes unconscious responses in religious ceremonies, education (including what teachers do not teach), and television scripts. He suggested that the fact that speech plays a role in social conditioning cannot be enough to justify regulation. Quite true, but beside the point. Religious ceremonies like pornography create unconscious conditioning, but unlike religious ceremonies, the pornography that should be regulated is valueless and creates substantial harm. And education and television scripts also can create unconscious conditioning, but a ban on pornography provides no warrant for similar bans on teaching or television scripts in the absence of quite exceptional circumstances.

Easterbrook also made an argument that is superficially more appealing. He maintained that point-of-view discrimination is never permitted, and he suggested that the ordinance wrongly discriminates between forms of sexuality. Depiction of certain forms of graphic, sexually explicit subordination are forbidden, but forms of graphic, sexually explicit depictions that portray women in positions of equality are lawful. Thus, from Easterbrook's perspective, the ordinance sponsors an approved view of women and sexuality while penalizing another view. This, "thought control,"[17] he suggested, is point-of-view discrimination which, he asserted, is never permitted. What Easterbrook missed is that the ordinance prohibits subordinating speech because it causes harm and does not prohibit other sexually oriented speech because it does not cause harm. This is not discrimination; to prohibit speech that does not cause harm would sacrifice liberty in pursuit of false equality. Nor is this uncommon. If I say something injurious to your reputation, you might be able to sue me for defamation, but if I say something nice about you, you could not. Is this discrimination? If I advocate illegal action, I may under certain circumstances be punished. If I advocate complying with the law, I may not be. Is this thought control? Discrimination? Of course not. You get the point.

Easterbrook's final concern was that the ordinance is totalitarian because it interferes with "our absolute right to propagate opinions that the government finds wrong or even hateful."[18] This simply mischaracterizes the ordinance. Under the ordinance, people are free to publish their opinions of women and sexuality. And the government is not prohibiting pornography because it finds it to be wrong or hateful. It is prohibiting pornography because it, as Easterbrook conceded, "leads to affront and lower pay at work, insult and injury at home, battery and rape on the streets."[19] It is "central in creating and maintaining sex as a basis of discrimination."[20]

Even if Easterbrook had not engaged in mischaracterizations and exaggerations, his rendition of First Amendment doctrine faces a serious obstacle, namely, that obscenity is beneath the protection of the First Amendment. Obscenity is defined to include prurient, patently offensive depictions or descriptions of sexual conduct that lack serious literary, artistic, political, and scientific value.[21] The problem for Easterbrook was to explain why the pornography ordinance is unconstitutional if an obscenity ordinance would not be unconstitutional. To be sure, the Indianapolis pornography ordinance does not exempt works that have serious literary, artistic, political, and scientific value.

But Easterbrook could have ruled that the ordinance was unconstitutional to the extent that it did not exempt works that had such serious value. Even there, it is hard to claim that works with serious value should be constitutionally protected if the actresses for the films have been forced to participate by their pimps.

But let us suppose we concentrate on that part of the ordinance prohibiting speech without serious value. It seems to me that the ordinance to that extent actually meets the obscenity definition. It forbids prurient, patently offensive depictions or descriptions of sexual conduct that lack serious literary, artistic, political, and scientific value. Indeed, it seems to me that the ordinance has a firmer foundation than the obscenity exception.

It has always been something of a mystery as to why the obscenity exception exists. Initially, the Court in *Roth v. United States* said that obscenity's "slight contribution to truth was outweighed by the interest in order and morality."[22] As to the interest in order, the Court did not point to any evidence in support of the claim that obscenity affected the interest in order. As to morality, the Court did not explain why obscenity was immoral. Subsequently, in *Paris Adult Theatre v. Slaton*,[23] the Court tried again to justify the obscenity exception. The issue was whether consenting adults had a constitutional right to see obscene films at the Paris Adult Theatre in Atlanta, Georgia. The Court once again said that there was an interest in order. And, it once again deferred to the legislature without offering evidence in support of the contention that obscenity presents a threat to order. It did not explain why deference was appropriate in this context, but not, for example, in cases involving advocacy of illegal action.

Getting closer to the real issue, the Court insisted that for adults to witness obscene films in a place of public accommodations intrudes on the privacy of all and that the states have "the power to make a morally neutral judgment that public exhibition of obscene material, or commerce in such material, has a tendency to injure the community as a whole … or to jeopardize … the States' 'right to maintain a decent society.'"[24]

What is missing from this account is an explanation of why adults watching obscene movies in a theater intrudes upon us all and threatens to disrupt a "decent society." And is it at all plausible that these judgments are "morally neutral"? I do not think so, but it is plain that the Court was unprepared to develop the moral underpinnings of its conclusions.

In what precise respect is obscenity immoral? Frequently, religious bodies will speak of obscenity as filthy, indecent, debasing, and unclean, but these are epithets in search of a theory.[25] A traditional theory of sexuality posits that sexual relations should take place only within a heterosexual marital relationship and, even more narrowly, only if reproduction is possible. A less sweeping view is that sexual relations should take place only in committed relationships whether straight or gay. Related to these perspectives is the suggestion that sex in uncommitted relationships reduces human beings to brute animals. They are copulating rather than making love. Perhaps the Court had this in mind when it denied that Georgia was involved in mind or thought control. It said that outlawing material lacking serious literary, artistic, political, or scientific value did not interfere with appeals to reason and the intellect. The rhetorical appeal of this suggestion is clear. It resonates with a central part of the Kantian tradition, one supposing that the dignity of human beings derives from their capacities for reason and autonomous choice, capacities that the tradition maintains distinguishes us from animals. It, however, is not clear to me that the importance of human beings is best thought of in terms of how we differ from animals. What we share with animals strikes me as important. And we might think best about what is important about human beings without thinking about animals at all.

Wholly apart from the rhetorical appeal of the observation that obscenity does not appeal to reason and intellect, the implicit suggestion that only speech appealing to reason and intellect is worthy of First Amendment protection is a nonstarter. It drastically short changes the importance of the emotional life of human beings, and it casts a blind eye to the aesthetic workings of literature, painting, and sculpture. It also fails to notice that the distinction between reason and the passions is not clear cut. Speech cannot trigger desire without passing through the cognitive screens of the intellect.

Perhaps the moral idea here is that obscenity leads to masturbation, which is self-gratification unconnected with the kind of commitment that sexuality "naturally" (?) calls for. Of course, nature in this context is a moral term, not a biological term. Human beings have the natural biological power to masturbate. Moreover, many traditional moralists do not claim that masturbation is always unhealthy or immoral, believing that it depends on the context. Indeed to take one slice of the religious population, both a majority of Catholics and a majority of Catholic priests deny that masturbation is always wrong. Indeed, prominent moral theologians sharply question the traditional teaching. Margaret A. Farley in her award-winning *Just Love: A Framework for Christian Social Ethics*[26] maintains: "Masturbation ... usually does not raise any moral questions at all. ... [T]he norms of justice ... would seem to apply to the choice of sexual self-pleasuring only insofar as this activity may help or harm, only insofar as it supports or limits, well-being and liberty of spirit. This remains largely an empirical question, not a moral one."

Finally, the masturbation theory does not line up with the definition of obscenity. If material appeals to "good old fashioned, healthy interests"[27] in sex, it is not prurient within the meaning of the law. The Court has said that only shameful or morbid material is prurient. "Normal" material is not. Obviously, sexually explicit material appealing to normal interests in sex can play a masturbatory role. Indeed, for most people, it would be more effective in that respect than speech depicting shameful or morbid sex. It would appear that obscenity portraying sex that the Court finds disgusting is unprotected. But the existence of disgust is not a substitute for a moral argument. Many members of the Court might be disgusted by gay sex, but it would be odd to find that portrayals of constitutionally protected sex would be obscene without a showing of harm from those portrayals.

It should now be clear why there is a stronger case for a pornography exception than an obscenity exception. Obscenity regulation licenses point-of-view discrimination. It demands that distinctions be made between normal and abnormal sex; it insists that distinctions be made between speech that is patently offensive and speech that is not; it requires that distinctions be made between types of speech that have serious value and those that do not. It gives the lie to Easterbrook's suggestion that point-of-view discrimination is not permitted. Moreover, the obscenity exception has been supported without a showing of harm or a theory of morality that connects with the definition of the exception. By contrast, the pornography ordinance condemns speech because of the harm it causes. The case for its regulation is far stronger than the case for regulating obscenity.

Indeed, the case against pornography has firm moral roots. Even if sex for pleasure outside committed relationships is not immoral, it is far more difficult to defend the use of sex for the shameless exploitation and degradation of others, typically women. Pornography, as described in the ordinance, depicts, encourages, and often actually involves precisely such exploitation and degradation. If obscenity is an exception to First Amendment protection, it is hard to understand why those forms of subordinating sexual speech lacking value should merit protection.

Of course, there are many who think that obscenity should not be an exception to First Amendment protection. There are many who think that the term obscenity is too vague to satisfy First Amendment standards. Yet most of them do not believe the distribution of obscene material to children or to unconsenting adults should be protected. In order to enforce limitations on such distribution, the vagueness of the obscenity concept would have to be tolerated. The First Amendment does not bar all vague regulations. Otherwise defamation law with its reliance on terms like opinion, public figure, and defamation would not pass legal muster. Are these terms vague? Of course. But First Amendment law tolerates some vagueness when it is appropriate to do so. Justice Brennan thought obscenity law was too vague to justify bans on the distribution of the material to consenting adults, but clear enough to justify a ban on the distribution of obscene material to children and unconsenting adults. This is a reasonable compromise and it probably represents the overriding view of those on the left.

But pornography gives rise to an interesting split on the left. For many years led by the ACLU, the standard liberal position was that obscenity should be protected. By arguing that pornography contributed in significant ways to sex discrimination and sexual assaults, Catharine MacKinnon shattered this unanimity among liberals.

The split among liberals that interests me is this: there are some who I think of as in the Kantian tradition in the respect that they are deontological, who think the facts do not matter. There is an absolute right for people to decide whether they want to read this material (leaving child pornography to the side), and the government should deal with sex discrimination and sexual assaults by outlawing them. Others who I put in the John Stewart Mill tradition believe that if pornographic material harms the interests of women in the ways charged that it should be outlawed. The current state of American law is that obscene materials can be prohibited, however vague the definition of those materials might be, because of unspecified notions of privacy, decency, with a confused moral perspective lurking in the background. On the other hand, materials causing harm to women can form the basis of a multibillion dollar constitutionally protected industry.

ALTERNATIVE APPROACHES

Canada has a more attractive perspective toward sexually oriented speech than that on offer either in the Seventh Circuit's approach to pornography or the Supreme Court's approach to obscenity. In fact, Canada has transformed its obscenity statute into something like the Indianapolis antipornography ordinance. Unlike the Court in *Hudnut*, however, the Canadian Supreme Court has not resorted to wild exaggerations. It does not see a direct path from outlawing pornography to government "control of all of the institutions of culture, the great censor and director of which thoughts are good for us." It does not see the "end of freedom of speech," or a form of thought control that unfairly favors one point of view about sexuality over another. Still less does it see the ordinance as totalitarian. It does recognize that the Canadian definition of obscenity standing by itself needs to be confined and rendered somewhat more precise.

Canada's most significant obscenity case involved the Avenue Video Boutique in Winnipeg, Manitoba, a store that rented and sold "hardcore" videotapes and magazines as well as sexual paraphernalia. Like the Paris Adult Theatre in Georgia, neither nonconsenting adults nor children were exposed to the material. The store was for private members only and did not admit persons under the age of eighteen years. Nonetheless, in 1987, Donald Butler, the store owner, and Norma McCord, an employee, were arrested for selling obscene materials and possessing obscene materials for sale.

In *Regina v. Butler*,[28] they challenged the constitutionality of the Canadian definition of obscenity as it appeared in section 163(8) of the Canadian Criminal Code. That provision defined obscenity to include "any publication a dominant characteristic of which is the undue exploitation of sex, or of sex and any one or more of the following subjects, namely crime, horror, cruelty, and violence."[29] The Canadian Supreme Court rebuffed the challenge in an opinion by Justice John Sopinka who had come to the Court only four years before directly from private practice.[30]

Sopinka recognized that obscenity is the kind of term like many others in the law that escapes precise technical definition. Standards, such as undue exploitation, he said, are an "inevitable part of the law,"[31] and they can be given sensible meanings through the case law. For example, material could not be undue exploitation as a matter of law if it possessed scientific, literary, or artistic merit, and this "artistic defense"[32] must be generously construed. The term undue exploitation was to be understood by national community standards, and the question was not what Canadians would think it right for themselves to see, but what they would not tolerate others seeing. What would justify this lack of tolerance? Sopinka argued that the kinds of materials that would justify this lack of tolerance are those materials that are harmful to society, particularly to women. He distinguished between three classes of material: (1) explicit sex with violence; (2) explicit sex without violence but which subjects people to treatment that is degrading or dehumanizing; and (3) explicit sex without violence that is neither degrading nor dehumanizing. Sopinka argued that, in the absence of using children in the production, material in the third category would not qualify as undue exploitation of sex. But, as I read him, he argued that material in the first and second categories insofar as they are degrading or dehumanizing would fail the community standards test provided that they cannot produce an artistic defense and provided the exploitation of sex is the dominant theme of the material.

What kinds of material are degrading or dehumanizing? Drawing from another Canadian case, Sopinka described them:

> They are exploited, portrayed as desiring pleasure from pain, by being humiliated and treated only as an object of male domination sexually, or in cruel or violent bondage. Women are portrayed in these films as pining away their lives waiting for a huge male penis to come along, on the person of a so-called sex therapist, or window washer, supposedly to transport them into complete sexual ecstasy. Or even more false and degrading, one is led to believe that their raison d'etre is to savour semen as a life elixir, or that they secretly desire to be taken forcibly by a male.[33]

Or to put it another way, "Women, particularly, are deprived of human character or identity and are depicted as sexual playthings, hysterically and instantly responsive to male sexual demands. They worship male genitals and their own value depends on the quality of their genitals and breasts."[34]

Sopinka argued that materials such as these should not be protected under the Canadian Charter of Rights and Freedoms because of the harm they cause and not merely because they were immoral. In arriving at the standard of proof for determining the existence of and extent of harm, Sopinka argued that a high standard was not needed because obscenity was of low free speech value. In his view, pornography did not contribute to truth or participation in the political process. It did contribute to individual self-fulfillment, he admitted, but only in its most "base aspect" of physical arousal. Moreover, he pointed to the purely economic (as opposed to artistic) motivation for the publication. This analysis sidestepped that of some civil liberties groups who suggest that pornography prompts us to question conventional notions of sexuality and is therefore political in character – or at least importantly social, but this is hardly the purpose nor a common effect of the material. Moreover, from the Canadian perspective, any such value would need to be weighed in the overall balance.

As previously mentioned, Sopinka was prepared to protect some erotic material, though not all. Although he made the distinction turn on the harm caused, it seems clear that moral judgments are at play as well. The denigration of pornography as appealing to baser forms of self-fulfillment rings of moral judgment. Moreover, it seems clear that the condemnation of speech that eroticizes the domination, degradation, and dehumanization of women is partially moral. Sopinka did not deny this. Although he denied that speech could be restricted exclusively for moral reasons, he maintained that Parliament could legislate on the basis of a fundamental conception of morality in order to safeguard values "integral to a free and democratic society."[35] And this, he suggested, is particularly appropriate when the moral disapprobation has a basis in Charter values such as the commitment to gender equality. Given that pornography was well outside the core of free speech values, he argued that it was appropriate to give more deference to claims about the harm of pornography than would make sense if the speech carried greater value.

In terms of the harm, Sopinka recognized that the harm to society particularly to women was not capable of exact proof and the social science was inconclusive, but there was a substantial body of opinion as to the harm represented by task forces in Canada, the United States, Australia, and New Zealand, and the concern was sufficiently rational as to justify prohibition.

I find much to admire in this opinion: the sensitivity to equality, the understanding that vagueness cannot be wholly drenched from legitimate laws, and the recognition that morality can rightly play a role in supporting the regulation of speech though not a sufficient one. Most of all, I appreciate the comfortable discernment that the value of speech must be balanced against the harm the state wishes to avoid in order to arrive at a sensible judgment. These are lessons the United States has yet to learn.

5   VIOLENCE

Pornography is not the only form of entertainment involving violence or depictions of violence. Pornography is part of a larger entertainment industry that includes some forms of violence or depictions of violence that deserve no constitutional protection. Indeed, I count their protection as exhibit A in support of the contention that the United States has succumbed to an indefensible form of First Amendment idolatry. In particular, I have in mind the depictions of actual animal cruelty for the entertainment of consumers and the sale of gruesomely violent video games to children. These forms of entertainment are harmful in their creation (or lead to harm), are themselves morally dubious, and are bereft of redeeming value. Despite this, the Supreme Court treats these forms of entertainment as valuable speech, speech that cannot be regulated without meeting extremely demanding requirements.

Turning first to depictions of animal cruelty, the federal statute prohibiting the depiction of animal cruelty for entertainment purposes is based on the moral view that it is wrong to treat animals in an inhumane way, and it is wrong to market displays of their suffering for commercial gain. The United States has much to be ashamed of with regard to its treatment of animals. It permits unspeakable cruelty in the treatment of and slaughtering of animals for food. The consumption of animals treated in this way raises serious moral issues (indeed, many argue that the consumption of animals itself raises serious issues apart from cruelty in their treatment). Many consume meat *despite* knowledge of the horrible ways in which they have been treated. Regardless of the morality of that consumption, it strikes me that those who buy video tapes of animal cruelty precisely because they *enjoy* witnessing the torture of animals are sick, sadistic (or masochistic), and twisted.

Immanuel Kant once argued that the immorality of animal cruelty was not based on the suffering of animals, but on the brutalization of human beings.[1] Kant thought we owed no direct duties to animals because they lacked human dignity. This strikes me as a morally impoverished view. But Kant was right to argue that human participation in cruelty to animals is brutalizing and inconsistent with human dignity. In addition to the needless harm to innocent animals, the commercialization of the depictions of animal cruelty appeals to the baser side of human beings, a side inconsistent with their dignity. Of course, it can be argued that the latter concern is excessively paternalistic and not within the scope of appropriate government concern. As I suggested in the last chapter, however, when the government is regulating harmful conduct, the morality of that conduct is appropriately taken into account. My emphasis in this chapter will be to show how the Court reinforced and strengthened the nearly automatic privileging of speech over other interests.

You will recall that in prior chapters, I have argued that the Court has inflated the value of speech involving intentional infliction of emotional distress, invasion of privacy, and the undermining of fair trials. In considering depictions of animal cruelty for entertainment purposes and the sale of violent video games to children, the Supreme Court has gone even further and concocted an approach that assumes categories of speech possess important value even when the categories of speech are without any value that would be recognized by a reasonable person.

United States v. Stevens[2] was the first case to adopt this approach. The federal law at issue in *Stevens* criminalized the creation, sale, or possession for commercial gain in interstate commerce of depictions of animal cruelty that was defined to cover those depictions in which a living animal was "intentionally maimed, mutilated, tortured, wounded, or killed" if the conduct violated federal or state law in which the creation, sale, or possession took place. Such depictions, however, were exempted from the statute's reach if they had serious religious, political, scientific, educational, journalistic, historical, or artistic value.[3]

Although the *Stevens* case involved vicious dog fights, the federal law was initially drafted in response to so-called crush videos. In those videos, women are shown from the waist down (making police identification difficult) torturing small animals including mice, hamsters, cats, and dogs by crushing them with high heels. In some of the videos the women can be heard talking to the animals in a dominatrix patter. The painful cries of the animals can also be heard. Surprisingly, there are not only persons who have a sexual fetish for these materials, but enough of them to make for a profitable business. But the market for depictions of animal cruelty was broader than crush videos. The market embraced everything from cock fights to dog fights, and the legislation was designed to combat such commerce as well. As written, however, the statute read without attention to its obvious purpose, could be interpreted to regard films of hunting out of season as a core violation if the films were sold for commercial purposes, a violation that could be cured only if the serious value test were met. Given the origin and purpose of the statute, it seems clear that the statute was designed to outlaw those depictions of animal cruelty marketed to appeal to the sadistic or masochistic entertainment interests of a target audience. It did not mean to include, for example, the films of the humane society as a violation that could be rescued only by the serious value test. Nonetheless, the Court read the statute in a wooden way, but it is not clear the result would have been different if it had read the statute in a way that more closely fit its purpose.

In the actual case, the defendant Robert J. Stevens did not sell crush videos, but he did run a business, Dogs of Velvet and Steel, and an associated website in which he sold video tapes of pit bulls fighting each other and attacking other animals in gory, gruesome, and bloody fights sometimes to the death.[4] The Humane Society in its brief to the Court submitted a DVD that showed "an orchestrated fight to the death where tortured dogs and puppies rip the skin and ears off their opponents, and bite through each other's ears, paws, neck, and genitals in a desperate attempt to survive. To avoid impending death, one dog rips out the trachea of the other, leaving the dead dog sprawled on the ground covered in blood."[5] In preparation for these fights, the Humane Society reported that the dogs endure physical torture and emotional manipulation throughout their lives in ways that predispose them to violence. They are fed hot peppers and gunpowder. They are prodded with sticks; they are shocked with electricity.

Of course, these dog fights are illegal in every state. People are not admitted to the fights without being screened by a trusted associate. The results of these illegal fights are reported in underground publications such as the *Sporting Dog Journal*. These reports help facilitate the gambling that surrounds these events. The *Journal* also contains information about dogs that assists in creating and promoting matches as well as advertisements for dog fighting videos. Of course, subscriptions for the *Journal* are carefully screened in an effort to shield the dog fighting industry from police investigations.

Nonetheless, Pennsylvania State trooper, Timothy C. Knapp, acting as an undercover agent, obtained a subscription. Working with a postal inspector, Knapp eventually ordered three videos: Pick-A-Winna, Japan Pit Fights (dog fighting is apparently legal in Japan), and Catch Dogs and Country Living. The Pick-A-Winna video sold for $25; the Japan Pit Fights for $45; the price for Catch Dogs does not appear to be in the record. Records found in the home of Stevens indicated that he earned more than $55,000 in video sales over a twenty eight month period. The first two videos involved typical pit bull fights with the dogs heard screaming in pain in the Japan video. The Catch Dogs video featured a pit bull ripping the face of a hog apart. On the basis of these videos, Stevens was convicted on three counts of violating 18 U.S.C. § 48.

On appeal, Stevens argued that the statute was unconstitutional. In resisting this argument, the government argued that depictions of animal cruelty are of minimal constitutional value and that any value in such depictions was greatly outweighed by the government interests. The Court led by Chief Justice Roberts rejected the idea that First Amendment protection should be determined by balancing the value of the speech against the interests in regulating the speech. Indeed, Roberts insisted that the government's argument was "startling and dangerous."[6]

Instead of balancing, Roberts stated that the categories of unprotected speech were confined to a few limited areas: "From 1791 to the present … the First Amendment has 'permitted restrictions in a few limited areas' and has never 'include[d] a freedom to disregard these traditional limitations.'"[7] These "historic and traditional categories long familiar to the bar"[8] were said to include obscenity, defamation, incitement, and speech integral to criminal conduct. He concluded that the Court had no authority to add new categories of unprotected speech to those that were historically and traditionally unprotected.

Nonetheless, he suggested that a proposed new category of unprotected speech would be subjected to existing doctrine. Under that doctrine, a category of otherwise protected speech could lose protection if the government could show that prohibition was necessary to achieve a compelling state interest (the so-called strict scrutiny test). In other words, the categories of unprotected speech are forever frozen, and speech regardless of its lack of value will be protected under our Constitution unless a quite demanding test is satisfied.

A number of observations come to mind in responding to Justice Roberts's renunciation of balancing in favor of a historical approach. First, there was nothing at all "startling" about the government's call for balancing. Our prior chapters have discussed areas in which speech has been unduly protected, and this is one of them. But, as the *Stevens* case recognizes, there are a number of categories of speech that are not protected under the First Amendment. Occasionally, the Court has explicitly recognized that in determining that speech is unprotected, it is balancing speech against a governmental interest. More often, the Court in justifying rules of nonprotection of speech has not been explicit but has relied on a number of factors: the importance of the state interest, the extent to which the regulation advances the state interest, the possibility of less restrictive alternatives to restricting speech, the extent to which the regulation impinges on free speech or press values, and the nature of the free speech values implicated. So, in the defamation context, the Court considers reputation and free press to be important and fashions a complex set of rules designed to accommodate both. In the advocacy of illegal action context, the Court recognizes self-expression values, political, and cathartic values and fashions a test designed to protect those values insofar as the speech does not become dangerous. In the so-called fighting words context (which at least includes words likely to cause a fight), the Court is concerned about order and dignitary injury and obviously believes no serious First Amendment values are present. In the obscenity context, the

Court is rather fuzzy about the importance of the state interests, but obviously is not impressed with the First Amendment values involved. Finally, in the copyright context, the Court seeks to protect incentives to produce and safeguard against unjust enrichment while permitting the dissemination of ideas and fair use of some expression, but it generally does not believe that the copying of expression is rich with First Amendment value and offers only limited protection for such copying.

Roberts conceded that balancing language explicitly existed in some cases, but he said that the Court had not said balancing was the test to be used in those cases; the Court had merely concluded that the free speech interest was outweighed by other interests in those cases. I do not dispute that characterization of the Court's language in the prior cases, but the same could be said for references to history in prior cases, and in many cases no reference to a historical approach appears at all. The truth is that the Court has been irresponsibly sloppy about its general approach to the creation of unprotected categories of speech. Nonetheless, as I have argued for more than thirty years, the only way to understand the cases is to recognize that balancing has permeated the interpretive exercise. That Roberts would claim to be "startled" is itself startling.

Second, as I will elaborate in Chapter 10, the idea that there were a few limited categories of unprotected speech at the time of the founding is simply false. Leaving that aside for later discussion, it must be said that many of the current categories of unprotected speech are defined in ways that lack a historical pedigree of any kind. The categories of unprotected obscenity, defamation, and incitement, as defined today, are entirely different from the time of their original formulation. Indeed, their most recent definitions have been refined in a line of cases beginning in the 1970s. To be sure, these are more protective now than they were before, but they are the product of balancing, not a historical test. Moreover, there are categories of unprotected speech that were wholly unknown to the Framers and not developed until the twentieth century.

Snyder v. Phelps, which we discussed in Chapter 1, is an example.[9] In that case, the Court did not stop to inquire whether the intentional infliction of emotional distress through speech was one of those exceptions to First Amendment protection that were part of a long-settled tradition. If it had, it would have needed to explore what a long-settled tradition might be, and it would have needed to determine whether a long-settled tradition distinguished between infliction of emotional distress on public issues and infliction of emotional distress on private issues. Although the Court has protected some forms of intentional infliction of emotional distress, the Court has not disposed of this category of unprotected speech altogether even though the historical test would seem to require its burial. As we will see, the Court recently did not question federal statutes of even more recent vintage that could not possibly meet the historical test. Although Roberts renounces balancing as "free-floating,"[10] "highly manipulable,"[11] and even "dangerous,"[12] balancing has been routinely used not only to evaluate time, place, and manner regulations of protected speech, but also to determine the scope of categories of protected and unprotected speech. Finally, in this connection, the strict scrutiny test is itself a balancing test and it surely could not meet the historical test. Indeed, so far as I can determine, the strict scrutiny test was not used in the First Amendment context until the 1960s.[13]

Third, the historical test imagines that the Framers were intent on freezing the set of then unprotected categories. If the Framers thought that certain categories of speech should not be protected under the idea of freedom of speech, however, presumably they would not want similar categories to be protected. The categories ultimately developed under a common law process; there is little reason to believe that the Framers would want the common law process to be abandoned. Indeed, given that, there is good reason to believe that the "historical" approach is inherently *unhistorical.* In *Stevens,* the government argued that if it was constitutional to outlaw obscenity, it is constitutional to outlaw depictions of animal torture. Under the historical test, this argument is out of bounds. But it fails to credit the wisdom underlying the unprotected categories. It leaves the law in a chaotic state in which some categories are protected for no better reason than the technology giving rise to them was not in existence at an earlier point in our history.

Fourth, as I have suggested, the historical test assumes that proposed new categories of unprotected speech have enormous value.

They cannot be prohibited unless the government can meet the strict scrutiny test, which the Court well knows is almost impossible to meet.

Regrettably, the Court struck down the animal cruelty statute without reaching the question whether Stevens's activity could be regulated under the strict scrutiny test. It did so by interpreting the statute in a rather bizarre way. Recall that the statute prohibited depictions in which a living animal is intentionally maimed, mutilated, tortured, wounded, or killed. Roberts argued that wounding or killing an animal does not necessarily involve cruelty, and he is right. But, as the government observed, the clear purpose of the act is to reach only the wounding or killing of an animal that does involve cruelty, and the statute makes this clear by banning depictions of animal cruelty. Roberts refused to interpret the wounding or killing prongs of the definition in light of the clear congressional purpose and from there it was easy to argue that the statute was impermissibly overbroad. Before he was done, he imagined that the statute covered hunting magazines (despite the fact that the House Report specifically stated that the statute did not cover hunting!). Having rewritten the statute to cover abundant amounts of material that were never intended to be covered, the Chief Justice, who masquerades as an apostle of judicial restraint, had no difficulty in declaring that the statute was overbroad. Nonetheless, he did pause to observe that the Court had not decided whether a statute limited to crush videos or other forms of extreme animal cruelty could pass constitutional muster under strict scrutiny.

The same approach by the Court mars its handling of legislation designed to combat the marketing of violent video games to children. Of course, many video games are unremarkable. But some quite popular video games are shamefully violent. In Manhunt, the "player sneaks around a 3-D environment and commits heinous acts of murder as a sadistic form of entertainment. Decapitation, steel-object-to-the-brain impaling and even the ability to jam a sickle up an unsuspecting victim's ass" is part of the Manhunt experience.[14] Another popular game called Postal calls on players to "burn people alive with gasoline or napalm; decapitate people with shovels and have dogs fetch their severed heads; beat police to death while they beg for mercy; kill bald unshaven men wearing pink dresses (in an 'expansion pack' called *Fog Hunter*); slaughter nude female zombies; urinate on people to make them vomit; and shoot players with a shotgun that has been silenced by ramming it into a cat's anus."[15] And in Postal 2, players were called upon to step up the violence by

> torturing images of young girls, setting them on fire, and bashing their brains out with a shovel, for no reason other than to accumulate more points in the game. In one scene in [Postal 2], the player (who sees through the eyes of the shooter) looks through a scope of an assault rifle and sees a very realistic image of a person's face. The player then shoots the victim in the kneecap. As the player watches the victim attempt to crawl away, moaning in pain, the player pours gasoline on the victim and lights him on fire. As the burning victim continues to crawl, the player urinates on the victim, and says "That's the ticket." After noting that it "smells like chicken," the player again looks at the victim through the scope on the gun, and again sees a realistic human face, on fire, crawling toward him. The player then shoots the victim in the face, which turns into charred remnants of a human image. In another scene, the player hits a woman in the face with a shovel, causing blood to gush from her face. As she cries out and kneels down, the player hits her twice more with the shovel, this time decapitating her. The player then proceeds to hit the headless corpse several more times, each time propelling the headless corpse through the air while it continues to bleed.[16]

To be sure, the industry has a rating system designed to advise what games are appropriate at various age levels. Under this system, an M rating signals that a game is not appropriate for a child under the age of seventeen. But this system fails to operate well in practice. The Federal Trade Commission found that 69 percent of unaccompanied children between the ages of thirteen to sixteen were able to buy an M-rated game and 56 percent of thirteen-year-olds were able to buy such games.[17]

In response to the commerce in violent video games, California passed an act that prohibited the sale of particularly gruesome games to minors and required that such games be labeled "18." Specifically, the California law covered games

> 'in which the range of options available to a player includes killing, maiming, dismembering, or sexually assaulting an image of a human being, if those acts are depicted' in a manner that '[a] reasonable person, considering the game as a whole, would find appeals to a deviant or morbid interest in minors,' that is 'patently

offensive to prevailing standards in the community as to what is suitable for minors,' and that 'causes the game as a whole to lack serious literary, artistic, political, or scientific value for minors.'

The law did not prohibit the sale of such games to parents for the use of their children. It did not prohibit the playing of such games by minors. Rather the law was specifically tailored to prevent the sale of such games to minors.[18]

The video game industry challenged this law on First Amendment grounds, and the case ultimately landed in the Supreme Court. In *Brown v. Entertainment Merchants Association*,[19] Justice Scalia upheld the industry's First Amendment claim.[20] After the *Stevens* case involving depictions of animal cruelty, the argument was easy to make. Like depictions of animal cruelty, there was no history of prohibiting violent video games, however gruesome and inappropriate for children they might be. To be sure, there was a history of restricting the sale of obscene materials to minors, and the statute closely tracked the obscenity definition for minors though it substituted violence for sex.

Of course, there is not the slightest evidence that the Framers of the Constitution would have thought that violent video games should enjoy First Amendment protection. Similarly, there is no reason to believe that those who developed the obscenity exception thought that it should be restricted to sexual conduct when there are good reasons to expand the category to cover prurient violence. Scalia, however, slammed the door on any attempt to expand the obscenity category to cover violence, and he offered no rationale for the conclusion that commerce in graphic sexual materials was somehow more problematic than traffic in graphic violent materials. He, therefore, concluded that the statute could be justified only if it met the strict scrutiny standard.

Before commenting on the Court's strict scrutiny discussion, I want to make some observations about Justice Alito's concurring opinion, joined by Chief Justice Roberts. Alito concurred because he believed that the statute was unconstitutionally vague. You will recall that a central theme of my argument is that the Court engages in First Amendment idolatry. That idolatry is obvious in the frozen categories approach employed in *Brown* and its predecessor *Stevens*. But I think it is implicit in Alito's opinion as well.

Alito argues that California's violence statute is less clear than similar statutes prohibiting the sale of obscene material to minors. Given that those statutes have existed at least since 1968 when the Court upheld the child obscenity definition,[21] the courts have had considerable time to clarify the meaning of the obscenity statutes. And, of course, Alito is right that marketers will have difficult judgments to make in determining what is and what is not covered. As I have suggested, it is a pleasant falsehood that vagueness is impermissible in First Amendment law. Vagueness simply cannot be wrung out of the fabric of any area of law. Consider speech that assaults the reputation of a person. The concept of defamation is sometimes clear in application, but often not. Who is a public figure? Again, sometimes the application is clear, but often it is not. What is negligence? All these concepts are vague in application and none of them has been found to be unconstitutionally vague.

Alito shows that there is vagueness in the California statute, but he does not explore further. What are the consequences of the vagueness? Presumably, a merchant will steer clear of the danger zone. In other words, a merchant will avoid selling to minors materials that could be found by a " '[a] reasonable person, considering the game as a whole, would find appeals to a deviant or morbid interest in minors,' that is 'patently offensive to prevailing standards in the community as to what is suitable for minors,' and that 'causes the game as a whole to lack serious literary, artistic, political, or scientific value for minors.' " In so doing, the merchant might refuse to sell to a minor material that would, if litigated, fall outside the statute. So what? First, the parents could buy the game for the child in any event. Second, it is hard to believe that the minor would be missing material that is important from a First Amendment perspective. In other words, we are talking about the sale only to minors of speech of questionable value that the minors could obtain with parental consent. Finally, vagueness in this context seems far less damaging than the vagueness permeating the defamation context where valuable speech can easily be chilled. By cutting short his exploration of the vagueness argument, Alito assumes, but does not demonstrate, that the speech that might be chilled is valuable. He thus flirts with a form of First Amendment idolatry.

If Alito's assumption that the speech at issue is valuable is not explicit, Scalia's assumption is quite apparent. The very purpose of requiring the government to meet a demanding test to justify its regulation of speech is to protect valuable speech. Indeed, Scalia went out of his way to insist that the strict scrutiny test is extremely difficult to meet, and, therefore, just how high on the value pedestal violent video games are presumed to be. Indeed, Scalia not only said that the strict scrutiny standard is demanding, he also observed that "'It is rare that a regulation restricting speech because of its content will ever be permissible.'"[22] One might think, however, that this might be one of those rare cases. The American Academy of Pediatrics, the American Academy of Child & Adolescent Psychiatry, the American Psychological Association, the American Medical Association, the American Academy of Family Physicians, and the American Psychiatric Association have issued statements deploring the developmental effects of violent video games on children.[23] The American Psychological Association and the American Academy of Pediatrics in separate statements have expressed the view that some of the effects on aggression are unique to interactive violent video games as opposed to the depiction of violence in other media.[24]

Scalia was unimpressed. In contrast to the conclusions of the professionals,[25] he engaged in an independent amateur analysis and declared that his nearly impossible standard of proof had not been met. So too, the claim that social science evidence demonstrates that violent video games cause violence has not impressed the lower courts. My reaction to this is threefold. First, we should not have to wait for social scientists to meet the difficult task of showing causation in a multifactor environment. It is massively counterintuitive to claim that games like Manhunt and Postal do not desensitize children to the horror of violence. Second, even if such games did not cause violence, it is dubious that they contribute in a positive way to the development of children. Indeed, some might argue that parents who permit their children to play such games are guilty of child neglect. Finally, the creation of a high standard of proof assumes the value of this speech, a wholly unsupported assumption.

Scalia argues that even if the conclusions of mental health professionals were correct, the law is under inclusive in that parents can purchase the material for their children. The latter is, of course, true. California compromised by allowing parents to permit their children to play these violent games. But, again, that has constitutional force, if, but only if, the material is regarded as being constitutionally valuable in the first place. When California is precluded from attacking a problem that medical professionals regard as serious, even in a compromised way, I think it is fair to conclude that the frozen categories approach to First Amendment interpretation is a crippling barrier to the implementation of wise public policy.

Fortunately, there are some signs that the frozen categories approach will not invariably be employed. Cracks in support of the approach were exposed in *United States v. Alvarez*.[26] The case arose out of statements made by board member Xavier Alvarez at his first public meeting of the Claremont, California Three Valley Water District Board. He introduced himself in this way: "I'm a retired marine of 25 years. I retired in the year 2001. Back in 1987, I was awarded the Congressional Medal of Honor. I got wounded many times by the same guy."[27] These statements were false, and Alvarez was indicted under the Stolen Valor Act, 18 U.S.C. § 704, which provides that "Whoever falsely represents himself or herself, verbally or in writing, to have been awarded any decoration or medal authorized by Congress for the Armed Forces of the United States ... shall be fined under this title, imprisoned not more than six months, or both."[28] The Act further provides that if the false representation relates to an award of the Congressional Medal of Honor, the possible imprisonment could rise to a year. Alvarez challenged the statute on First Amendment grounds.[29]

Four justices on the Court led by Justice Kennedy stuck with the frozen categories approach to interpreting the First Amendment. They said: although falsely making such claims is indefensible, there is no long history of outlawing false autobiographical statements of military honors, and prohibiting such representations is not necessary to achieve a compelling governmental interest. That was not a difficult argument to make. But an embarrassing challenge to the frozen categories approach was presented in the case. It turns out that other significant statutes outlaw the making of false statements. In particular, 18 U.S.C. §1001 forbids the making of materially false statements to government agents whether or not the misrepresentation misleads.

The statute is a major tool in the arsenal of federal law enforcement. For example, Martha Stewart and thousands of others have gone to jail and/or been forced to plea because of the statute. There is no way the Court will declare that statute unconstitutional, and the plurality made clear that it was not questioning 18 U.S.C. §1001. But it is hard to see how those justices could uphold that statute using the frozen categories approach. It meets neither the long history test, nor the strict scrutiny test. It richly demonstrates the need for more sensitive interpretive tools than the frozen categories approach can provide.

Fortunately, Justice Breyer, concurring, joined by Justice Kagan, appreciated the deficiencies associated with the frozen categories method. Instead of strict scrutiny, they argued for intermediate scrutiny or proportionality. In other words, they thought the Court should take account of the seriousness of the speech-related harm the provision will likely cause, the nature and importance of the provision's countervailing objectives, the extent to which the provision will tend to achieve those objectives, and whether there are other, less restrictive ways of doing so. In other words, Justice Breyer insisted on the kind of balancing that the majority in *Stevens* tried to marginalize with the epithet of "startling and dangerous." Breyer wisely observed that some such approach is necessary if the First Amendment is to offer proper protection in the many instances in which a statute adversely affects constitutionally protected interests but warrants neither near-automatic condemnation (as strict scrutiny implies) nor near-automatic approval (as is implicit in rational basis review).

The opinion of Justice Alito, joined by Justices Scalia and Thomas, dissenting, is more ambiguous, but I do not think it sits easily with the frozen category approach. Although General George Washington warned of punishment for those who wore a badge of honor that had not been earned, there is obviously no First Amendment tradition holding that lies about military honors are a category of unprotected speech. Alito argued, however, that the First Amendment has accepted punishment for fraud and defamation that do reach back to the founding, for false statements of fact regulated by tort law of comparatively recent vintage, and for violations of twentieth-century statutory law prohibiting false statements of fact under certain circumstances such as 18 U.S.C. §1001. He also pointed to a line of cases beginning in the

1960s denying the First Amendment value of false statements of fact. Alito's arguments raise interesting issues in support of the view that lies about military honors or knowingly false statements that inflict some sort of harm without some supporting interest should be regarded as an unprotected category. But my point is that he was not relying on the frozen category approach. He relied on recent common law, statutes, and cases not connected to a long historical tradition. Although fraud and defamation were categories of unprotected speech at the beginning of the republic, the Stolen Valor Act does not involve fraud or defamation. Moreover, the frozen category approach does not authorize drawing analogies from historical categories. I do not regard what Alito is doing as sinful. Indeed, like Breyer's approach, it is a sensible way to argue. I welcome the departure from the approach taken in *Stevens* and *Brown*.

Nonetheless, I wonder whether much optimism is warranted. Justices Breyer, Kagan, Scalia, and Thomas joined Roberts's opinion in *Stevens*. Similarly, with the exception of the vagueness opinion by Alito and Roberts, the various opinions in *Brown* either endorse Scalia's majority opinion and its frozen category approach or are compatible with it. Even Breyer applies strict scrutiny though he maintains the test is satisfied. There is no telling which direction the Court will go in future cases. Even if the frozen category approach is rejected, as we have seen in prior chapters, there is every reason to think that the Court will inflate the value of speech at the expense of other significant interests.

ALTERNATIVE APPROACHES

Outside of the United States, the frozen category approach is not to be found. Courts around the world (including the European Court of Human Rights, the European Court of Justice, Germany, Canada, Israel, and South Africa) are committed to an entirely different perspective. In these courts and elsewhere, freedom of speech is respected, but it is clearly recognized that when speech conflicts with other important interests, it is necessary to engage in a balancing of factors that they call proportionality. Proportionality is not a method of interpretation confined to free speech or press. It is a general method applied to all rights. The method is well discussed in an important book by Moshe Cohen-Eliya and Iddo Porat.[30] As they describe it, proportionality was first systematized in Germany as a method structuring the inquiry when judges need to decide conflicts between rights and other rights and interests. As they put it, the stages of the inquiry are "first, that its objective is legitimate and important; second, that the means chosen were rationally connected to achieve that objective (suitability);[31] third, that no less drastic means were available (necessity); and fourth, that the benefit from realizing the objective exceeds the harm to the right[32] (proportionality in the strict sense)."[33]

Many American scholars criticize proportionality as a form of discretionary balancing threatening the protection of rights. Courts around the world reject that perspective. For example, as proportionality developed in its German home, it was a doctrine fashioned to protect rights. The state's power to act was limited by the extent to which its action was necessary to meet its goals. Since at the time there were no written rights, the doctrine of proportionality served to keep the state within limits that did not unnecessarily encroach on rights, which were conceived to be natural in character. Moreover, the courts were deemed to be the appropriate fora to reign in excessive state power because the Parliament was thought to be reactionary and subservient to the government.

Similarly, after the disaster of World War II, it was widely believed that popular democracy fueled by nationalism had failed. So too, government institutions had caved in the face of dictatorial regimes in Spain, Italy, France, and Germany. The Courts were not sufficiently independent. What was needed to assure that such dictatorships never took power again were strong constitutional courts filled by able jurists immune to popular currents to support strong constitutions fashioned to promote the public interest while respecting the dignity of each individual. New constitutional courts were established in many prominent European countries and new constitutions were written. The principle of proportionality was seen as integral to the German Constitution. That Constitution regarded its citizens as members of a community with shared values, values that recognized human dignity as a shared right. Although human dignity was the paramount constitutional value, the Constitution recognized that even in a community of shared values, rights and interests inevitably clashed. It was the task of the courts using the doctrine of proportionality to assure that those rights and interests be realized to the fullest extent possible. In Germany and elsewhere, proportionality is seen as a methodology calculated to protect human rights and interests, not to water them down.

At least prior to the frozen categories approach, I think it is fair to say, however, that American courts have applied similar factors in considering whether speech involving advocacy of illegal action, obscenity, or libel should be protected. But in a proportionality analysis, the factors are systematically applied; American free speech balancing to produce categories of unprotected speech by comparison has been slipshod and sloppy.[34] On the other hand, there is no formal basis to suppose that balancing should lead to different results than proportionality. If the important factors are considered whether systematically or not, nothing in the factors themselves should tip toward different outcomes. Nonetheless, different cultures, history, and politics may well have a substantial influence on how the factors are weighed and applied.

No European high court has yet considered violent video games from a free speech perspective. But regulation is extensive.[35] For example, the British Video Recording Act of 1984, as amended, subjects a video game to a licensing regime if a game depicts the "humiliation or torture of, or other acts of gross violence toward other human beings or animals." *Regina v. Video Appeals Committee*[36] has interpreted the licensing statute in a violent video games case, but no free speech issue was considered. In addition to the United Kingdom, Ireland, Germany, and Italy all regulate video games. For example, Manhunt in various forms has been prohibited in these countries either altogether or for children. Lower courts in Germany have upheld the actions. I think it very likely that the European Court of Human Rights would give deference to these attempts to regulate violent video games if a case should arise. In any event, unlike the approach taken in the United States, it is nearly certain that the European Court of Human Rights would consider a challenge to a ban of a game like Manhunt under a balancing regime that fairly considered the relevant interests.

6   COMMERCE

For most of the history of the United States, commercial speech in general and commercial advertising in particular has been bereft of constitutional protection. Commercial advertising has no obvious connection to democratic life. Instead, advertising ordinarily involves corporations seeking to promote their products by manipulating consumers with irrelevant, nonverifiable, noninformational appeals, appeals frequently designed to attach an erotic connection (created out of whole cloth) to their message. Nor is this a new phenomenon. About the period from 1880 to 1930, T. J. Jackson Lears writes: "[T]herapeutic advertising became a method of social control – a way to arouse consumer demand by associating products with imaginary states of well-being."[1] To make matters worse, commercial advertisers frequently corrupt the communications media in which their advertisements appear by insisting that material be sanitized in ways that will offer a noncontroversial home for their products or a place free of material that might otherwise threaten their profitability.[2]

Of course, commercial advertising serves an economic purpose in creating demand, and it is understandable why, in the absence of more explicit fraud and deception, a legislature would decline to regulate. But it is unclear why this deluge of manipulation should enjoy constitutional protection. Indeed, whatever the economic advantages associated with commercial advertising, it comes with cultural and political costs.

When US advertisers spend in excess of $180 billion dollars on media advertisements in a single year,[3] they inevitably promote a materialistic, hedonistic culture.[4] It encourages human beings in that culture to focus on possessing objects (and to revel in sensations) at the center of their lives. This conception of the good life might comport with the crassest form of hedonism, but there is more to life than pleasure seeking including the serving of others, the nurturing of relationships, the cultivation of character, and the development of a mature personality. In the end, it is preposterous to suppose that human beings achieve their dignity by securing material goods. What John Dewey observed is certainly true – at least at funerals, "We praise even our most successful [people], not for their ruthless and self-centered energy in getting ahead, but because of their love of flowers, children, and dogs."[5] Moreover, you do not have to be a Catholic to see the point of Pope John Paul II's observation: "When individuals and communities do not see a rigorous respect for the moral, cultural and spiritual requirements, based on the dignity of the person ... then all the rest – availability of goods, abundance of technical resources applied to daily life, a certain level of material well-being – will prove unsatisfying and in the end contemptible."[6]

Consumer culture also has problematic political effects as many have observed. John Kenneth Galbraith argued that consumer culture undermined needed public sector spending on everything from public streets to hospitals.[7] Similarly, Daniel Bell argued that consumer culture encouraged personal gratification over social solidarity and public regarding interests.[8] Herbert Marcuse maintained that consumerism promoted complacency at the expense of democratic participation and resistance to injustice.[9] Surely, a consumer culture also makes political appeals for material sacrifice beyond the realm of the feasible. To the extent political steps to avoid serious environmental problems would require economic sacrifice, a culture of advertising creating new materialistic desires and demands surely stands in the way. Moreover, a materialist, hedonistic culture presses politicians toward imperialistic adventures designed to sustain the high standard of living consumers have been persuaded to crave. It seems to me that what Reinhold Niebuhr says of the Christian has far broader application: "To know both the law of love as the final standard and the law of self-love as a persistent force is to enable the Christian to have a foundation for a pragmatic ethic in which power and self-interest are used, beguiled, harnessed and deflected for the ultimate end of establishing the highest and most inclusive community of justice and order."[10] Achieving justice is a tall order; moving closer to justice is difficult; it is far more difficult in a society filled with self-absorbed consumers.

So understood, the exclusion of commercial speech from the scope of the First Amendment comports with the Civic Republican theme of the Constitution. Although the nature of Civic Republicanism is contested[11] and although the Framers understood that the People were not saints, there is no doubt that the Framers sought to achieve a Republican form of government, to institute a government that would promote the public interest, and so far as possible virtuous[12] public spirited citizens who would make such a government possible.[13] Commercial advertising is deeply at odds with the goals of a Republican form of government.

I say this not to suggest that consumer advertising should be outlawed, but to insist that the Constitution was on sound footing when it was interpreted to permit legislatures to regulate commercial advertising without fear that judges would subject their regulations to some form of First Amendment scrutiny. It was easy to believe that the regulation of speech in the economic sphere including advertising was just not the kind of speech with which the First Amendment was concerned. But the long history in which we knew that commercial advertising was outside the scope of the First Amendment is now gone.

That history ended in 1976 when the Court decided *Virginia State Board of Pharmacy v. Virginia Citizens Council.*[14] Virginia prohibited pharmacists from advertising the prices of their drugs despite quite substantial price variation, sometimes as much as 300 percent. This law against "unprofessional conduct" obviously had the effect of favoring one group of pharmacists over another. It might be argued that it is reminiscent of *Ferguson v. Skrupa,*[15] a case where the Nebraska legislature required that "debt adjusters" be lawyers. There the Nebraska legislature likely dominated by lawyers froze nonlawyers out of the debt adjusting field even though it is preposterous to suppose that a person needs to go to law school for three years and pass a bar examination to work in that narrow field. In *Virginia Pharmacy*, one group of pharmacists captured the legislature for its own ends; in *Skrupa*, lawyers captured the legislature for their own selfish ends.

Regrettably, however, the analogy to *Skrupa* would not have been helpful to the pharmacists even if it were convincing. Why? Because the legislation was upheld in *Skrupa*! The Court held in *Skrupa* that neither constitutional liberty nor equality was violated when an interest group captured a legislature for its own ends so long as a public purpose, however implausible, could be advanced to support the regulation at issue.

The Court was influenced by its own repudiation of many prior cases in which the Court had invalidated economic liberty regulations as violations of constitutional liberty or equality. In particular, the Court had come to realize that this line of cases rested upon implausible exaggerations about the healthy functioning of markets and that if the line of cases were respected, it would have been impossible to deal with the great depression effectively. It resolved to abandon any serious review of economic liberty or equality claims. This carried a good idea too far. When a legislature passes licensing requirements like those in *Skrupa*, requirements that exclude a person from a job, the Court should have taken the claim against the requirements seriously. One might extend the point to prohibitions on price advertising as infringing on the liberty to make one's business known for what it is. But there appears to be no wiggle room. The Court has slammed the front door on economic liberty claims.

In *Virginia Pharmacy*, however, a bright young lawyer working for Ralph Nader's Public Citizen named Alan Morrison persuaded the Court to let a variant of the economic liberty claim in through a side door by holding for the first time in American history that the First Amendment protected the rights of consumers to receive some forms of commercial advertising.[16] Although *Virginia Pharmacy* involved prescription drug prices, Morrison's motivation for the law suit was ultimately to afford constitutional protection to attorney advertising. He believed, however, that the claim of constitutional protection for attorney advertising would be a harder sell to a Court composed of lawyers who had been raised in a system that precluded such advertising, had not themselves needed to advertise in order to thrive, and who might be sympathetic to the idea that lawyer advertising was unprofessional.

Persuading the Court to protect prescription drug advertising was difficult enough particularly since the Court was previously on record as stating that commercial advertising was not the kind of speech the First Amendment was designed to protect.[17] But that position had been subjected to substantial criticism in the law reviews;[18] some subsequent cases gave room to argue that the audience for messages had rights; and the Virginia statute in question was not a model of appealing policy. Senior citizens on fixed budgets were being denied access to important information that could not be easily gathered any other way.

Instead of bringing the case on behalf of pharmacists wanting to advertise, therefore, Morrison and his then colleague Raymond Bonner brought the case on behalf of consumers, arguing that the state should not be able to prevent them from receiving true and useful information without substantial justification. As a matter of first impression, the argument sounds plausible on First Amendment grounds. But this was not a matter of first impression. The First Amendment had not initially been conceived to cover commercial advertising; it had never been interpreted to cover commercial advertising; indeed, the contention that commercial advertising was covered by the First Amendment had been precisely rejected.

How then could the Court decide in favor of the consumers without resorting to arguments from language, history, or judicial precedent about commercial speech? Essentially, the Court argued that the First Amendment unquestionably protected political speech and that it would be inconsistent to protect political speech without protecting commercial speech. In support of this surprising contention, the Court offered several arguments.

First, it suggested that the interest in the free flow of commercial information may be "as keen, if not keener by far than his interest in the day's most urgent political debate."[19] This argument took on a special poignancy in the context of the particular facts before the Court. It is easy to imagine a struggling impoverished aged couple studying the drug price ads as they struggle with the spiraling costs of medical care. Suppose, however, that the case involved the issue of alcoholic beverage price advertising, an issue the Court confronted somewhat later. There instead of the elderly impoverished couple, we might think of an alcoholic studying the paper for a low-priced jug wine. Although I do not want to minimize the interest of consumers generally, it is not clear that their interest in prices or other commercial information speaks to the heart of the First Amendment. As William Van Alstyne wryly puts it, "After all. As the National Enquirer likes to observe, 'Inquiring minds want to know.' They 'want to know' about the kind of crème rinse Cindy Lauper uses, as much as, perhaps even more than, they want to know whether the CIA may have helped to bring down the government in South Vietnam."[20] In other words, First Amendment values might not be determined by public opinion polls reflecting the views of focus groups.

The Court had other arguments up its sleeve. Not only did it argue that the interests of consumers might be more important than commercial speech, but also that commercial speech *is* political speech. The argument observed that we have a predominantly free enterprise economy, maintained that in such an economy the allocation of resources will be privately made, argued that it is in the public interest that such private decisions be made intelligently and in a well-informed way, and concluded that the free flow of information is "indispensable to the proper allocation of resources in a free enterprise system."[21] But it did not stop there. Without taking a breath, it apparently thought it followed that "[I]t is also indispensable to the formation of intelligent opinions as to how that system ought to be regulated or altered. Therefore, even if the First Amendment were thought to be primarily an instrument to enlighten public decision-making in a democracy, we could not say that the free flow of information does not serve that goal."[22] Let's stop with that conclusion and work our way backward.

Is commercial advertising containing factual information really indispensable to the formation of intelligent opinions concerning how the economic system should be regulated or altered? Has it ever occurred to you to vote for a candidate based on factual information you gleaned from a commercial advertisement? So far as I am aware, no political scientist has ever claimed, let alone determined, that the factual content of commercial advertisements has played even a minimal role in American political elections. I conclude that the Court's breathtaking assertion is simply false.

It seems plausible, however, that truthful information in advertisements can and does play some role in the economic allocation

of resources albeit a slight role given that the overwhelming majority of advertisements are bereft of factual information (we will be
back to that). Nonetheless, the suggestion that the private allocation
of resources is part of public decision making in a democracy is a
bit fast and loose. Of course, government allocation of resources
is an important part of public decision making. For many wealthy
corporations, John Kenneth Galbraith's quip that we have socialism for the rich and capitalism for the poor seems apt. That the
private allocation of resources predominates over government allocation of resources seems quite beside a First Amendment point.
Even if we suppose that commercial advertising is political, protection of "political speech" in this context seems dramatically less
important than in others if all that is stake is the efficient allocation of resources. Since government so frequently departs from the
model of a free enterprise economy with constitutional blessing,
perhaps the "proper" allocation of resources as seen by the market
should not be privileged at all. If we focus, for example, on the sale
of tobacco, which government taxes to discourage sales, we might
legitimately wonder why facilitating a market-driven allocation of
resources should be a First Amendment worry at all.

Having said that commercial speech is more important than political speech and that commercial speech is political speech, the Court
also took a different tack: it suggested that it could not tell the difference between commercial and political speech by suggesting that "no
line between publicly 'interesting' or 'important' commercial advertising and the opposite kind could ever be drawn."[23] In support of
this suggestion, the Court provided examples of advertisements that
might have political import, for example, an advertisement for abortion clinics, or an advertisement for artificial furs advocating the sale
of the product as an alternative to contributing to the extinction of
fur-bearing animals. The abortion example can be handled without
resort to the First Amendment. Without regard to the First Amendment,
if the government blocks consumers from gaining information about
access to abortions, it is placing an undue burden on that constitutional right. The artificial fur example would gain more traction if
commercial advertisements in general had a public interest element,
but the fact is they clearly do not, and it makes sense to create a general

rule that commercial speech is not political speech rather than having the courts examining individual advertisements on an *ad hoc* basis to decide whether they have enough of a public interest element to render them political.

Nonetheless, the Court had said commercial speech is more important than political speech, that it is political speech and that no line could be drawn that would distinguish between the two. It all made for splendid chamber music. But before the opinion was published, someone at the Court realized that distinguishing between commercial speech and political speech was a legal necessity. Here's why. It is a constitutional given that government may not generally outlaw false political speech. Generally, it is up to the people, not the government, to decide the truth or falsity of political speech. But the same conclusion does not apply to commercial advertising. The Federal Trade Commission and its counterpart agencies in the states regularly bring advertisers to court for engaging in false or misleading commercial advertising. If political and commercial speech cannot be distinguished, the bread-and-butter regulation of the Federal Trade Commission and integrity of the market (such as it is) would be imperiled.

So the Court had to drop an embarrassing footnote. Having claimed that political and commercial speech could not be distinguished, the Court in footnote 24 stated that commonsense differences existed between commercial advertising and other forms of speech and that government could restrain commercial advertising in ways that would never be contemplated with political speech.[24] The Court did not admit that these differences involved a difference in value between the two forms of speech. It claimed that commercial advertising was more objective and more verifiable by the disseminator than political speech. And it claimed that commercial speech was more likely to be chilled than political speech because of an advertiser's use of the speech for profits. These alleged distinctions are by no means obvious; indeed legal commentators have barbequed them in the law reviews.

Be that as it may, *Virginia Pharmacy* provided a measure of protection for truthful statements made in commercial advertisements while adhering to the view that false and misleading commercial advertising were not protected. But the opinion suggested that the value of political and commercial speech was comparable or that commercial speech was political speech. The Court quickly backed away from these suggestions in a case where an attorney named Ohralik showed up offering his services in the hospital room of an eighteen-year-old girl who had been injured in an automobile accident.[25] In a subsequent visit, she signed a contingent fee agreement. Subsequently, she discharged Ohralik, and he sued her for breach of contract. When the State Bar of Ohio got wind of this behavior, they disciplined Ohralik for violating rules against soliciting clients. Ohralik defended on free speech grounds all the way to the Supreme Court. Ohralik argued that he was simply advertising the availability of his services in a nonmisleading way.

In a companion case arising in South Carolina, Edna Smith Primus made a similar argument.[26] On behalf of the ACLU, she had advised a group of allegedly illegally sterilized women of their rights and had written a letter to one of the women offering to represent her free of charge though reserving the right to collect attorney's fees if the lawsuit was successful. Relying on rules similar to Ohio, South Carolina sought to discipline Primus under its antisolicitation rules. Of course, Ohralik was a less sympathetic party than Primus. Primus was not seeking to make a personal profit, was motivated by the enforcement of constitutional rights, and had proceeded by letter, which gave the prospective client time for reflection. Ohralik sought personal gain, in a garden variety automobile accident case, and solicited the client face to face when she was in a vulnerable position. Although unsympathetic parties often win in free speech cases (recall Nazis and pornographers), only a fool would bet that an attorney had a constitutional right to solicit accident patients in their hospital rooms. It was no surprise that Ohralik lost and Primus won.

The particular approach employed in *Ohralik*, however, was of constitutional significance. In determining what standard to apply in *Ohralik*, the Court abandoned the pretense that commercial and political speech were of equivalent constitutional value. Unlike *Primus* where the Court applied a demanding test on the premise that the ACLU was seeking to further political and ideological goals, the Court in *Ohralik* stated that commercial speech enjoyed only "a limited measure of protection, commensurate with its subordinate position in the scale of First Amendment values."[27] The Court did not claim that pharmacists could advertise, but not lawyers, nor did it deny that

Ohralik had communicated information worthy of a degree of constitutional protection. But it concluded that speech associated with a business transaction was traditionally subject to regulation, and protecting vulnerable persons from possible exploitation was an important state interest.

It is hard to resist the conclusion (and I will not resist) that the commercial speech doctrine was a mess from the outset. The "commercial is political" premise was bankrupt from the start. The backing and filling began in footnote 24 and the retreat was completed in *Ohralik* with the recognition that commercial speech was lower in the hierarchy of First Amendment values. The problem is that this recognition was unaccompanied by any discussion of what values informed the hierarchy or why commercial speech should enjoy any protection under the First Amendment.

Nonetheless, protected it was. But what degree of protection? *Central Hudson Gas and Electric Company v. Public Service Commission*[28] announced a one-size-fits-all commercial speech test, a test that on its face is less demanding than the test used in political speech cases: "In commercial speech cases, then, a four-part analysis has developed. At the outset we must determine whether the expression must be protected by the First Amendment. For commercial speech to come within that provision, it at least must concern lawful activity and not be misleading. Next we ask whether the asserted governmental interest is substantial. If both inquiries yield positive answers, we must determine whether the regulation directly advances the governmental interest asserted, and whether it is not more extensive than is necessary to serve that interest."[29] The strength of this test, of course, depends on the sympathies of the judge applying it. For some time, the Court applied the test like a bad parent: strict one day, lax the next. For example, in *Central Hudson* the Court struck down a New York energy conservation statute prohibiting promotional advertising by utility companies. On the other hand, when Puerto Rico prohibited promotional advertising of casino gambling directed to its residents while permitting such advertising directed to tourists, the Court upheld Puerto Rico's scheme of regulation. Whether or not the results are consistent, it is clear that *Central Hudson* was applied with a heavier hand to the utility than to the gambling casino.

In the past twenty years, however, in a step-by-step process expertly analyzed by David Vladeck, the former Director of the Bureau of Consumer Protection of the Federal Trade Commission, the Court has toughened the *Central Hudson* test to the point that it "results in the virtually automatic invalidation of laws restraining truthful commercial speech."[30]

A victory for truth you may say. But a victory for "truth" may be quite damaging to the public health: 480,000 people die every year because of tobacco.[31] Yet the Court's application of *Central Hudson* makes it virtually impossible to ban truthful tobacco ads unless they are directed to children.[32] A key case is *Lorillard Tobacco Company v. Reilly*[33] where Massachusetts prohibited the advertising of cigarettes, smokeless tobacco, or cigars within one thousand feet of a school or playground. Although the Court held that the ban on cigarettes was preempted by federal law, its analysis of the other restrictions would have been the same as applied to cigarettes in the absence of preemption. Basically, the Court held that there were so many schools and playgrounds that in many areas of Massachusetts, the restriction functioned as a complete ban. This was thought to be problematic because adults have an interest in receiving truthful information about tobacco products.

I find it difficult to believe that any adult interest in receiving such ads outweighs the state interest in protecting children. Indeed, I see strong reason to doubt the significance of the adult interest. Oh, of course, I recognize the strong need of many tobacco smokers to have a cigarette in the morning and many other times in the day. But it would be the rare smoker who would leap out of bed needing to see a cigarette advertisement. To be sure, some might not know precisely where cigarettes are sold, but virtually everyone knows the kind of establishments that sell cigarettes. Honest and intelligent people might disagree whether retail establishments should be able to have signs indicating that cigarettes are sold inside, but if the restrictions go too far in regulating such signs, they could be declared unconstitutional in that specific context. In general, however, when tobacco products create a massive public health problem and they do, I think banning tobacco advertising to adults is wise public policy and not a constitutional affront.

Despite the language in *Lorillard*, about the audience interest, I think the driving force of the opinion is about the speaker's interest, *not* the audience interest. The Court specifically refers to the interest of tobacco manufacturers and retail establishments in conveying truthful information to adults. This reference involves no small shift in commercial speech doctrine. *Virginia Pharmacy* was all about protecting consumers. *Lorillard* asserts that consumers have a corresponding interest to those of the tobacco companies, but the assertion rests on imagining consumers anxious to read their daily tobacco ads, and we all know those consumers do not exist.

If my claim about the predominance of the speaker's interest in *Lorillard* is unconvincing, the Second Circuit Court of Appeals decision in a New York attorney advertising case involving a personal injury law firm is absolutely clear cut.[34] The law firm of Alexander and Catalano ran ads in which they called themselves the "heavy hitters." The firm's commercials contained jingles and special effects including wisps of smoke and electrical currents surrounding the firm's name. Alexander and Catalano were sometimes depicted as giants towering above local buildings rushing to a client's house so quickly that they became blurs. Not to be outdone, their legal assistance was portrayed to extend to space aliens. New York passed a series of regulations that would clamp down on this kind of advertising. Alexander and his firm sued to invalidate the regulations, and the case was decided by the Second Circuit Court of Appeals, the federal appellate court with jurisdiction over New York.

As Circuit Judge Calabresi, former Dean of the Yale Law School, saw it, the issue was whether speech that is "irrelevant, unverifiable, and non-informational"[35] is protected under the commercial speech doctrine. By focusing on language in cases that did not remotely present the question, Calabrese concluded that noninformational speech of this character was commercial speech subject to the *Central Hudson* test. In doing so, he did not pause to consider which First Amendment values were being advanced. I have argued that the Court exaggerated the First Amendment values in *Virginia Pharmacy*, but conceded that listeners had interests that could be cognized in First Amendment terms. It is hard to understand what listener interests are present in *Alexander*. Of course, consumers have an interest in knowing that

Alexander and Catalano provide legal services as well as any information that could help them assess their quality. But blue smoke? Electric currents? Appearing larger than buildings? Being described as the Heavy Hitters? I can see why Alexander and Catalano want to advertise in this way. The commercials are funny (at least, the first time); the Heavy Hitters motto is sung with a catchy tune; the commercials grab attention. In this respect, these commercials are part of a much larger picture than attorney advertising. US advertising expenditures exceeded $180 billion in 2008. And most of that advertising was decidedly not informational.

Some advertising is entertaining. I, for example, love the commercial in which we are told that an unknown actor is the most interesting man in the world and that when he is thirsty he drinks Dos Equis. Nonetheless, commercials such as these are a far cry from the advertisements in *Virginia Pharmacy*. These commercials are not informational. They are manipulative. They are nonrational. They sell products through stealth. Of course, most people maintain that they are not influenced by such ads. But the same people are attached to Colgate or Crest and many other products by osmosis. Indeed, 40 percent of urban children are strongly attached to automobile brands by the seventh grade if not well before.[36] Those who think that manipulative advertising is unsuccessful might ask themselves just why corporations spend so many billions on these communications.

I supported *Virginia Pharmacy* when it was decided. If I had known that *Virginia Pharmacy* would have led to the support of tobacco advertising, it would never have occurred to me to support it. Similarly, if I had known that *Virginia Pharmacy* would have led to a right of business corporations to manipulate the public, I would never have gotten on that bus.

Of course, we can take some solace in the fact that false and misleading commercial speech is not protected though the concept of misleading speech is insufficiently rigorous. It fails to protect consumers from irrational manipulation. It protects even knowingly false opinions under the so-called puffery doctrine.[37] And surprisingly after all these years it is still not clear how commercial speech is defined. The narrow view is that commercial speech is that speech that proposes a commercial transaction. Supporting the narrow view is the fact that for some time even after *Virginia Pharmacy* most important economic regulation of speech was not vulnerable to First Amendment attack. As the Court recognized in *Ohralik v. State Bar Association*,[38] government may regulate "the exchange of information about securities, corporate proxy statements, the exchange of price and production information among competitors, and employer's threats of retaliation for the labor activities of employees."[39]

But in *Sorrell v. IMS Health Inc.*,[40] the Supreme Court held that a Vermont law prohibiting the sale of pharmacy records for marketing purposes that revealed the prescribing practices of individual doctors without their consent violated the First Amendment. The law permitted the sale of the records without the names of patients for other purposes such as health care research or law enforcement. Under prior law, this would have been regarded as a garden variety form of economic regulation.[41] It sought among other things to lower health care costs by making it difficult for pharmaceutical companies to hawk more costly branded drugs to doctors who did not consent to have their prescribing practices made known to the companies.

But the Court stated that "Speech in aid of pharmaceutical marketing ... is a form of expression protected by the Free Speech Clause of the First Amendment."[42] The Court maintained that the regulation wrongly discriminated against a class of speakers, that is, pharmaceutical marketers and by favoring noncommercial speech over commercial speech and generic drugs over branded drugs, the regulation discriminated on the basis of content. The Court ruled that the regulation could not be upheld under the test ordinarily applied to commercial speech regulation or to the more stringent test applied to noncommercial speech. It did not precisely rule whether this regulation amounted to commercial speech or noncommercial speech though portions of the opinion seemed to suggest the Court thought of it as commercial speech.

Sorrell seems to be a marked departure from prior law with disturbing implications for the future.[43] The Court had previously ruled that commercial speech is lower in the hierarchy of constitutional values. To be concerned that commercial speakers are being treated differently from health researchers is to cast a blind eye at that hierarchy, and by stubbornly adhering to a blind faith that best results will emerge in this market despite abundant evidence that consumers will pay higher prices for drugs with no medical advantage, privileges the hawkers of drugs over the consumers.[44] To be concerned that the regulation is aimed at particular speakers is to threaten the whole terrain of economic regulation. The FDA, SEC, and the FCC to mention a few each regulate companies in particular industries and no others. They are in the business of regulating ("discriminating" against?) particular speakers. Any serious suggestion that their efforts involve impermissible speaker discrimination would wholly disrupt our current system of economic regulation. And at the heart of *Sorrell* is the supposition that economic regulation involving direct regulation of speech content, at least in the absence of false and misleading content, should be presumptively unconstitutional. This ignores or deliberately strikes at contemporary economic regulation because it frequently regulates the use of information in the market through default rules.

To be sure, *Sorrell* could be read narrowly as a case involving the shutting off of information for a form of commercial advertising that receives a degree of First Amendment protection. But the broad sweep of its language suggests otherwise, and court dockets are now filled with claims challenging economic regulations involving speech.[45] If the Court applies *Sorrell* broadly or otherwise is receptive to those claims, it could transform the commercial speech doctrine from a doctrine primarily designed to protect consumers into a sword threatening many hundreds of regulations designed to protect consumers.

ALTERNATIVE APPROACHES

As I have suggested in previous chapters, the law in other Western jurisdictions is more sensible. The European Court of Human Rights finds that commercial advertising is within the scope of freedom of speech, but has for the most part found regulations of that speech to be justifiable.[46] Moreover, the handling of tobacco advertising is more sensible than that in the United States. In 2003 the European Parliament and Council issued a directive regarding tobacco advertising.[47] The directive emphasized that tobacco was an "addictive product responsible for over a half a million deaths in the Community annually."[48] It sought to regulate the promotion of tobacco "thereby avoiding a situation where young people began smoking at an early age as a result of promotion and become addicted."[49] Accordingly, with minor exceptions, it prohibited tobacco advertising in social media, radio, newspapers, and periodicals.[50]

As we have seen, in the United States, general prohibitions of tobacco advertising are unconstitutional. But the European Court of Justice made short work of the claim that the directive violated freedom of expression. It observed that freedom of expression can be limited in pursuit of the public interest in certain circumstances and intimated that deference to public authorities to be the balance between the public interest and freedom of expression was particularly appropriate with respect to commercial expression.[51] The advocate general put it well in discussing a previous tobacco directive: "Commercial expression does not contribute in the same way as political, literary, or artistic expression do, in a liberal democratic society, to the achievement of social goods such as, for example, the enhancement of democratic debate and accountability or the questioning of current orthodoxies with a view to promoting tolerance or change."[52] Thinking along these lines, the burden to justify restrictions on commercial speech is considerably less than needed to justify restrictions on political expression and, of course, nowhere near as great as that thought to be constitutionally required in the United States.

For well over 150 years, commercial advertising has stood outside the scope of the First Amendment. *Virginia Pharmacy* took us down a new path and the road has been too rocky. It is often excessively nostalgic to yearn for the good old days, but in this respect, those days were far better.

7   DEMOCRACY

It is deeply problematic that speech is privileged over privacy, fair trials, racial and sexual equality, and the public health, to take a number of the examples we have discussed. But it may be even more bothersome that the First Amendment is interpreted in ways that are at odds with any sensible understanding of democracy.

I do not mean to suggest that the First Amendment is the only problem by any means, but its interpretation has deepened our democratic difficulties. Even before the Court decisions I criticize in this chapter, it has been the case that our "democracy" has given undue weight to the input of wealthy individuals and of business corporations. This kind of weight does not fit with any of the wide array of democratic theories. Edmund Burke,[1] Walter Lippman,[2] and Joseph Schumpeter,[3] among others, have argued for a form of elitist democracy. They recognized that elections are necessary to determine who shall rule, but in various ways, they suggested that citizens do not know enough to otherwise rule. So elites need to rule in ways that further the public interest. Nothing in their various theories, however, suggested that the elites were confined to the wealthy, let alone to the notion that corporations were wise members of the elite.

James Madison seemed to favor a form of pluralist democracy in which the people were to take a stronger rule than suggested by the conception of elitist democracy,[4] and Robert Dahl maintained that pluralism better described American democracy than the elitist approach.[5] On this understanding, people's interests were represented in groups or factions. And those groups applied pressure in the political sphere to advance their interests. In turn, leaders made

decisions designed to bring about the best resolution of those conflicting interests. To the extent, groups were unrepresented or victims of prejudice, John Hart Ely argued that courts did and should
protect their interests.[6]

Various other theorists advanced forms of Civic Republicanism
or Deliberative Democracy that challenged aspects of Dahl's pluralist
picture. First, the pluralist picture seems to assume that citizens exclusively advanced their own interests as opposed to the public interest.
Some theorists maintained that the pluralist theory exaggerated the
degree of conflicting interests. They argued that there was frequently
a common good that could be arrived at through public dialogue.[7]
Second, some argued that whether or not a common good could be
arrived at, the legitimacy of government depended upon a vital open
and public sphere in which public dialogue was an important part of
the formation of the public will.[8] Third, instead of taking the interest
of groups as given, as the pluralist theory appears to do, some theorists
suggested that government and other institutions had a role to play in
encouraging civic virtue[9] or a sense of justice.[10]

John Dewey advanced a form of Social Democracy that was
broader than the other theories. He contended, for example, that it
was not enough in a democratic society for citizens to be active in
groups that influenced government. A true democracy from his perspective involved self-government across a broader cultural and economic range in which political participation extended to the church,
business, workplace, and school.[11]

Although these democratic theorists have quite different views,
most, if not all, would share the assessment of Jeffrey Stout: "If a
[wealthy and powerful class] were to gain control of government, it
would then be able to use all available constitutional means, including
taxation, expenditure, and regulation, to rule plutocratically. It might
then succeed in fostering conditions in which gaps between classes
would widen and democratic participation would atrophy. These conditions, in turn, could strengthen a potential oligarchy's hold on power
while weakening the people's ability to resist. The result could hardly
be termed democratic. It could be more accurately described as a
caste system in modern dress – a feudal regime without the grace of
chivalry."[12]

Stout's picture of an undemocratic society strikes me as having an all too familiar resemblance to the society in which we live. And the main point of this chapter is that the First Amendment that should serve as a bulwark of democracy instead functions to undermine it. As is now well known, it has been twisted to permit the wealthy and business corporations to spend unlimited sums of money to influence the outcome of election campaigns. Less well known are the arguments used by the conservatives to justify their position. Those arguments rest on a fusion of unbridled capitalism and liberty and the perverted assumption that such a fusion *is* democracy. Many of the arguments seem to be no more than Machiavellian maneuvers. Some are based in a general vision of the First Amendment that is quite unattractive.

As a preliminary matter, it should be observed that the First Amendment is not the only culprit in the story of how the wealthy and business corporations exercise undue power in our political system. Even before *Buckley v. Valeo*, which we will soon discuss, the system of campaign finance already allowed individuals to pour large amounts of money into federal election campaigns, and the amounts have been systematically raised over the years to account for inflation. So for the 2013–2014 election cycle, legislation permitted individuals to give $2,600 to a candidate in a primary and $2,600 more in the general election and $48,600 to all candidates, $32,400 to a political party in a calendar year, $10,000 combined to party committees at the local level, $5,000 to any other political committee up to $74,600 for all parties and political action committees. Over a two year period, an individual could give up to $123,200 in campaign contributions.[13]

Prior to First Amendment intervention, the scheme imposed sharp limits on corporate and union spending. Corporations and unions were prohibited from making direct campaign contributions to candidates or political organizations, and they were prohibited from advertising on behalf of candidates. On the other hand, they were permitted to solicit voluntary contributions to political action committees that in turn could make contributions to candidates and political organizations and could engage in independent advertising on behalf of candidates.

The Supreme Court has interpreted the First Amendment to undermine this already awkward scheme.[14] The most prominent cases accomplishing this democratic distortion are *Buckley v. Valeo*[15] and

Citizens United v. Federal Election Commission.[16] Of lesser import, but nonetheless revealing, is *McCutcheon v. Federal Election Commission.*[17]

Buckley involved a broad scale challenge to the Federal Election Campaign Act of 1971 as amended in 1974. The amendments were passed in reaction to the Watergate scandal in which Republican operatives broke into Democratic National Committee headquarters at the Watergate complex funded through a slush fund of the Committee to Reelect President Nixon. The investigation into the break-in revealed widespread corruption in funding federal election campaigns. Substantial public pressure for campaign finance reform emerged, and Common Cause spearheaded a battle on Capitol Hill for responsive legislation. Legislators were attracted to reform to curb the costs of election campaigns and the effort involved in raising money, and Democrats were particularly attracted to reform because Republicans had a fundraising advantage with the wealthy. More generally, reformers hoped to address corruption in the democratic system and to promote equality in American politics.

Most important for our purposes are three amendments. One limited campaign contributions to federal election candidates to $1,000 per election. If there were no cap on contributions, the dangers of corruption and its appearance were manifest. The other amendments were designed to promote equality by limiting the amounts candidates could spend in an election and limiting the amounts that individuals could spend on advertisements on behalf of a candidate. The latter provision was also designed to close a possible loophole. It would do little good if a person could contribute only $1,000, but could then turn around and buy $1 million worth of advertisements on behalf of the candidate. So Congress limited independent expenditures on behalf of candidates to $1,000 per election. If expenditures on behalf of candidates were coordinated with their campaigns, the expenditures would be classified as contributions.

These amendments and others were challenged by Senator James Buckley of New York and Senator Eugene McCarthy of Wisconsin. Buckley had won his seat by raising large contributions from relatively few supporters. McCarthy had relied on large contributions in successfully opposing President Lyndon Johnson in the primaries during the Vietnam War. The forces against the legislation regarded it as a form of incumbent protection, and the ACLU joined those forces primarily out of a concern that the independent expenditures provision would stifle public criticism.

On the other side, Francis R. Valeo was the named defendant because he was the Secretary of the Senate, but the defense of the law was led by the Federal Election Commission and Common Cause. President Ford's Justice Department filed a friend of the court brief, purportedly offering neutral advice on the law to the Court, but hostile to the legislation in tone.[18]

The Supreme Court's treatment of the issues resulted in a compromise pleasing no one. To put it simply, the Court upheld the contributions limitations, but struck down the spending restrictions. As a threshold matter, it seems to me that the Court was right to conclude that First Amendment interests were implicated by both types of restrictions. It is easy to mock the idea that money is speech. Of course, money is not speech, but restricting the amount of money a person can spend on speech undeniably limits speech. Suppose, for example, a legislature told a newspaper that it was free to publish, but could not spend more than $1,000 per day in publishing the paper. Clearly, freedom of press would be abridged.

Moreover, at least in some dimensions, the restriction on contributions is less problematic than the restriction on expenditures. A restriction on expenditures limits the self-expression of the speaker in ways that a restriction on contributions does not. Speech resulting from contributions is the self-expression of the candidate, not the contributor. Nonetheless, the Court wrongly downplayed the effect of contribution limitations on political campaigns. It suggested that contribution limitations would simply force candidates to build a stronger base of support, but would not reduce the total amount of money available to support political expression by the candidate. This sets a blind eye to those candidates who need seed money in large contributions to build that stronger base. Moreover, it underestimates the harm done to the democratic process when candidates spend more time raising money and less time attending to the public's business. And it fails to appreciate the extent to which the positions of candidates are developed to make their overall candidacy appealing to wealthy interests.[19]

By playing fast and loose with the genuine workings of campaign finance, the Court obscured the reality that one has to balance First Amendment interests against the interests of democratic equality and the integrity of the democratic process. Although the Court wrongly minimized the impact of the contribution limits on freedom of speech, I think it properly recognized that any free speech impact involved was outweighed by the paramount concerns of combating corruption, restoring faith in the integrity of democratic elections, and promoting a sense of equal citizenship in the elections process.

There was a case to be made against an aspect of the spending restrictions. There was a plausible argument that the restriction in dollar amount on independent expenditures was too low. At the time, as applied, as the Court pointed out, an individual would not have been able to purchase a quarter-page advertisement in a major metropolitan newspaper. On the other hand, the overwhelming majority of citizens could ill afford to buy such an advertisement. To permit such purchases would give the wealthy few an advantage based on their wealth rather than their political sagacity.

The Court's discussion and ultimate dismissal of the spending restrictions, however, was more sweeping and deeply flawed than permitting a single quarter-page advertisement in a major metropolitan newspaper (per wealthy person). Indeed, the Court was tone deaf to the equality concern.[20] It seemed to dismiss the concern out of hand: "[T]he concept that government may restrict the speech of some elements of our society in order to enhance the relative voice of others is wholly foreign to the First Amendment."[21] That is one way of putting the issue. The lower court put it a different way. Can "the wealthy few [claim] a constitutional guarantee to a stronger political voice than the unwealthy many because they are able to give and spend more money, and because the amounts they give and spend cannot be limited?"[22] One thing that cannot be said in defense of the Court's abrupt dismissal of the equality concern is that the wealthy deserve political privileges. Undoubtedly, some people because of their knowledge or experience might gain a more respectful audience than others. Perfect equality is not possible, nor is it desirable. But the mere acquisition of wealth bears no necessary relation to political merit.

More consistent with First Amendment traditions is the Court's faith in the ability of an audience to discern the truth regardless of the quantity of inputs from a particular side. But this faith simply substitutes ideology for social science. The scientific and marketing research plainly shows that people come to believe many things for reasons wholly unrelated to their truth. Among these are the personal characteristics of the speaker, the relationship of the view to their prior set of beliefs,[23] the extent to which the view conforms with what other hearers are likely to believe, the frequency with which the claim is uttered, the visual background in which the claim is presented, and the extent to which the belief makes the listener happy or unhappy.[24]

Finally, if we shift our focus from the audience to the candidate, the equality claim becomes sharper. If you were a candidate, would it be a matter of indifference to you if the opposing candidate could spend much more money to get elected? One does not have to believe that the candidate who spends the most always wins to believe that the candidate who can spend more has an advantage. That advantage is undeserved when the opposing candidate happens to be wealthy. It is undeserved when the opposing candidate appeals to wealthy interests. The equality claim did not deserve to be dismissed in so ham-handed a fashion. It is difficult to persuade candidates and voters that our democracy deserves respect when it is rigged from the outset in favor of the wealthy.

Even if the equality concern were illegitimate, shouldn't the independent expenditures provision have been upheld as a loophole closing device? After all, if a supporter wanted to curry favor with a potential officeholder, spending vast sums in expenditures to elect the candidate might be more welcome than lesser sums given in the form of contributions.

The Court resorted to some fancy statutory interpretation to get around this argument. The independent expenditure limitation referred to expenditures relative to a clearly identified candidate. It would have been sensible to maintain that expenditures intended to support the election or defeat of a clearly identified candidate were expenditures within the meaning of the act. Instead, in order to avoid a vagueness problem of its own making, the Court ruled that nothing was an expenditure unless it specifically advocated the election or defeat of a clearly identified candidate. So if you paid for an advertisement saying that candidate X robbed banks on Thursday nights, no expenditure would be implicated, unless you added magic words like "Do not vote for candidate X." In the absence of using the magic words, individuals could spend unlimited sums of money to influence the outcome of election campaigns.

Without any apparent sense of shame, the Court recognized that its limiting construction had undermined the effectiveness of the independent expenditure restriction's utility as a loophole closing device: "It would naively underestimate the ingenuity and resourcefulness of persons and groups desiring to buy influence to believe they would have much difficulty devising expenditures that skirted the restriction on express advocacy of election or defeat, but nevertheless benefitted the candidate's campaign."[25]

Having made mincemeat of the independent expenditures provision, there was now a credible argument that the contributions limitation was unconstitutional on the ground that it could be so easily circumvented. In an apparent answer to this argument, the Court stated that the "absence of prearrangement and coordination of an expenditure with the candidate or his agent not only undermines the value of the expenditure to the candidate, but also alleviates the danger that expenditures will be given as a quid pro quo for improper commitments from the candidate."[26] So, in one paragraph, the restriction on independent expenditures fails as a loophole closing device, and we are cautioned not to be naïve about the ingenuity of those who spend. In another paragraph, we are told that the restriction is in fact effective. When historians search Supreme Court opinions for examples of fine legal reasoning, these passages will not make the cut.

In fact, the ruling left the act in shambles. It not only opened the way for wealthy individuals to spend unlimited sums in the political process, but also for business corporations as well. Business corporations' participation in federal election campaign had previously been sharply limited. They have been permitted to solicit voluntary contributions to political action committees that could then spend money in the electoral process. But they have been prohibited from using their treasury funds to contribute to federal election candidates since 1907 under the Tillman Act and from using their treasury funds for independent expenditures on behalf of candidates since 1947 under the Taft Hartley Law.

Buckley did not authorize business corporations to contribute to candidates or to purchase advertisements that explicitly advocated the election or defeat of a candidate. But its interpretation of the independent expenditures amendment to the Federal Election Campaign Act of 1971 opened a loophole large enough for any fool to see, and the business corporations had their eyes wide open. So long as they did not use the magic words specifically advocating election or defeat, they could spend millions on attack ads. Thus, as *Buckley* managed to overturn central aspects of the Federal Election Campaign Act of 1971 as amended, it also implicitly rejected the Taft Hartley Act's long-standing rejection of direct corporate participation in the political process.

Note that the rise of ads not using the magic words, but otherwise intended to affect the outcome of elections – so-called issue ads – were entirely outside the scheme of campaign finance regulation. Not only was there no ceiling on the amounts that could be spent, no disclosure or reporting requirements applied either. Consequently, no precise measurements of the amounts spent on these ads are available. But knowledgeable observers of election campaigns agreed that "issue" ads had become an important factor in election campaigns[27] and the corrupting power of money was infecting the body politic.

In order to combat these "issue" ads (and other campaign finance abuses), Congress passed the Bipartisan Campaign Reform Act of 2002. With the exception of news stories, commentaries, editorials, and the like, the Act prohibited corporations and unions from engaging in "electioneering communications" – any broadcast, cable, or satellite communication with an audience of fifty thousand people or more that referred to a clearly identified candidate for a federal office within thirty days of a primary or sixty days of a general election. On the other hand, corporations or unions could establish a Political Action Committee fund by the voluntary contributions of stockholders or employees in the case of corporations or members in the case of unions to make such expenditures. This Act struck at the heart of the abuse. It was easy to craft an ad for or against a candidate without using the magic words asking the voter to vote for or against a candidate. It was far more difficult to spend for or against a candidate without using his or her name.

The Supreme Court upheld this provision in *McConnell v. Federal Election Commission*.[28] It argued that the provision did not raise the vagueness issues that gave rise to the express advocacy interpretation employed in *Buckley* and that the express advocacy interpretation as applied to corporations failed to promote the congressional interests in combating corruption or the appearance of corruption.[29] *McConnell's* reign was short lived. Justices Stevens and O'Connor left the Court only to be replaced by Chief Justice Roberts and Justice Alito.

This set the stage for a case that deserved widespread political attention, attention it did not receive. *FEC v. Wisconsin Right to Life, Inc.*,[30] narrowly interpreted *McConnell* and rewrote the Bipartisan Campaign Reform Act in a way that tore the heart out of the Act and elevated corporate free speech rights to new heights. Ironically, Russ Feingold, a coauthor (with John McCain) of the Bipartisan Campaign Reform Act was a central figure in the case. Wisconsin Right to Life, a nonprofit corporation, was opposed to the reelection of Feingold. In 1998, it spent $60,000 to oppose him. In 2004, the election year giving rise to the case, Wisconsin Right to Life through its PAC again opposed Feingold and tied its opposition to Feingold's use of the filibuster to block judicial appointees of President Bush: "Send Feingold Packing."[31]

Wisconsin Right to Life ran three different television advertisements from its general treasury (not its PAC) within the time frame prohibited by the Bipartisan Campaign Reform Act. Relying in large part on $50,000 of contributions from business corporations, Wisconsin Right to Life sharply criticized the use of the filibuster for judicial nominations (an issue upon which Feingold's position was well known), urged the audience to contact him, and referred it to a website that criticized Feingold specifically. The ads were run when the Senate was not in session, nor were they resumed when the Senate came back into session. They were timed to affect the campaign in which the filibuster was a major issue.

The case against Wisconsin Right to Life was straightforward. It had run ads mentioning Feingold with the prohibited period, and *McConnell* had declared the Act constitutional. When the case reached the Supreme Court, however, Chief Justice Roberts argued that *McConnell* only decided that the Act was constitutional on its face; it did not decide that the First Amendment would not protect any ads during the prohibited periods. In other words, the Act might be unconstitutional as applied in some cases. But surely the filibuster ads were transparently pieces of electioneering: written by a group opposed to Feingold's reelection and timed to affect the election rather than any vote on filibustering.

One might have argued that Wisconsin Right to Life was a nonprofit and, therefore, not covered by the Act, but the Act had previously been interpreted to apply to nonprofits using the contributions of business corporations. Otherwise business corporations could pour millions through dummy nonprofits. One might argue that the ads criticized filibusters not Feingold; they merely asked the audience to contact Feingold about his vote on the issue. But this ignores the fact that the Wisconsin electorate knew Feingold's position and his opponent's position and the fact that the ads pointed the audience to a website reinforcing the point. One would have to be wilfully blind not to recognize the intent of these ads.

Nonetheless, Chief Justice Roberts declared that the ads were issue ads, not electioneering ads. He said that neither intent nor effect were standards relevant to determining whether an ad was an issue ad or an electioneering ad. They were insufficiently clear to be useful as tests (even though the intent in this case would be hard to deny with a straight face). Having interpreted *McConnell* to allow ad hoc determinations whether the Act was constitutionally applied and having cast aside intent and effect as relevant factors, the Chief Justice said the Act could constitutionally be applied, if, but only if, ads were "susceptible of no reasonable interpretation other than as an appeal to vote for or against a specific candidate."[32] Before this case the Act as interpreted in *McConnell* surely blocked the overwhelming majority of ads by business corporations, unions, and wealthy individuals in the period prior to elections including the Feingold advertisement. After Roberts had rewritten the statute, campaign strategists had considerable room to evade the Act's provisions.

There was one aspect of the opinion that might give a corporate strategist pause. Roberts's opinion observed that the filibustering ads did not attack the character of the candidate or even mention the election. This left the door wide open to discuss how a particular candidate has voted on taxes or business favors, but it might suggest that the Act has some teeth with respect to character attacks. It is hard to say that a character attack is an issue advertisement. Nonetheless, Roberts's opinion authorized the spending of unlimited sums to elect or defeat candidates so long as they were not foolish enough to say so in their ads or brazen enough to attack a candidate's character.

As we shall see, the distance between *Citizens United* and *Wisconsin Right to Life* is not great. Yet outside legal circles, the Roberts's opinion did not ignite any substantial political criticism. On the other hand, *Citizens United* ignited a firestorm. *Wisconsin Right to Life* accomplished its campaign finance revolution through legal sleight of hand. Its shameless character could not be easily explained in a sound bite. *Citizens United*, however, was an unnecessary slap in the face; the public has not turned the other cheek.

Citizens United could and should have been an unremarkable case. Citizens United, a nonprofit corporation that received small amounts of contributions from business corporations, produced *Hillary: The Movie*, a documentary arguing that she was an unsuitable candidate for President. The film was released in theaters and on DVD, but Citizens United wanted to make the film available through video-on-demand in cable and to advertise on broadcast and cable television. The Federal Election Commission, apparently out to show that its zeal outstripped its common sense, argued that this was illegal under the Bipartisan Campaign Reform Act. To my mind, this is the kind of interpretation that gives administrative agencies a bad name. The Act was designed to combat the flood of corporate money producing campaign ads designed to elect or defeat candidates. There was no evidence in the legislative record that documentaries were a part of the problem. Even if the Act were interpreted to apply to this documentary or promotions for it, I would think that freedom of press should have protected Citizens United.[33]

Alternatively, the Court had already held that campaign expenditures of nonprofit corporations were protected under the First Amendment unless they had received contributions from business corporations raising the possibility that they were shells designed to evade the campaign finance laws. But the contributions by business corporations to Citizens United were small enough that they should not have altered its nonprofit status under the campaign finance laws. Under either of these arguments, Citizens United should have won and the case could have been filed away in the department of insignificance.

But the conservative majority, led behind the scenes by Chief Justice Roberts, reached out to decide an issue that had not been even suggested by Citizens United. The Court directed that the case be held over for the next term to determine whether cases like *McConnell* should be overturned and that corporations be determined to have the same free speech rights afforded to ordinary citizens.[34] In other words, the Court was not forced into a corner where it had to decide this issue. It created the issue out of thin air. The term "judicial activism" is generally not very useful, but if it had never been used before, it might have been generated to accurately characterize the Court's action in this case.

Nonetheless, the issue confronted in *Citizens United* should be placed in perspective. Free speech rights for corporations were not invented in this 2010 case. Media corporations had long been afforded First Amendment protection. Nonprofit corporations had also been afforded free speech rights in and out of the electoral process. Importantly, even the right of business corporations to speak out on political issues of the day and, as we have seen, in their commercial advertising had been previously settled, however wrongly. The limits that had been placed on business corporations were in the elections process, limits that we have traced in this chapter. At the time of *Citizens United*, their capacity to give campaign contributions was foreclosed except through PACS, but thanks to *Wisconsin Right to Life*, they could freely spend to elect or oppose federal election candidates so long as they discussed issues, did not use the magic words, and did not focus on the character of candidates.

Citizens United retained the contribution limits, but allowed corporations to discuss the character of candidates and to use the magic words. Allowing corporations to discuss character in their ads could prove significant in some campaigns; allowing corporations to use the magic words seems to be of trivial importance. I cannot avoid the conclusion that despite all the public attention and backlash, from a legal perspective, *Citizens United* is really not a major case.

Nonetheless, it is a case of major symbolic importance and it raises issues of profound importance as did the earlier corporate speech cases. One of the major arguments used to defend limits on corporate speech is that corporations have amassed vast sums of money for reasons that have no relationship to their political views.[35] For them to be able to spend this money in political campaigns unfairly distorts the political process. For reasons such as this, long ago Charles Lindblom concluded that the disproportionate power of corporations excludes them from any sensible democratic theory or vision.[36] The picture the Court tries to paint in opposition to this is that a group of people are being discriminated against because they elected to use the corporate form. After all, wealthy people ordinarily amassed their fortunes for reasons unrelated to their political views, and they are permitted to spend unlimited sums on independent expenditures. So, too, media corporations often have raised money for reasons that are not related to their political views, and they are permitted to devote vast sums of money in expressing their views.

The argument about wealthy people is certainly accurate, but it does not provide a justification for compounding the felony. It speaks loudly and clearly for limiting the amounts that wealthy people can spend in the political process. As to media corporations, I can imagine a strong argument against permitting them to engage in independent expenditures outside their own media business. That is, I see no reason why the New York Times Company should be able to spend unlimited sums buying television advertisements for the candidate of its choice. If the *New York Times* editorializes in its own pages, however, I see a significant difference. The press clause marks out protection for a largely governmentally unregulated set of institutions whose purpose is to provide information, opinion, and vision for challenging or supporting government and private centers of power and to participate in building the culture.[37] When the Court suggests that preventing business corporations from buying ads in the media would license closing down the media, it indulges in the non sequitur.

One further aspect of the picture the Court tries to paint does not ring true. It is the picture of a group of people who decided to take on

a corporate form. The suggestion is that a business corporation selling tobacco, for example, is just a group of people trying to get their
message heard in the political marketplace. In fact, it is hard to identify
what people's political views a tobacco corporation is promoting when
it buys a political advertisement. In truth, a tobacco company, or any
other business corporation buying an ad, is not representing any individual or individuals' political views. It is rather promoting the view its
managers believe will best promote profits for the company whether
or not that message conforms to the political views of its managers,
its employees, or its shareholders. The company's ad represents a
political interest, but it is not the interest of human beings, and it is not
an assessment of anyone's view of the public interest. With occasional
exceptions, it represents an economic guess as to what will profit an
artificial entity that is not a human being, let alone a citizen.[38]

The most remarkable aspect of the *Citizens United* decision, however, is its cavalier claim that when corporations spend millions of dollars on behalf of a candidate, there is no basis for the worry that our
democracy is compromised. The claim proceeds from an eccentric,
indeed perverse, understanding of democracy. According to Justice
Kennedy, who authored the opinion, democratic concerns are triggered by demonstrable bribes, but not otherwise: "The fact that speakers may have influence over or access to elected officials does not mean
that these officials are corrupt: 'Favoritism and influence are not …
avoidable in representative politics. It is in the nature of an elected
representative to favor certain policies, and, by necessary corollary, to
favor the voters and contributors who support those policies.'"[39] Get
it? Buying influence and access is part of our democracy. The Court
calls it democracy. Others could be forgiven for calling it bribery. More
generally, this impoverished conception of democracy exhibits a fundamental departure from a basic theme of the Constitution. A central
goal of Civic Republican government is to assure that the government
represents the public interest, not particular factions. To favor contributors (i.e., particular factions) is to risk departing from the public
interest particularly because there is no reason to believe that contributors are striving for the public interest,[40] let alone accurately perceiving
the public interest. James Madison and the Framers identified the phenomenon of representing factions at the expense of the public interest

as corruption.[41] It was a crucial goal of the Constitution to achieve a form of government that would *not* be corrupt in this way.

Equally remarkable is Kennedy's assurance that the appearance of access or influence "will not cause the electorate to lose faith in our democracy."[42] Why not? Because a voter knows that his or her fellow citizens will not be influenced by a blizzard of ads unless the ads speak the truth? Really? I wonder if Justice Kennedy and his conservative cohorts were surprised when the overwhelming majority of American voters opposed the decision.[43] Do they still think that the appearance of access or influence has not caused the electorate to lose faith in our democracy?

I very much doubt it, but they made a similar claim in the *McCutcheon* decision four years after *Citizens United*. McCutcheon complained about the aggregate limits in the campaign system. Recall that the campaign finance system permits an individual to give $2,600 to a candidate in a primary and $2,600 more in the general election and $48,600 to all candidates, $32,400 to a political party in a calendar year, $10,000 combined to party committees at the local level, $5,000 to any other political committee up to $74,600 for all parties and political action committees. Over a two year period, an individual could give up to $123,200 in campaign contributions. McCutcheon did not question the contribution limits to individual candidates, parties, or party committees.

What he challenged were the so-called aggregate limits: $48,600 to all candidates, $74,600 for all parties and political action committees, and the $123,000 overall limit. I find it hard to feel sorry for McCutcheon's plight. Indeed, the overwhelming majority of Americans would regard the permitted amount as already excessive (if not obscene) and threatening to the democratic process. Not so with the Court. The Court concluded that these limits seriously restrict participation in the democratic process. This process you will recall is one in which rich people buy access and influence from "responsive" politicians. The Court even went on to insist that removing these limits would not create an appearance of corruption. That the Court could maintain that these limits impair rather than further the democratic process, that it believes the wealthy have a constitutional right to buy more influence and access, that it has the gall to insist that no appearance of corruption is created shows a cynical disregard for the general population, an all-too-cozy responsiveness to the wishes of the wealthy, a perverse conception of democracy, and a bizarre view that the First Amendment value of every dime spent outweighs the value of a process in which citizens rule over the wealthy few.

But suppose we give the conservatives the benefit of the doubt. Suppose money given to politicians does not bribe them to change their views. Even if that were true, even if the line between influence realized from contributions and bribery were significant and clear, it is obvious that politicians crafting an election campaign must develop a message that will attract wealthy contributors to their campaigns. Politicians know they need that money to get elected or reelected. This would be less of a problem if the views of the wealthy invariably corresponded with the public interest. Perhaps that is why Justice Kennedy and his pro-business allies on the Court do not see the corruption. Perhaps they believe that the views of business correspond with the public interest. But surely they know that it is not the function of the Court to constitutionalize that view. Perhaps they are aware of that and in the tradition of party hacks have proceeded anyway. Perhaps the conservative majority believes that the institutional forces that represent their views have been discriminated against and the discrimination needs to be remedied. I do not know. What should be clear is that in this area, the Court has made the First Amendment an enemy of any sensible view of democracy.

ALTERNATIVE APPROACHES

Campaign finance in other countries is not unflawed.[44] Politicians everywhere have incentives to construct election systems that smooth the path to their reelection. Nonetheless, governmentally subsidized access to television is common in European elections. Moreover, in Europe, free speech is not transformed into an absolute barrier to electoral reform. The European Court of Human Rights, for example, has endorsed both free speech and free election rights and unlike *Citizens United*, it has recognized that those two rights can come into conflict. Moreover, it is prepared to uphold restrictions on free speech before and during elections that would not otherwise be appropriate outside the elections context.[45]

The Supreme Court of Canada is especially concerned about the kinds of dangers so cavalierly put to the side by the US Supreme Court in *Buckley* and *Citizens United*. In the context of examining restrictions on spending in referendum elections, it embraced the goals of preventing "the most affluent members of society from exerting a disproportionate influence by dominating [election debates] through greater access to election resources" of promoting a "sense of equality of participation and influence between the proponents of each option," and of assuring that "the system is designed to preserve the confidence of the electorate in a democratic process that it knows will not be dominated by the power of money."[46] In applying these principles, the Canadian Supreme Court has upheld quite severe restrictions on independent expenditures.[47]

To be sure, the US Supreme Court is divided over this particular issue, but the conservative majority purports to believe that when the wealthy few spend vastly disproportionate amounts in the election process, those expenditures are of no political importance and do not undermine confidence in the electoral process. It is hard to nurture the belief that the conservative justices are quite so naïve and when justices make politically important rulings with arguments that lack credibility, they lead us to believe that arguments they cannot speak aloud are actually guiding their views.

PART II

8   DISSENT

To this point, I have argued that a commitment to free speech is carried to an extreme when it jeopardizes privacy, justice, equality, and democracy or when it promotes animal cruelty and downplays the serious impact of violent video games on our children. Regrettably, this severely libertarian approach to freedom of speech is allied with a marked insensitivity to the protection of free speech when it most matters. Freedom of speech is most important when it challenges existing customs, habits, institutions, traditions, and authorities.[1] These forms of dissent implicate virtually all of the values that have been associated with free speech including liberty, freedom, equality, justice, tolerance, dignity, self-government, democracy, truth, marketplace values, the checking value, associational values, communitarian values, and cathartic values. Dissent deserves special protection not merely because it consolidates so many important values, but also because the natural reaction of those who are attacked is to censor the speech that offends.

Although many values support protecting dissent, one particularly important value is justice. In any large-scale society, hierarchies will persist.[2] Those who are powerful within hierarchies frequently perceive that those perceptions or policies that reinforce their power are the right ones. Moreover, many in power try to preserve or enlarge their power even without such rationalizations. Those in power are not always corrupt, but corruption is not rare and all of us see the world through a partial perspective. I think it inevitable that some degree of injustice permeates societal hierarchies. We will always need dissent to combat injustice because injustice will always be present.[3] As Reinhold Neibuhr put it, "We cannot fully trust the motives of any ruling class or power. That is why it is important to maintain democratic checks upon the centers of power."[4]

As will become clear, I do not maintain that dissent should always be protected. Sometimes, dissenting speech is uniquely harmful (consider, calculated defamatory lies about those in powerful positions). Nor do I contend that the United States has done a particularly poor job in protecting dissent in comparison with other countries. Indeed, its record in this area may be better than any other country in the world. But I do maintain that its record is far weaker than it should be.

In particular, I want to explore six areas in which dissent is inadequately safeguarded. First, government can make dissent difficult by unreasonably regulating its time, place, and manner. Second, our defamation laws discourage important dissent. Third, when government acts as a manager in controlled environments such as the workplace and the schools, it is permitted to smother dissent. Fourth, the Court unreasonably defers to government claims of national security without appropriate independent scrutiny. Fifth, the ability of the press to provide a check on powerful institutions is unreasonably compromised. Finally, the structure of our Constitution itself discourages important dissent.

TIME, PLACE, AND MANNER

The Court has rigidly provided formal protection to freedom of speech when government has attempted to regulate content. So it has protected violent video games, depictions of animal cruelty, and speech invading privacy or the administration of the criminal justice system. When government moves to block demonstrations without regard to the content of the demonstrations, however, the protection for freedom of speech, not to mention freedom of assembly and the right to petition for the redress of grievances, is insubstantial.

A good example of this impoverished protection was on display in *Clark v. Community for Creative Non-Violence* ("CCNV").[5] As Justice Marshall stated in dissent, "The Court's salutary skepticism of governmental decision making in First Amendment matters dissipates once it determines that a restriction is not content-based ... What the Court fails to recognize is that public officials have strong incentives to over-regulate even in the absence of an intent to censor particular views."[6] Justice Marshall was reacting to the squelching by the National Park Service of a demonstration in a small part of Lafayette Park across the street from the White House and a small part of the Washington Mall. One could read the majority's opinion without the slightest clue, let alone appreciation, of the fact that Lafayette Park and the Mall have been historically important sites for powerful political demonstrations throughout our nation's history.

As it had the year before, CCNV sought in the dead of winter to dramatize the plight of the homeless by sleeping in the park in "tent cities." In applying for a permit, CCNV observed that the demonstration would permit the homeless to "communicate their humanity, their need, and their plight to the government and the public in the *only* real way open to them."[7] And CCNV informed the Park Service that unless the homeless could sleep in the park, they would not be able to participate. The Park Service granted a permit that would allow CCNV to erect tents, and to *feign* sleep within the tents, but denied the demonstrators permission actually to sleep inside the tents. From the perspective of the Park Service, this would constitute "camping," which is forbidden in the National Parks except in designated areas. The Park Service was well aware that this condition would undermine the demonstration, yet it refused to grant an exemption.

First, it should be noted that the characterization of the demonstration as camping is contestable. CCNV did not propose to dig, make fires, or even cook; nor did it request permission to establish medical or sanitation facilities or to store personal belongings. Nonetheless, in support of the antisleeping condition the Park Service advanced an interest in keeping the parks in an attractive and intact condition and argued that permitting the demonstration could trigger numerous similar demonstrations that would aggravate the effect on the Park system. With respect to the aesthetic interest, the Park Service had already approved the erection of tent cities for the demonstrations on the Mall and in Lafayette Park on a twenty-four-hour basis for a week's time. It is hard to understand how the aesthetic interests of the parks would be compromised if the demonstrators actually slept in the tents as opposed to feigning sleep.

The government argued that a precedent would be set in which many other groups would seek to sleep in the park as a part of demonstrations, but this argument assumes a demand for sleeping demonstrations in the winter that is difficult to credit. Indeed, absent from the Park Service's argument was the recognition that that CCNV had engaged in the same demonstration the year before without the feared plethora of other such requests and without any demonstrable negative impact on the enjoyment of Lafayette Park or the Mall by its many visitors.

In upholding the Park Service's regulation as applied to CCNV, Justice White observed that the Constitution has not assigned the authority to the judiciary to replace the Park Service as the manager of the National Parks. Fair enough. But the judiciary has been assigned the task to enforce the First Amendment, and the performance of the Court in *Clark* was woefully deficient.

Not only did the Court exaggerate the governmental interests put forward by the Park Service; it cast a blind eye on the seriousness of the First Amendment interests as well. If the First Amendment recognition of the right to petition government for redress of grievances is to be taken seriously, it must take on special force in preventing government stifling of demonstrations in the nation's capital and particularly in the public spaces near the seats of government. Regrettably, *Clark* is not an isolated example. Many lower courts followed it in repressing the Occupy movement.[8] And local governments with court blessings have constructed so-called free speech zones permitting demonstrators to assemble far from the people with which they wish to communicate. So governments have kept demonstrators far removed from the Democratic and Republican conventions, from the World Trade Organization meetings, and from various public officials. They have utilized cages and cocoons for demonstrators to stay in, erected metal barricades, and utilized "restricted zones" as large as twenty-five blocks. If demonstrations are the life blood of social movements, governmental power to use force in ways that restrict their effectiveness should be subject to significant constraints.[9]

As we have previously seen, the Court has been assiduous in protecting corporations in their ability to throw money into the political
system to have their way, but when the methods of real people are at
issue, particularly poor people, the Court has the empathy and the
understanding of a brick wall.

DEFAMATION LAW

Defamation law, which includes libel and slander, is particularly
important in a democracy because it imposes sanctions against those
who criticize others, who are often powerful people. The Court fares
better in the area of defamation than it does in dealing with demonstrations, but the progress here has fallen far short of what would
be required if the Court took dissent more seriously. On the bright
side, one of the great First Amendment cases is *New York Times Co.
v. Sullivan*.[10] The Court there, as we have seen, pronounced that we
have a "profound national commitment to the principle that debate
on public issues should be uninhibited, robust, and wide-open."[11] In
applying that principle, the Court overturned the common law, which
permitted a public official to recover in a libel suit merely by showing
that a defamatory statement had been made against him or her. Falsity
was presumed; substantial damages were presumed; and malice was
presumed. The defendant could prevail only by proving that the statement was true or by showing that a "privilege" to make the statement
applied.

Instead of the common law, the Court held that a public official
could not recover in a libel suit unless he or she demonstrated that the
defamatory statement was made as a knowing or reckless falsehood.
No longer could a newspaper be subjected to a crippling damage suit
because of a careless error. The case stood for the idea that critics in
a democracy should not be easily punished for freewheeling criticism.
The burden was on the public official to show a serious breach of
integrity.

In a series of cases, the holding of *Sullivan* was extended to public
figures. The notion was that public figures were able to influence the
affairs of society and had ready access to the mass media to influence

policy and to counter criticism of their own conduct despite their failure to hold a government position. As Chief Justice Warren remarked, "the distinction between governmental and private sectors are blurred."[12] Although the Court does not impose the same requirements on private persons who are not public officials or public figures, at least with respect to defamatory statements that relate to public issues, the private person does not have the presumptions of the common law. The private person must show fault or negligence on the part of the defendant and may not recover presumed or punitive damages without a showing that the statement was issued as a knowing or reckless falsehood.

From a dissent-based perspective, there is much to praise. The system is designed to prevent a chilling effect on the criticism of particularly powerful people in the society and assures at least with respect to public issues that even private persons will have to show negligence before recovering actual damages. The problem with this First Amendment scheme is that its determination of who counts as a public figure is both too broad and too narrow. The standard for determining who is or is not a public figure was set out in *Gertz v. Robert Welch, Inc.*[13] Elmer Gertz there sued Robert Welch, Inc., for a statement in *American Opinion* magazine to the effect that he had a criminal record, was the architect of a communist frame up, and had been an officer in a communist front organization.

The statements were false, but the defendant argued that Gertz was a public figure who had to prove that the statements were published as knowing or reckless falsehoods. The Court stated that there were two kinds of public figures: (1) "An individual may achieve such pervasive fame or notoriety that he becomes a public figure for all purposes and in all contexts";[14] or (2) "More commonly, an individual injects himself into the forefront of a particular public controversy and thereby becomes a public figure for a limited range of issues."[15]

It strikes me that the first category is too broad. It is not clear that a truly famous person should be treated as a public figure for all purposes and in all contexts. Suppose defamatory statements are made about the sexual tastes of Derek Jeter (now retired), LeBron James, Stephen Colbert, or Wolfgang Puck. Unquestionably such statements would cater to the curiosity of baseball fans, basketball fans, television watchers, and lovers of food, but it is not clear that fame should impose heavier requirements in a libel suit for statements that relate to subject matter that has no bearing on why they are famous. On the other hand, if it were claimed that Jeter or James used productivity enhancing, but illegal drugs, or it were asserted that Colbert plagiarized jokes from another comedian, or Puck used questionable tactics in acquiring produce or made false statements about his workplace, then treating them as public figures would make sense.

The more serious problem, however, is that, as interpreted, the public figure category is too narrow. Take the case of *Tavoulareas v. Piro.*[16] William P. Tavoulareas was the Chair of Mobil Oil. He was accused of setting his son up in a shipping management company that did business with Mobil. According to the definition of a public figure set out in *Gertz*, those facts in and of themselves are insufficient to make the case that he is a public figure. Although Tavoulareas was an extremely powerful and important executive, it is unlikely that most people would know him by name or by sight. He had not achieved pervasive fame or notoriety. Thus, in order for him to be a public figure, it would have to be shown that he thrust himself to the forefront of a particular public controversy in order to influence the outcome.

But I would argue that the Chair of Mobil Oil should be regarded as a public figure with respect to any statement that relates to his job performance whether or not he is famous and whether or not he thrust himself to the forefront of the particular public controversy at issue. The point of the public figure doctrine is not to chill criticism of powerful people in our society, and the Chair of Mobil Oil surely meets that description. As Sheldon Wolin observed, and as we saw in the last chapter, the influence of large corporations "extends beyond the merely economic sphere, penetrating legislatures, governmental agencies, and political parties."[17] There is something seriously wrong with a doctrine that regards Wolfgang Puck (or in former days Julia Child) as a public figure, but not the Chair of one of the largest oil companies in the world, at least with respect to his business activities.

But my criticism of the public figure doctrine goes deeper still. Its focus seems to be on national fame or injection into a particular public controversy. It seems to me that the focus should be on power, and hierarchies of power can be local, state, or national. Take the Dean of the Cornell Law School. The Dean is a powerful figure within the

Cornell Law School. It seems to me that if the local newspaper were to criticize him, he should be treated as a public figure. The same applies to a teacher who exercises power over students who is called out in the local law school newspaper. On the other hand, if the *New York Times* attacks a law teacher, in the absence of more facts, there is no basis to treat the professor as having power in the national society. The basic idea is that we want to encourage the criticism of injustice in local, regional, and national hierarchies of all forms and descriptions. Regrettably, our defamation law has no such focus. Indeed, in its fascination with fame and notoriety, it seems to have lost contact with important First Amendment values.

DISSENT BY WORKERS AND STUDENTS

The lack of constitutional respect for dissent in the workplace is particularly disquieting. Most important, the First Amendment does not apply at all to the private workplace. So far as the Constitution is concerned, a private employer can fire any employee because his or her views are not liked by the employer.[18] This leaves millions of citizens constitutionally defenseless in combatting discrimination on account of their speech in a vital sphere of their lives.

Even when the First Amendment does apply as is the case with public employers, protections for dissent are weak. *Connick v. Myers*[19] well illustrates the difficulty. Harry Connick Sr., the District Attorney of New Orleans, transferred Assistant District Attorney Sheila Myers to a different section over her strong objection. In response, Myers distributed a questionnaire to her fellow attorneys asking about their attitudes to the transfer policies of the office, office morale, the need for a grievance committee, the level of confidence in various supervisors, and whether they felt pressured to participate in election campaigns. Connick fired Myers for distributing the questionnaire. He regarded the distribution as a "mini-insurrection"[20] and an act of insubordination. Myers argued that her speech was protected under the First Amendment.

When the Supreme Court approached the issue, it regarded it as crucial to determine whether the speech of Myers was of public concern. One might think that any dispute in a public agency over its management should be classified as a matter of public concern, but the Court thought otherwise. It suggested that the questions about transfer policy, office supervisors, the desirability of a grievance committee, and office morale were indicative of a single employee being dissatisfied with the status quo rather than a matter of public concern. On the other hand, it concluded that the question whether employees felt pressured to participate in political campaigns did implicate a matter of public concern. Nonetheless, the Court concluded that the other questions predominated and it deferred to Connick's judgment that Meyers's action tended to undermine his authority and to disrupt personal working relationships within the office.

Beyond *Connick*, the Court held in *Garcetti v. Ceballos*[21] that speech made on the job within the scope of employment receives no First Amendment protection at all (though the Court may make an exception to support the academic freedom of professors).[22] The case is particularly appalling because Caballos as a supervising district attorney was criticizing a search warrant on the ground that it contained false representations. The case licenses retaliation against government employees when as part of their job they expose and criticize the abuse of power by government officials. On the other hand, as the Court held in *Pickering v. Board of Education*,[23] employees who criticize an employer in the newspaper on a matter of public concern may be protected if the contribution to public discourse is not outweighed by the interests of the public employer. So, if it is part of your job to give critical feedback to your employer, you may want to go to the newspaper in order to have any constitutional protection. In sum, private employees have no free speech protection; public employees do not have enough.

The situation for students is bad as well. In private schools, students have no applicable First Amendment rights. In public schools, there was once substantial respect for a student's right to speak. In 1969, the Court held in *Tinker v. Des Moines School District*[24] that a school child in a public school had a constitutional right to wear a black armband to school in protest of the Vietnam War. The Court ruled that public schools are not "enclaves of totalitarianism"[25] and denied that school

children shed their First Amendment rights as they pass through the
schoolhouse gate. The Court noted that the speech was not disruptive
and did not interfere with the rights of others. Nonetheless, in subsequent years, as Jamin Raskin observes, Tinker has been eroded by
the "sharp undertow of sympathy for authoritarian structure on the
Burger, Rehnquist, and Roberts Courts."[26]

A good example of this erosion involved the Olympic Torch Parade.
The parade passed through Juneau, Alaska, in front of a high school.
Deborah Morse, the principal of the school, decided to let students and
staff stand across the street from the school during school hours so they
could watch the televised event. In an effort to appear on national television, Joseph Frederick and some other students unfurled a fourteen-foot
banner that read "BONG HITS 4 JESUS." Morse ordered that the banner be
taken down. Frederick refused, and he, but not the other students, was
suspended for ten days. Frederick argued that the suspension violated his
First Amendment rights. In *Morse v. Frederick*,[27] Chief Justice Roberts
upheld the actions of the principal on the ground that Frederick's speech
was "reasonably viewed as promoting illegal drug usage."[28]

An alternative reading, of course, is that the message is gibberish,
silly, meaningless, and intended to be funny. Assuming that the slogan
was advocating drug usage, however, the message addresses a matter
of public concern and might implicate serious First Amendment principles. These concerns would give way if the message were directed
to inciting imminent lawless action and likely to incite such action.
And perhaps the imminence standard could be relaxed in the school
context. But it is utterly unlikely that any student would be moved by
this vague slogan to smoke dope. The slogan neither caused disrup-
tion of the school environment nor interfered with the rights of others. *Morse* simply backed away from *Tinker's* perspective that students
should be free to dissent from authoritarian dictates, and *Morse* is part
of a pattern in which the Court has bent over backward to uphold
censorship by school authorities of student speeches and the student
press. Indeed, as Raskin explains, the "conservative court has carved
out major exceptions to *Tinker* in the contexts of social conformity,
sexual prudishness, protection of adult's feelings, and promotion of
ideological unity for drug prohibition."[29]

NATIONAL SECURITY

One of the long-standing battles between the conservatives and the liberals in free speech cases is that the former have tended to bend over backward in deferring to the executive and legislative branches when national security is claimed to be at stake. *Holder v. Humanitarian Law Project*[30] is a conspicuous example. Some of the plaintiffs in the litigation to take a representative example wished to train members of the Partiya Karkeran Kurdistan (PKK) in ways to petition the United Nations and other representative bodies for relief. The US government maintained that such training would provide material support to a foreign terrorist organization in violation of a federal criminal statute.[31] The plaintiffs argued that the statute could not be applied in this fashion without violating the First Amendment.

The conservative majority disagreed even though it did not suggest that the plaintiffs intended to further the terrorist aims of the organization, even though it recognized that the speech involved was political, and even though it determined that a rigorous and demanding standard was required. The Court claimed that assistance in formulating peaceful petitions would support the terrorist aims of the organization. In so concluding, the Court respectfully deferred to the executive and legislative branches. This language of deference seems quite incompatible with rigorous scrutiny. Recall that in the violent video games case, the Court gave the back of its hand to professional mental health organizations rather than respectful deference. Justice Breyer in dissent complained that neither the legislature nor the executive had provided any empirical support for the claim that the speech would further the terrorist objectives of the organization.[32] The worry that the PKK would use peaceful means to further violence in his view was too speculative to justify censorship.

To be sure, *Humanitarian Law Project* is a single case in the national security area, but it does continue the theme that the Court will defer to authorities at the expense of dissenters – whether those authorities are the Park Service, a public employer, a school principal, or the executive branch even when its support for censorship is generalized and speculative.

THE PRESS CLAUSE

Because the institutional press continues to reach a broad audience[33] and because it plays a special role in reporting the news and exposing injustice, a system of freedom of expression designed to combat injustice would recognize the need for recognizing its role in some circumstances.[34] Yet, members of the Court have denied that the press clause confers any special privileges on the press.[35] From this perspective, the Press Clause apparently means no more than the notion that the right to free speech includes the right to use a printing press or other technological means of reaching a broad audience. It is not at all clear that this claim accurately describes all of the case law.[36]

Nonetheless, the First Amendment is not adequately structured to permit the press to serve as a check on powerful institutions. If the press is recognized as an institution with a special responsibility to report the news and to expose wrongdoing by powerful individuals and institutions, it should be given special rights of access to gather news by entering prisons, protest sites, scenes of disaster, witnessing the return of war casualties, executions, public meetings, and the like. For example, it makes sense that the general public has no general right of access to prisons, but denying access to reporters is a prescription for inhumane punishment.[37] Under existing law, access is too often the exception and not the rule. Of course, access needs to be limited in reasonable ways. But the rule that wholesale denials of access are consistent with the First Amendment is convenient, but it protects injustice.[38]

So too, the law needs to recognize that law enforcement cannot treat press institutions as if they are ordinary businesses. The *New York Times* is not a fertilizer factory. Searches of press rooms and press material should be permitted only on a showing of pressing necessity.[39] The confidentiality of sources should be respected except in the rarest of cases.[40] Moreover, government should not be able to circumvent statutory restrictions protecting reporters from divulging the names of their sources by the dragnet approaches they might take in getting the telephone, bank, and e-mail records of a suspected drug dealer. In each of these areas, press institutions are treated by the Constitution in ways that would not distinguish them from ordinary businesses, and members of the press are sometimes treated in ways that would not distinguish them from criminal suspects.[41] Denying access protects injustice from being discovered, and treating members of the press in ways that compel them to be adjuncts of law enforcement undermines any confidence that confidential sources are participating in a secure system.

Underlying these failures to support those who would provide information and commentary of potential importance to public dialogue is a sense that those who work for the press should not have special privileges in a democracy. But the public loses, for example, if those who work for the press are shut out of a public meeting because of a first-come-first-served rule. Refusing to make a distinction when genuine differences exist creates a false equality, an equality that serves neither the press nor the public.

Perhaps more important is a concern that the term *press* is too difficult to define. There is no question that defining the press involves difficulties that are compounded by the rise of the Internet, and it may be that the term press might need to be applied in different ways in different contexts. But the difficulties are not insuperable.[42] Regularity of publication, the size of the audience reached, the nature of the subject matter, and possible delegation of decisions away from governmental actors to press organizations and the like (as is often done when press galleries are created) are each considerations that make the inquiry less difficult. Moreover, the consequences of making a mistake are not as severe as those involved in censorship. Someone who is not classified as press still maintains free speech rights. Most important, if a distinction is not made between the public and the press, the public will lose the benefits of information and criticism that press institutions can provide.

GOVERNMENTAL STRUCTURE

The Constitution protects freedom of speech; yet at the same time it discourages much speech. In this respect, our Constitution is not unique. All constitutions discourage some types of speech. I do not mean to suggest that this is necessarily bad. For example, our Constitution discourages, but does not prohibit, speech that would try to institute slavery or abrogate the Bill of Rights. It discourages this because the Constitution places formidable barriers to engaging in a successful effort to amend it. This often is a good thing. I doubt we would welcome a national movement calling upon us to reinstitute slavery or one that would call upon us to eliminate freedom of press.

On the other hand, one of the difficulties of mobilizing a movement to overturn *Citizens United* is the widespread view that the movement could not succeed because of the difficulty of amending the Constitution. I do not see that as a good thing. Nonetheless, one must take the bitter with the sweet. And the difficulty of amending fundamental rights is something to be celebrated, not denigrated even though it discourages much speech on public issues.

There is a deeper aspect of the Constitution discouraging speech that is more problematic. Even beyond the difficulty of the amendment process, the constitutional structure makes it difficult to achieve national change. This is deliberate. Alexander Hamilton argued in *The Federalist Papers*, No. 73, that making change difficult restrained the "excess of lawmaking" and "kept things in the same state in which they happen to be at any given period." He argued that "the injury which possibly may be done by defeating a few good laws will be amply compensated by preventing a number of bad ones."[43] Underlying this sentiment is a fear of popular democratic movements that, if not checked, could sweep in a number of "bad laws." Thus, as every school child knows (or should know), a measure in most cases cannot become law without passing the House and the Senate and not being vetoed by the President (in the absence of an override), or struck down by the courts. The House was initially designed to be the voice of the people, but gerrymandering has made it possible (as was the case in 2013) for a majority of the representatives to be elected by a minority of the electorate.

This antipopulist feature is compounded by what has come to be called the "winner take all" system combined with the districting system. So, if a party candidate wins a congressional district by 51–49 percent, the candidate wins the seat. If the same party carried every seat by the same margin, the party would have 100 percent of the representation with only 51 percent of the vote. Of course, that does not happen. But even without gerrymandering, representation can fail to reflect the interests of voters.

By contrast, suppose members of Congress ran in statewide races without a winner take all system (and then were assigned districts by the party) and suppose further that seats were assigned on a proportional basis, the result would be a representation more reflective of the attitudes of the electorate and a more politically diverse political spectrum.

The spectrum would be more politically diverse because third parties could achieve a measure of representation proportional to their earned vote. No longer would those who voted for third party candidates be casting their votes for candidates without a plausible electoral chance. And the press, an institution that covers the powerful, would have an incentive to cover the issues raised by third parties because they would become political actors. I mention this not to suggest that proportional representation is just around the corner, but to indicate that the structure of our political system operates to channel political discussion by powerful institutions in the system of political discourse.

Even more obviously, the Senate is deliberately structured not to reflect the voice of popular movements. States with small populations like Mississippi and Alabama each get two representatives in the Senate; so do heavily populated New York and California. To get an idea of the impact of this structure on popular representation, consider that according to the 2000 Census, senators from the twenty-six smallest states, who represented only 17.8 percent of the nation's population, nonetheless constituted a majority of the Senate.[44] This one-state – two votes – feature of the Constitution cannot even be amended. In addition, only one-third of the body is up for election at any time making it difficult for a popular majority to transform the body in a single election. Moreover, the blocking feature of the Senate is compounded by the existence of the filibuster in which a small minority of a body that already represents a minority of the population can in many circumstances prevent a measure from becoming law.

One other feature greatly aggravates the problem. Political campaigns are not funded by the government; they are primarily funded by contributions from the private sector, and politicians typically want to be reelected. The costs of campaigns are skyrocketing and that means money must be raised, not only from the grassroots, but also from the wealthy. Obviously, the wealthy include business corporations, and, as we discussed in Chapter 7, the wealthy include business corporations that invest in politicians who will pass or resist legislation protecting or increasing their profits wholly apart from whether those actions will help the public interest or reflect the interests of popular movements. This, of course, leads to the power of the lobbies representing moneyed interests on Capitol Hill. A politician who does not cater to moneyed interests is unlikely to get reelected. This means that to get a measure through Congress requires getting it through the House and the Senate that in turn requires getting past the moneyed interests that bankroll campaigns of politicians.

What impact does this have on contemporary politics? If you believe that government should be small, that taxes should never increase, that the poor should not be assisted financially, that new efforts to ensure worker safety, higher wages, and stronger legislation in favor of unions, and that strong environmental legislation should be blocked, the structure of the Constitution makes it difficult for opponents of your beliefs to prevail because they need congressional action and the system is deliberately designed to make that action difficult. In other words, Republicans are favored by these structural features. Moreover, Democrats in order to be elected or reelected have to cater to moneyed interests as well. One of the most interesting questions in politics is which moneyed interests favor which parties and why. Knowing that would tell us much more about the plans of a politician than a dozen campaign speeches. As my colleague Aziz Rana remarks in a forthcoming book, "[T]he very effect of the framers' structure of divided government was that it allowed socio-economic elites to dominate quietly the instruments of statecraft while making it very difficult for poor citizens – whose only meaningful resource was sheer numbers – to use elections and mass pressure to overcome the variety of veto points embedded in political decision-making."[45]

None of this means that change cannot occur. Change is not impossible, and great victories have been achieved. It does mean that when change is difficult to achieve, dissent is discouraged. Indeed, somewhere between one-half to two-thirds of qualified voters do not vote in the United States.[46] Those Americans doubt their vote makes a difference. When change is so difficult to achieve, it becomes more understandable how our structures tend to create a "democracy" – presiding over avid consumers rather than engaged citizens.

ALTERNATIVE APPROACHES

In prior chapters I have argued that other countries have adopted approaches that are superior to those employed in our country in dealing with free speech issues. In many respects, I believe the United States despite its deficiencies generally does a better job of protecting dissent than other countries. For example, the Supreme Court has held in *Brandenburg v. Ohio*[47] that advocacy of illegal action is permitted unless it is "directed to inciting or producing imminent lawless action and is likely to incite or produce imminent lawless action."[48] As Eric Barendt has observed, courts in England, Germany, Turkey, and the European Court of Human Rights have far less protection for this brand of dissent.[49] Similarly, as discussed earlier in this chapter, the Supreme Court held in *New York Times Co. v. Sullivan*,[50] that a public official (and subsequently a public figure) could not recover in a defamation suit in the absence of a showing of a knowing or reckless falsehood. Here again Canada, England, Germany and the European Court of Human Rights have refused to go as far. In the absence of certain privileged situations (e.g., speaking on the floor of a legislature), the protection they have been willing to afford in cases involving statements of fact is a defense of truth or something on the order of reasonable care under the totality of circumstances.[51] Regrettably, Europe's handling of issues involving demonstrations is no better than the United States and in some cases worse.[52]

The employment context is somewhat more nuanced. The European Court of Human Rights has held that the European Convention's free speech protections extend to public *and* private employees. I think it fair to say that Europe provides at least as much free speech protection to public employees as does the United States and substantially more to private employees under the European Convention of Human Rights. It has not formulated a ruling regarding on-the-job speech along the lines of *Garcetti*. Hopefully, it will permit employers some discretion while not affording them plenary power to fire employees in retaliation for their critical speech.

One area in which Europe is better in the dissent department is that the structure of most of its governments is somewhat more encouraging of social change affording incentives to dissent. As we have seen, the US Constitution is structured to avoid political change and, therefore, tends to support the status quo. Not so with European governments. In addition, other features of the governmental structure in the United States produce two parties and highly discourage third parties. Many European countries by contrast have proportional representation. This broadens the political spectrum and gives incentives for more principled criticism of the status quo.

In the end, I conclude that neither the United States nor the European countries have a standout record in protecting dissent. In my view, the United States has better doctrine in this area, and Europe has better structure. Both need to improve.

9   RELIGION

In the previous chapter, I argued that the Court's libertarian approach to speech protection faltered when it was called upon to protect the speech that matters the most. In other words, it casts a blind eye upon the needs of the subordinated, the vulnerable, and the minority. Just as the Court is not sufficiently sensitive to the importance of protecting those who use speech to dissent, the Court is insensitive to those whose religions mark them out as different from others. First, in the absence of malicious intent, the Court has developed a constitutional doctrine that does little to protect religious liberty. In addition, in the system of freedom of expression, the Court permits government speech about religion that marginalizes the nonreligious and those of minority religions. In many of the chapters we considered in Part I, I suggested that better approaches could be found in other Western countries. But here, European approaches in this area are differentiated and disappointing. On the whole, those approaches are somewhat worse than those taken in the United States.

The First Amendment addresses religion in two ways. First, it protects the free exercise of religion. Second, it prohibits the establishment of religion by the state. Taken together, these clauses should protect important values. Ideally, the Free Exercise Clause would stand for religious liberty, particularly freedom of conscience;[1] it also would protect equality by guarding against discrimination on the basis of religion; it would safeguard freedom of religious association, which is vital to many forms of free exercise; it would bind together a strong political community committed to protecting religious freedom. The Establishment Clause should also promote important values many of which are also supported by the Free Exercise Clause. Ideally, the Establishment Clause would protect equality by steering clear of religious positions, so that some religions would not be favored over others, and so that the nonreligious would not be relegated to unequal citizenship; by protecting equality, religious liberty would also be promoted; by treating all citizens as insiders, the Clause would foster an inclusive political community in which political divisiveness triggered by religion would be minimized; by recognizing that religious issues are not the province of government, the Clause would protect the autonomy of government, and it would protect religious institutions from politicians who historically have harmed religions even when they have purported to help them;[2] finally, it is conceivable that by separating religion from the governmental sphere, religion would actually be promoted.[3]

Led by the conservatives on the Court, however, both the Free Exercise Clause and the Establishment Clause have been narrowly interpreted without sufficient attention to the important values they ideally would protect and promote.[4] Room has been left for statutory protections such as the Religious Freedom Restoration Act, but the Court's interpretations of our Constitution have surgically removed the teeth from constitutionally grounded protections of religion.

Although the Constitution's Free Exercise Clause has never been interpreted in a way that provided generous protection for religious liberty, *Employment Division v. Smith*[5] sharply narrowed the protections previously afforded and stands as the landmark case today. At the time of the facts leading to the decision, Alfred L. Smith was a sixty-six-year-old Klamath Indian and a member of the Native American Church. The use of peyote in the Native American Church as part of its religious ceremonies dates back to the middle of the sixteenth century in Mexico and was well established by the nineteenth century. Its use in religious ceremonies is akin to the sacrament of communion in Christian churches except that peyote is itself an object of worship. Prayers are devoted to it in the same way that prayers are directed to the Holy Spirit. Although the use of peyote is optional at such services (as is the taking of communion by congregants in Christian services), a prohibition of its use would strike at the "theological heart"[6] of the religion.

Peyote is a hallucinogen (giving rise to perception anomalies), but without the addictive craving of a narcotic. It takes the form of small buttons on a spineless cactus primarily found in Texas and northern Mexico. Its hallucinogenic effects vary with the person, but it can be marked by bright colors, geometric shapes, and visions involving humans or animals. It induces a feeling of comprehension and friendliness toward others. On the other hand, it can induce symptoms of schizophrenia or paranoia.

It is widely outlawed though, as we will see, the prohibitions often make exceptions for bona fide religions that use peyote as a sacrament. Smith, however, worked in the state of Oregon, and the state of Oregon made no such exception. To students of Oregon history, this should not be surprising because Oregon was not traditionally welcoming to nonwhites. Oregon's original territorial constitution barred black people, "Chinamen," and Hawaiians from the state, a provision that was not changed until 1922, and even then the Ku Klux Klan remained a major power in the state. As late as 1974, a so-called "Indian War" took place in which Indians protested their treatment by white bartenders in Klamath Falls. After two Indians in separate incidents were charged with murder, the mayor of Klamath Falls observed that "Indians as a whole – with few exceptions – are a pretty irresponsible group."[7] And the state of Oregon had a project of selling off Indian lands and attempting to substitute "American" culture for "Indian" culture.

Al Smith's tribe was one of the first tribes to have its land sold in an effort to Americanize the tribe and free the lands for private loggers. Smith's cultural transition was troubled and he became an alcoholic. He recovered, however, and devoted a substantial part of his life to helping others who were dependent on drugs. He ultimately worked as a rehabilitation counselor at the Douglas County Council on Alcohol and Drug Abuse Prevention and Treatment ("ADAPT"), a private organization.

And here is where Mr. Smith's journey to the Supreme Court begins. Smith was a member of the Native American Church when he was hired by ADAPT in August of 1982, but he had not previously ingested peyote. So far as the record shows, Smith ingested peyote on only one occasion at a religious full weekend ceremony in

March, 1984. Even then he ingested a nominal amount of peyote, an amount insufficient to produce a hallucinogenic effect. Why did he do so? Apparently, Mr. Smith ingested peyote in religious solidarity with a friend and coworker who previously had been fired for ingesting peyote at a religious ceremony. Smith had been warned not to ingest peyote because ADAPT had a policy that prohibited the use of alcohol or any nonprescription drugs by staff members who were former substance abusers.

He was fired for this, and he applied for unemployment compensation. The Oregon Employment Division denied his application on the ground that he had been fired for misconduct. Smith maintained that this denial violated his right to the Free Exercise of Religion, and strong Supreme Court precedent supported his view. *Sherbert v. Verner*[8] and *Hobbie v. Unemployment Appeals Comm'n*[9] upheld the First Amendment right of Seventh Day Adventists to unemployment compensation when they had refused on religious grounds to work on Saturday. *Thomas v. Review Board*[10] upheld the First Amendment right of a Jehovah's Witness to unemployment compensation who had refused to accept a transfer that would have required him to assist in the production of tanks in violation of his religious views. In rejecting Smith's First Amendment claim, Justice Scalia distinguished those cases on the ground that the employees in those cases had not violated a criminal law.

It is not clear why this distinction made a difference. Oregon might have said that criminal misconduct was special for purposes of its unemployment compensation system; however, it explicitly rejected that view. In considering whether a religious exemption was required, Oregon sought to determine whether granting the exemption would create fiscal issues for its system. It determined that it would not. Peyote is not marijuana. The ingestion of peyote induces nausea. It is not fitting for recreational use. The number of marijuana users consequently dwarfs those who use peyote. An exception for the religious use of marijuana could induce false claims that might present difficulties for the Oregon system in a way that was not remotely threatened by peyote. The criminal aspect of the misconduct was wholly irrelevant to the Oregon scheme.

Nonetheless, for Scalia, the issue was whether freedom of religion required an exemption from the criminal statute outlawing the ingestion of peyote. Scalia denied that it did. He purported to be frightened of a system in which "each conscience is a law unto itself."[11] He insisted that a system in which judges balanced the government interests against the interest in religious freedom would be unworkable. Indeed, Scalia concluded that when a statute applicable to a general category of conduct happens to burden religion, that result would ordinarily require no constitutional inquiry at all.

Embarrassing Scalia's constitutional conclusion were a number of cases in which the Court had squarely held that a generally applicable statute that burdens religion in fact does require a strong justification to pass constitutional muster. For example, *Wisconsin v. Yoder*[12] involved a compulsory education statute requiring that parents – religious or not – send their children to high schools accredited by the state. The Amish religion required parents to keep their children out of schools after the eighth grade. The Amish believed that high school attendance was contrary to the Amish religion and way of life and that they would endanger their own salvation and that of their children by complying with the law. The Court upheld the religious right of the Amish to keep their children within the community. Scalia primarily distinguished *Yoder* and other similar cases by noting that there was another constitutional interest involved as well.[13] So *Yoder* also involved the right of parents to raise their children. Scalia maintained that where religion rights were accompanied by other constitutional interests, a searching inquiry was appropriate, but ordinarily not otherwise.

What emerges is this patchwork: if a law is of general application (i.e., nondiscriminatory) and burdens religion, no freedom of religion issue exists unless it is in the area of unemployment compensation where no criminal conduct is involved and unless no cognizable other constitutional interest is present. By contrast, if a generally applicable statute burdens speech, the statute as applied is unconstitutional unless it meets a constitutional test. Go figure.

Aside from the reckless disregard for freedom of religion that this case manifests, it is important to notice who is likely to be harmed by it. Scalia notes that his rule applies to all religions regardless of their majority or minority status. For example, during Prohibition, laws against wine consumption threatened to burden the central religious ceremonies of some important Christian denominations. But, unlike the Native Americans in Oregon, they had no trouble securing an exemption. Scalia, of course, knew that religious minorities could be disadvantaged by his cavalier rewriting of existing precedent. As he put it, "[L]eaving accommodation to the political process will place at a relative disadvantage those religious practices that are not widely engaged in," but that, he claimed, was the unavoidable consequence of democratic government.[14] Really? I would have thought that democratic government did more for minorities than requiring them to beg for exemptions at the whim of a majoritarian legislature. I would have thought that a democratic government would have a Bill of Rights designed to protect minorities and a Court prepared to enforce it.

Fortunately, as has been true in a number of instances in which the discrimination against religious minorities was accompanied by substantial publicity, *Smith* ignited a firestorm of political reaction. The State of Oregon under broad pressure from religious groups enacted an exemption,[15] and the US Congress passed the Religious Freedom Restoration Act,[16] an Act designed to guarantee those religious liberties by statute that the Court had dismissed in constitutional law. Congress was only partly successful. Although the Court upheld the statute as applied to federal law and programs,[17] it ruled that the Congress had no power to guarantee religious freedom of this type against the actions of states and localities.[18] Accordingly, many states have passed their own anti-*Smith* statutes.[19] Nonetheless, as Justice Blackmun observed in dissent, the Founders thought that religious freedom was an indispensable part of constitutional liberty, and that freedom was not to be confined to the religious majority. Under the leadership of Justice Scalia, the Court for the most part left religious protection to the vagaries of the political process.[20]

One case brought under the federal statute merits our attention. Even though the decision is statutory, the statute is designed to restore constitutional rights, and it speaks volumes about the politics of religious freedom. The case is *Burwell v. Hobby Lobby Stores, Inc.*[21] Hobby Lobby challenged a regulation of the US Department of Health and Human Services requiring that employers with fifty or more employees provide health insurance that included forms of contraception the owners of Hobby Lobby believed were tantamount to abortion. Hobby Lobby is a company with more than five hundred stores and thirteen thousand employees, but the corporation and an affiliated business are entirely owned by a family of five, each member of which is religiously opposed to these contraceptives.[22]

The conservative majority ruled that the government had to meet an even more stringent test than had been employed under the religious liberty the legislation was merely designed to *restore*[23] and ruled in favor of *Hobby Lobby* over the dissent of the four more liberal justices. This lineup appears to turn the *Smith* decision upside down. There the conservatives denied the freedom of religion claim despite liberal dissents. Here the conservatives *champion* freedom of religion despite liberal dissents.

Most liberals deplored the result in *Hobby Lobby*. They did so despite the Court's assurance that none of the involved employees would be denied access to insurance coverage for contraceptives. It turned out that the Court's assurance was overdrawn. The Court did not take into account that it would take time for the administration to fashion a rule in response to the decision, and the rule was not applied retroactively. So presumably some women were harmed by the delay, and, at a minimum, the Court in my view should have made sure that no woman was negatively affected.[24]

Nonetheless, the main opposition to the decision relied on three main arguments that were independent of the interim effect of the decision on women. The first argument is that a corporation is not a human being. A corporation, after all, has no conscience. On the other hand, religious organizations including corporations (think of churches organized as corporations) have freedom of religion rights.

The real question is whether a for-profit corporation (which many liberals want to engage in some social responsibility activities) should have freedom of religion rights (or standing to raise the rights of shareholders) when all of the shareholders object to an activity on the basis of conscience. Of course, it is arguable that shareholders should not be able to make selective use of the corporate form. If Hobby Lobby is sued, corporate law insists that the company is a person and that it is separate from the shareholders. So a plaintiff cannot reach the assets of corporate shareholders to enforce a damage award. Liability is limited to corporate assets. When religious rights of the shareholders are claimed, however, the shareholders maintain that they and the company are inseparable.[25]

In my view these positions are not incompatible. The limited liability of shareholders is not designed as a favor to shareholders. It is calculated to encourage investment. Encouraging investment, however, need not and should not require the waiving of religious rights. To deny the freedom of religion right on the ground that the business is a corporation rather than a partnership elevates form over substance.[26]

The second argument maintains that the law here does not impose a substantial burden.[27] In the end, however, the argument ultimately rests on a simple disagreement with the owners' views. Of course, it is easy to disagree with those views. The owners in the end are being forced by the government to make funds available in the form of insurance for medical care including contraceptives. The contraceptives at issue would be used if, but only if, women make the choice to use the particular contraceptives to which the owners object. Making money available for immoral purposes is a part of our daily tax life. To conclude that obeying this government regulation is foreclosed as a matter of conscience is morally precious to say the least. And the argument that notifying the insurance company of the moral objection is also morally foreclosed strikes me as what Catholics would ordinarily characterize as an excessively scrupulous conscience.

My point, however, is that even if the moral claim is crazy, it is still a substantial burden to force someone to engage in conduct that violates their conscience. There should be room in non-conscience cases for government to argue that a burden is not substantial so long as the theology of the claimant is not questioned. But it is not up to the government to officially declare that a conscientious religious objection is a false objection. Please understand. I am not saying that freedom of conscience should always prevail. Freedom of conscience should give way in the face of a significant interest in many cases. If women, for example, would have been denied access to contraceptives (the ones at issue would cost a month's pay of a Hobby Lobby worker), that interest in my view should have overridden the freedom of conscience claim. But that ultimately was not the case here.[28]

The third argument relies on the fact that taxpayers with religious objections to the uses to which their money is put cannot successfully claim that such taxation violates their rights to religious liberty. The reason they have no claim is not that no religious burden exists. Many, for example, have been forced to support wars to which they are conscientiously opposed. One problem is that if government had to accommodate every religious or moral objection to the uses to which taxation is put, the administrative burden would be impossibly difficult. This would be compounded by the issue of sincerity. Policing the sincerity of objecting taxpayers would be a monumental task, and the promise of accommodation would encourage false claims.

I have gone back and forth on the wisdom of the outcome in *Hobby Lobby*, but I have come to believe it was wrongly decided. Properly understood, the system at issue in *Hobby Lobby* involves a tax. To be sure, the compelled extraction would have gone to an insurance company and not the government, but the taxation system the government adopted was simply more efficient than having the money go to the government and then back to the insurance company. Either way the employer would be forced to fund a disfavored use.

Moreover, the approach in *Hobby Lobby* raises substantial sincerity issues for the future. To be sure, everyone on the Court agreed that the owners of Hobby Lobby are sincere, and in considering the argument I will accept that assumption. Nonetheless, it should be noted that Hobby Lobby's 401K plan has $73 million invested in mutual funds that include investments in the very contraceptives to which they morally object. I would like to hear an explanation of why the owners are morally precluded from offering insurance that includes certain contraceptives, but not precluded from offering investments in which employees make money off the sale of those contraceptives. Perhaps, a fiduciary obligation requires making such funds available, but that would raise the question why the fiduciary obligation itself does not create a religious burden.

I also worry that the sincerity of many on the right is politically corrupted. I think the hatred for Obama has helped fuel the religious objections, which does not mean that the objectors are insincere. It does mean that many objectors got to these views by a corrupt process.

As I have suggested, the larger point goes well beyond the question whether the owners of Hobby Lobby are sincere (I believe they are); the problem is that the decision requires the government to set up an administrative apparatus to judge the religious sincerity of an untold number of claimants. I believe this was justifiable and necessary with respect to conscientious objectors to the military draft. But it is hard to ignore the substantial administrative burden created by the system.

In the end, we are left with an apparent ideological shift by conservatives and liberals. What about the conservative justices? Why do they reach out to defend a religious claim in *Hobby Lobby*, but not in *Smith*? Here I can only speculate. *Smith* called upon the Court to engage in what they regard as difficult form of balancing and doing so to support drug use. It declined to enter the thicket. *Hobby Lobby* involved a case in which the statute forced the Court to enter the thicket. When it entered, some might say that it protected a religious minority. As a mathematical demographic matter, this is unquestionably correct. But it bears noting that with the exception of Justice Kennedy,[29] each member of the majority was a conservative Catholic. It would not be a surprise to learn that they shared the theological views of the Bishops on contraception and abortion. It is entirely conceivable that they were part of the minority they protected in *Hobby Lobby*. Moreover, as conservatives, they were hostile to the Affordable Care Act, could be expected to be generally hostile to taxation, and were likely to associate forced financial extractions with denials of freedom. They also may have had little empathy for Native Americans and a religion that appeared strange to them, but they regularly attend church with many who share the views about contraceptives held by the owners of Hobby Lobby.[30]

What about the liberal justices? Their views did not depend on the taxation argument. So, why protect those who traffic in depictions of the abuse of animals and the like, but not protect the conscience of conservative Christians? From the perspective of the liberals, it was easy to support the earlier religious claims of Native American religious believers, the Amish, the Quakers, and other objectors to war as a matter of conscience. But supporting the religious claims of powerful political enemies whose claims threatened to harm the reproductive rights of women combined with acceptance of religious rights for business corporations was too much to swallow. Alternatively, it might be argued that the government interest in *Hobby Lobby* was simply stronger than in the prior cases, but that interest might have been furthered in ways that do not impinge on the religious interest – at least in the long run.

However one characterizes the result in *Hobby Lobby*, the general rule promulgated in *Smith* guarantees that the freedom of religion claims based in the Constitution will rarely have any legal purchase. Religious minorities are left to pursue their claims in a political process that is ordinarily responsive to money, powerful interest groups, and majorities.

In *Smith*, as we have seen, Justice Scalia recognized the disadvantages religious minorities faced, but he wrote it off as an unavoidable consequence of the democratic process. This insensitivity to religious minorities pervades the Establishment Clause context as well, but it plays itself out in a different way. In the Establishment Clause context, however, the Court is even more polarized than in the Free Exercise arena. The most significant of the recent cases is *Town of Greece v. Galloway*.[31] The case involved prayers employed to open the monthly Town Board sessions in a town of ninety-four thousand residents located near Rochester, New York. The town is predominantly Christian. Approximately twenty-eight hundred of the residents are Jewish with lesser number of Buddhists and Hindus. The number of atheists and agnostics is unclear.

With the exception of a single Buddhist temple, all of the religious buildings in Greece are Christian churches, although several Jewish synagogues are situated across the border in Rochester. During the period relevant to the litigation, there were approximately 120 board meetings. At the invitation of the board, during this period, 116 monthly meetings were led by Christian ministers who were called the chaplain of the month. Only four prayers were led by non-Christians, and those four took place only after the litigation was filed in 2008. Thereafter, from 2009 through June 2010 when the record closed, only Christian ministers led prayers. Apparently, all of the prayers were delivered by the chaplains facing the audience present with their backs to the board.

The board maintained it had a nondiscrimination policy, and that it would permit anyone of any faith tradition to lead a prayer if they asked, and the record shows that the board did invite those who asked to give a prayer to be the chaplain of the month. But this policy was not mentioned in any board meeting, in any board publication, or even on its website.

Although both houses of Congress advise guest chaplains that they should bear in mind that the members of Congress adhere to a variety of faith traditions, the Town of Greece gave no such admonition. Chaplains in Greece quite frequently prayed in ways that were not mindful of the possible presence of those who were not Christian. Indeed, the typical prayer invoked the name of Jesus. Some of the prayers could not even have been shared by all Christians. There were references in some of the prayers to the doctrine that Christ died for our sins. This atonement doctrine, although probably adhered to by most Christians, is nonetheless a controversial feature of Christian theology. Many liberal Protestant theologians think the picture of an angry God so upset about the Divine affront implicated by human sin that he could only be satisfied by the torture, suffering, and death of a Divine human involves a distortion of the meaning of the Crucifixion and of the nature of God. Instead these theologians see the Crucifixion as standing for God's empathizing with the suffering of humanity, its repudiation of the embrace of worldly power and prestige, and its siding with the poor and vulnerable.[32]

The plaintiffs, of course, argued that the Town of Greece had sponsored sectarian prayer in violation of the Establishment Clause, and they also contended that the overall context in which many of the prayers were delivered impermissibly pressured audience members to indicate their joining in the prayer by standing, bowing heads, saying Amen, or, as some of the board members did, making the sign of the cross. Unlike observers of congressional sessions who are simply spectators, those present at the Town of Greece meetings were typically there to ask the board to do something. They might reasonably fear that open disagreement with the prayer could alienate one of more of the board members.

It is easy to understand how one might think that the Town of Greece had run afoul of the Establishment Clause. The Court has stated that the "clearest command of the Establishment Clause is that one religious denomination cannot be officially preferred over another."[33] As I have indicated, there are many reasons for this position. First, the Clause stands for equal citizenship regardless of religious faith or lack of it. Jews, Hindus, Buddhists, Christians, atheists, and agnostics stand equal before the law. If government favors any of these deep positions on the meaning of life over another, the outsider is relegated to second-class citizenship and there are risks that the liberty of the outsider might be compromised because of his or her marginalized status. In addition, if religious doctrine becomes part of politics, the risks of political division marked by religious differences become more acute with the potential for instability such divisions have brought in their wake.

The Establishment Clause stands opposed to religions dominating government. This does not mean that the Constitution stands against religious opposition to government policies, such as those involving war, capital punishment, poverty, or abortion. Such involvement may carry risks, but that sort of democratic involvement is quite different from government determinations whether Jesus Christ died on the cross for our sins. There is no necessity for the government to address such an issue; no reason to think that the government has any special theological expertise; and every reason to think that the preferred theological outcome would closely track what would be likely to get politicians reelected. At the same time, the Establishment Clause is historically opposed to government attempts to "help" religious groups by, for example, giving subsidies to churches, let alone selective subsidies. European history is rife with examples of the prophetic mission of churches being compromised by the desire for monetary favors. James Madison in particular eloquently spoke out against this form of corruption. It has been a historic theme of the American Baptist Church (not to be confused with the Southern Baptist Church) and other churches of the religious left.

This is not to say that the Constitution stands for an impregnable wall of separation between church and state because the Constitution itself is compromised. For example, "In God We Trust" appears on our coins and currency. The motto discriminates against Buddhists, Hindus, atheists, and agnostics. But no justice has argued that the motto violates the Establishment Clause. Some have sought to explain this by the claim that the motto has lost its religious meaning. Admittedly, it would be a rare phenomenon if a person were to look at a dollar bill and be inspired to pray. But the motto is not bereft of religious meaning. It asserts the theological proposition that God exists and it asserts that the God that exists is one we can trust. Moreover, if the phrase has lost religious meaning, it stands as a poster child for the notion that government efforts to assist religion end up harming religion.

I think it unavoidable that this exercise of religion by government is a limited exception to general Establishment Clause principles. I wish we lived in a country where such discrimination against religious and nonreligious minorities was unconstitutional, and where citizens did not cling to the view that religion is assisted by an alliance, however superficial, with government. But I think we do not. It is fair to say that our Constitution is embedded in a religious culture, and the best we can hope for is that the increasingly pluralistic character of the society will lead the Court to a jurisprudence that is more respectful of the diversity of religious and nonreligious views held in the country. Nonetheless, it would be folly to hope that such respect will come from the current Court. It is doubtful whether the current majority subscribes to each of the principles I have described. Even if it did so subscribe, the *Greece* Court pointed to another exception to these Establishment Clause principles.

Throughout our nation's history, legislative prayer has traditionally been employed to open its sessions, and the Court has upheld its constitutionality.[34] Justice Kennedy in writing for the Court relied on the long history of legislative prayer as confirming the absence of an Establishment Clause violation in *Greece*. He insisted that the principal audience for the invocations was the lawmakers, not the public. It is hard to credit this claim given that the ministers in Greece regularly faced the public with their backs to the lawmakers! Even more important, the minister in *Marsh v. Chambers*,[35] the case that upheld legislative prayer, had removed all references to Christ after a Jewish lawmaker complained. The Court observed that the content of the prayers was of no concern so long as the occasion was not exploited to advance one faith over another.[36] Indeed, the lower court declared the prayer practices of Greece to be unconstitutional precisely because a reasonable observer would find that the town prayer program conveyed the message that it endorsed Christianity. When government chooses to have ministers start its sessions with full knowledge of the Christian content of the prayers week after week after week, it is fatuous to suggest that government is not significantly involved in promulgating a sectarian religious message.

Justice Kennedy seemed to accept the idea that a legislature could not advance a particular faith, but he stressed that prayers at legislative sessions need not be bland or nonsectarian. He argued that the intent of the legislature was not to discriminate, that the content embraced by the ministers was not endorsed by the legislature, and that the legislature had no obligation to find ministers outside the borders of the town to produce greater diversity. Even if one accepts Justice Kennedy's position as to the *intent* of the Town Board,[37] it seems obvious that Justice Kennedy is insensitive to the *effect* of the prayer practice on those citizens who attend its sessions.

As Justice O'Connor had argued in many prior cases and as Justice Kagan argued in an eloquent dissent, government involvement that a reasonable observer would recognize as an endorsement of a particular religious tradition creates insiders and outsiders on the basis of religion in a country where citizens are constitutional equals regardless of their religious faith. As Justice Kagan remarked, our "public institutions belong no less to the Buddhist or Hindu than to the Methodist or Episcopalian."[38] Justice Kennedy recharacterized this demand for religious equality into an insistence that there is a right not to be offended. From there, it was easy to claim that citizens are frequently exposed to ideas with which they disagree. With this turn, he transformed a claim for religious equality into an assault on freedom of speech – as if limiting government endorsements of religion was an attack on freedom of speech.

It makes one wonder how Justice Kennedy would apply this principle if Congress decided to change "In God We Trust" on the coins and currency to "In Jesus We Trust" or how he would react to a town that put up a banner at City Hall stating "In the Devil, We Trust." My guess is that Justice Kennedy would balk at these government actions. He would observe that legislative prayer has a long history, that Christian prayers were heard in the Congress early in the Republic, and that they were heard in Nebraska before the Jewish legislator objected. His primary argument would be that the prayers were those of the ministers, not the government despite the deep governmental involvement. He would not simply dismiss the argument against such governmental actions as a mere right not to be offended. Nonetheless, *Town of Greece* exhibits a good-old-boy insider insensitivity to the concerns of religious minorities. If the case were an aberration, it would not be terribly problematic, but it is the dominant motif in cases involving the Establishment Clause, the Free Speech Clause, and for that matter across the constitutional spectrum.

Finally, it is worth contrasting the model of government embedded in free speech regulation and that involved when government speaks. When government regulates speech, the First Amendment is stated to be value free. For example, the Court says, "There is no such thing as a false idea." The attitude is one of tolerance and neutrality. This trope, however, is contradicted by doctrine that treats much speech as protected or subject to less protection because its value is not as great as other forms of speech such as political speech. So too, when government speaks, and governments spend millions, if not billions, of dollars in publications, public service announcements, monuments, and subsidies of speech that it supports, it takes positions on ideas; it repudiates the notion that there is no such thing as a false idea. But there are limits on government speech. Although the Court has yet to say so, presumably it would say that Massachusetts would violate the First Amendment Free Speech Clause if it spent millions of dollars on partisan advertisements urging citizens to reelect Democrats. And, it would similarly say that Boston would violate the Establishment Clause if it were to declare that Boston was a Catholic city even though the Court is dominated by Catholic conservatives.

My claim in this chapter is not that the Court finds no substance in the Religion Clauses. But in the run of the cases that actually come before them – not unlikely law professor hypotheticals, the Court has upheld government activities that burden dissenters and religious minorities.

DIFFERENT APPROACHES

In many respects the approach taken in Canada and European countries is even worse. Although established churches are no longer the norm in Europe, they had been a dominant tradition in European history, and they had been a significant part of the tensions leading to wars between and within countries. Although the violent consequences of these connections between religion and the state are now isolated, other consequences of those tight and cozy connections between religion and the state persist.

It is well known that the role of religion in European beliefs and daily life has long been in serious decline. As Basil Hume has remarked, "It would not be unduly dramatic to observe that Europe … is suffering from a spiritual and moral crisis of immense proportions."[39] To be sure, the sociological factors contributing to religiosity or its decline are complicated and controversial. But James Madison was prescient when he observed that supported churches become dependent, compliant, lazy, bloated, and corrupt. Moreover, when churches are tied to unpopular and dictatorial governments, there is substantial reason to doubt their commitment to moral values and good reason to think that these ties erode support for the churches in question.

So it seems obvious that the Catholic Church did itself no favors when it supported or was perceived to support Franco, Salazar, Mussolini, and Vichy France. Similarly, the Church's quiescence with respect to Hitler's Germany has been been subject to significant criticism. At the same time, the Church sided with the people against the Polish dictatorship and stood on the side of Irish nationalism, and its prophetic stance resonates even today though other factors have since undercut the moral force of the Church primarily in Ireland.

This historical background plays out in diverse ways in Western countries. I will argue that the rights of religious minorities are not properly respected in Europe. But Germany's Federal Constitutional Court is better in this respect than most of the other countries, though its conclusions are arrived at in a manner that would not be contemplated in the United States. Indeed, the relations between religion and the state in Germany offer a revealing contrast from those in the United States.

As part of its Basic Law, Germany prohibits an established church, and it requires that the state remain neutral in matters of faith and religion. One of the reasons for this is the desire to preserve stability in a pluralistic society. Germany, after the integration of West and East Germany, is a country of Protestants, Catholics, atheists, and agnostics, and to a lesser extent Jews and a rising number of Muslims. All are guaranteed freedom of belief under the Basic Law. Despite the prohibition on the establishment of religion, however, religions are supported in ways that would be unthinkable in the United States.

For example, if a religion is organized as a public corporation, the religion can levy taxes on its members and state taxing authorities will collect taxes on its behalf. In the United States, parents have a right to send their children to private religious schools if they can afford it. Moreover, the Supreme Court over a powerful dissent ruled that state scholarships could be provided to students who attend private schools whether or not the schools are religious. On the other hand, direct subsidies to private religious schools are for the most part prohibited, and religion may not be advocated in public schools though it is permissible to teach about religion.

In Germany, many state-supported public schools are denominational, for example, Protestant or Catholic, and it does not violate German law if the only public school available to some parents and their children is a public denominational school. Nor does it violate German law for religion to be taught as a matter of faith in public schools. Indeed, either a course in religion that is faith-based or a course in Ethics is a mandatory subject in German schools. Even stronger, the right to be taught a faith-based course in religion is a German right (though it can be waived). None of this violates the German rule prohibiting the establishment of religion.

Although the German conception of establishment is even narrower than that of the United States, its understanding of freedom of faith and conscience is broad. The German Classroom Crucifix Case II[40] strongly illustrates this point though, as we will see, the approach taken in other Western countries is often different. The case centers on a Bavarian requirement that a crucifix be displayed in every elementary school classroom. Parents who were adherents to a humanistic philosophy or religion called anthroposophy objected to the display on behalf of their children.

The Federal Constitutional Court ruled, not that the display violated the establishment prohibition, but that it compromised the children's freedom of belief and conscience. It spoke against "state-enforced 'learning under the cross' with no possibility to avoid seeing it."[41] The Court recognized that there were crosses all over the heavily Catholic state of Bavaria, but it distinguished those encounters on the ground that they were fleeting and not backed by state-enforced sanctions in contrast with the sanctions for not respecting the demands of compulsory education. Moreover, the Court observed that those displays were not consciously directed at young and impressionable children who had yet to develop their critical capacities.

In defense of the ordinance, Bavaria argued that the cross was a historical symbol and a cultural artifact of the Western tradition. Or as the dissent put it, the cross "is less a symbol of the Christian faith than of the values reflected in the Christian community school, namely those values associated with a Western culture deeply rooted in Christian ideas."[42] This is the kind of argument mustered in defense of the motto "In God We Trust." The suggestion is that the motto has been secularized or drained of spiritual meaning. It emphasizes the nonreligious aspect of a symbol that has been utilized precisely because it is religious.

The Court was rightly not impressed. It recognized that the cross is the most significant faith symbol of Christianity: "It symbolizes man's redemption from original sin through Christ's sacrifice just as it represents Christ's victory over Satan and death and his power over the world."[43] To downplay the religious significance of the cross as a cultural artifact amounted to a "profanation contrary to the understanding of Christians and the Christian church."[44] There is a double irony here. Those who want the crosses deny their religious significance when the energy behind the display is religious in character. The Court in defending religious liberty asserts a theological position about the meaning of the cross, and in doing so, unwittingly supports one Christian view over another in defining its meaning.

In comparing the action of the German Court with US jurisprudence, the Supreme Court majority would find an Establishment Clause violation without reaching the Free Exercise issue. The German

Court finds a religious liberty violation without discussing the establishment prohibition issue. The distinction is important because the decision has been interpreted to permit the continued display of crucifixes in German classrooms so long as there is no objection. And, given concerns about bullying and retaliation, objections require courage. The absence of an expressed objection may evidence compromised acquiescence rather than affirmative consent.

The idea that the religious freedom can be threatened when students are compelled to study under the cross is not confined to Germany. The presence of religious symbols in state schools is forbidden by regulations in the former Yugoslav Republic of Macedonia, in France with some exceptions, and in Georgia. In addition, the Swiss Federal Court has held that a requirement of crucifixes in primary school classrooms was unconstitutional, but suggested that crucifixes in other parts of the schools might be permissible. And in Spain, the High Court of Castile and Leon ruled that religious symbols should be removed from schools if they received an explicit request from the parents of a pupil.

On the other hand, in most other European countries, religious symbols have been displayed without legal contest. In Poland, Romania, and Italy the display of religious symbols has been ruled to be consistent with the principle of religious freedom. In the United States, the conflict in views among these jurisdictions would be resolved one way or another by the Supreme Court. In Europe, however, the European Court of Human Rights has determined that the countries are permitted to act on their different theories of religious freedom. The Court affords deference or a margin of appreciation to the legal, political, and cultural traditions of the different countries. This does not mean that the Court is a rubber stamp. Far from it. But the Court does not insist on the uniformity of rights interpretation that dominates US jurisprudence.

So the German Crucifix Case is consistent with the European Convention on Human Rights, but so is the different treatment afforded by Italy in the *Case of Lautsi and Others v. Italy*.[45] Italian law required that crucifixes be displayed in state school classrooms. Mrs. Soile Lautsi and her two sons challenged the presence of crucifixes in a state school in Abano Terme in the province of Padua. Initially, her husband complained at the school level and the school's governors rebuffed the complaint by a vote of ten to two. Mrs. Lautsi and her children took the case to the Veneto administrative court insisting that the crucifix display violated principles of equality, of impartiality by administrative authorities, and religious freedom. The administrative court rejected the complaint and in so doing embarked on a lengthy disquisition as to the meaning the crucifix should be understood to convey. The Court did not deny that the crucifix is a religious symbol. It did deny that the crucifix was a Catholic symbol.

The latter claim would be difficult for many Protestants to credit. For many centuries, Catholicism has been dominant in Italy. In 1929, Catholicism was declared to be Italy's official religion. This state of affairs persisted for more than fifty years when the Protocol between the Italian State and the Catholic Church was revised in 1985. Nonetheless, Catholicism remained dominant, and close ties between the government and the Church persisted. In addition, the crucifix, which contains a representation of the body of Jesus, not a bare cross, has been a required presence for a Catholic mass since 1570, and most Protestant denominations explicitly use a cross in their devotions and not a crucifix. So the assertion by the administrative court might surprise both Catholics and Protestants.

The description of the meaning of the crucifix as developed by the administrative court though learned and intriguing could not plausibly be understood to describe a consensus. Indeed, the description is Catholic in character, but not a description that would be uniformly shared among Catholics. In the hands of the administrative court, the crucifix stands for love of one's neighbor, and it exalts charity over faith. So understood, the crucifix stands for the "ideas of tolerance, equality and liberty which form the basis of the modern secular state, and of the Italian State in particular."[46] To be sure, this understanding of the crucifix evolved through various stages of history. It moved through the inquisition, anti-Semitism, and the crusades, but it has culminated in the "principles of human dignity, tolerance, and freedom, including religious freedom, and therefore, in the last analysis, the foundations of the secular state."[47] The Court capped off this discussion with this bit of analysis: "In Christianity even the faith in an omniscient god is secondary in relation to charity, meaning respect for one's fellow human beings."[48] From this perspective, the crucifix cannot deny equality because it stands for equality.

Much could be said in response to this, but two criticisms stand out. First, as the German Court observed, interpretations of this sort secularize the central symbol of Christianity. In celebrating virtues like tolerance, Christ is relegated to the background. Second, the notion that charity is valued over faith repudiates the heart of the Protestant reformation in its emphasis on faith over good works. From the Protestant perspective, it may be galling to be told that the right way to interpret the crucifix is to recognize that charity transcends faith; it is downright insulting to be told that this understanding does not privilege the Catholic view over the Protestant.

In the face of this, Lautsi pressed on. She prevailed before a Chamber (seven judges) of the European Court of Human Rights, but Italy appealed to the Grand Chamber (seventeen judges) of that Court. There twenty countries supported Italy, and the Grand Chamber denied Lautsi's claim. Lautsi's claim before the Grand Chamber was that the display of the crucifix violated the right of parents to ensure that the education of their children was "in conformity with their own religious and philosophical convictions."[49] In addition, she maintained that the display violated freedom of thought, conscience, and religion.[50] Such rights could be limited only to the extent that they are "prescribed by law and necessary in a democratic society in the interests of public safety, for the protection of public order, health or morals, or for the protection of the rights and freedom of others."[51]

The right of parents, the Court held, did not mean that the parents could require a particular form of teaching or even that information of a religious or philosophical character need be excluded. It did require that such information be imparted in an objective manner without proselytizing and with respect for the pluralistic character of the students in a manner that cultivates a critical mind. And it recognized that the presence of the crucifix falls within an area in which there must be respect for the parents' right to educate their children according to their own religious and philosophical convictions. Moreover, the Court acknowledged that the crucifix is predominantly a religious symbol.

Nonetheless, the Court found no violation. It pointed to the absence of record evidence of any religious influence on pupils.

Although it understood Lautsi's view that the school's actions did not afford her the parental respect demanded, it denigrated her belief as subjective in character and insufficient to make out a violation. It accepted the government's view that the crucifix was being used to advance the values underlying the democracy and Western civilization, and that goals of that sort fell within the "margin of appreciation."[52]

Clearly, the crucial move of the Court was its requirement of record evidence of religious influence on the students, but it took an entirely different approach when it dealt with a case involving a Muslim teacher wearing an Islamic headscarf in a primary school in Geneva, Switzerland. The teacher, who had converted from Catholicism to Islam, was ordered not to wear the scarf despite the absence of any complaint from a parent or student. In *Dahlab v. Switzerland*,[53] the Federal Swiss Court maintained that the teacher "may have interfered with the religious beliefs of her pupils, other pupils at the school, and the pupil's parents."[54] The Court acknowledged the absence of any record evidence of interference, but concluded that absence did not mean there was no influence, and it speculated that some parents or children might have refrained from action in the hopes that the education authorities would act on their own.

The Federal Court did not merely hang its hat on the speculation of religious influence. It pointed to the requirement that the state be neutral on religious matters. It also argued that the wearing of the headscarf was inconsistent with the principle of gender equality, which is part of the Swiss Constitution. The gender equality claim is open to question. To be sure, for many, the wearing of a headscarf symbolizes the subordinate position of women. On the other hand, many Islamic feminists embrace the headscarf as making clear that women are not to be regarded as available sex objects, a message entirely consistent with gender equality.

On appeal, the European Court of Human Rights said, "It cannot be denied outright that the wearing of a headscarf might have some kind of proselytizing effect"[55] on children of a tender age and affirmed that the wearing of a headscarf was inconsistent with gender equality. In addition, the Court held in *Dogru v. France*[56] that the wearing of a headscarf by a school child interfered with the rights of others in that it could be a source of pressure and exclusion. Moreover, its purportedly ostentatious character contravened the French government's commitment to secularism. On the other hand, the wearing of a Christian cross was deemed permissible so long as it was not ostentatious. This formulation has a clear discriminatory effect since the wearing of crosses in France routinely does not involve the wearing of large crosses.

In sum, the European Court of Human Rights seems to regard a crucifix in a predominantly Catholic country ostentatiously present every minute of the day in every classroom as bereft of religious influence. But the wearing of a religious symbol by members of a religious minority is a matter of deep concern to protect the religious rights of others even though they are permitted to wear the symbols of their faith. It is difficult for me to see this as anything other than discrimination against Muslims. I conclude that the US law protecting religious minorities needs substantial improvement, and the European law is even worse.

PART III

10 HOW DID WE GET HERE?

We have seen that Western countries treat speech regulation in far different ways than the United States. For the most part the approaches taken in Europe and Canada are similar to those taken in Israel, South Africa, and other countries. We have yet to explore why the United States is so different from the rest of the world when it comes to protecting speech. To put it another way, we have not yet explored the phenomenon of US free speech (including free press) exceptionalism. Many point to deep-seated cultural differences. I want to explore that, but I will ultimately argue that the differences arise from political, ideological, and interpretive disagreements – disagreements that are historically late-breaking.

Most of the literature on US exceptionalism has emphasized general cultural differences between Europe and the United States.[1] And, of course, the differences between the United States and Europe range far beyond free speech. Consider our constitutional protection of the right to bear arms, our use of the death penalty, our failure to guarantee rights of food, clothing, housing, or medical care (and the degree we fall short in meeting these needs even for children), and the impossibility that an openly atheistic person could be elected to high political office. In assessing these differences, we might suppose that these general differences arise from large cultural distinctions that also affect free speech. Beyond freedom of speech, in terms of differences, as Stephen Gardbaum observes,

> the standard list of differences includes economic systems (free
> market capitalism versus a mixed economy), political traditions

(U.S. antigovernmentalism, top elective offices open to those with little or no political experience, and the absence of both a strong socialist movement and a professional, high-level civil service), work ethics and culture, moral and personal values, the contemporary roles of religion and extent of religious belief, attachment to firearms, unique team sports, senses of humor, and forms of self-presentation. The explanations of these differences are, of course, legion and much disputed, but they include the United States' newness, existence and status as the product of the first successful colonial revolution, geography, political isolation and isolationism, a long period of buoyant economic self-sufficiency, and demographics as a heterogeneous and non-organic immigrant society.[2]

I want to focus for a moment on an aspect of free market capitalism. Gardbaum is certainly right to suggest that the United States has a greater measure of free market capitalism than European countries. But the US market is not entirely free of governmental participation, and one of the most important aspects of that participation bears directly on the question we are pursuing here. The United States has a system of socialized education in grades K–12. Nearly 90 percent of American children attend public schools. In addition, the United States features a number of important public universities. Even in the case of private universities, federal aid is quite substantial, not to mention tax subsidies. Public education promotes values; it is designed to produce good citizens, and it endeavors to communicate constitutional values. In terms of the First Amendment, it does not communicate the complexity of the doctrine to the millions of students it reaches. That would be an enormously difficult task. It does, however, communicate to students that our country stands for freedom of speech in unique ways. American students leave school socialized to believe that protecting speech is an important part of our constitutional identity, and to believe that is an unqualified good. They are for the most part innocent of the idea that speech conflicts with other values in many complicated contexts, and that those value might outweigh the importance of speech in many circumstances. As I said in the introduction, they emerge as cheerleaders for the First Amendment, which they perceive as absolute or nearly so.

Given this pattern of socialization, one might expect that the United States would come to be more supportive of speech than other countries. Of course, education does not entirely stick. Students are encouraged not to smoke, to avoid drugs and excessive use of alcohol, and to abstain from teenage sex (or at least to use a condom). Perhaps that encouragement has some positive effects, but, if I may engage in euphemism, it is not an unqualified success. So, too, in the First Amendment area, polls sometimes show surprisingly disappointing results on the basic issues of free speech, but it is common in general for the public to be proud of the nation's commitment to free speech. If I am right about this socialization process and that it can explain part of the US privileged commitment to free speech, what still needs to be explained is how the country became committed to socialize children in this way. Of course, a nation committed to strong free speech will socialize its children to share the commitment, but that begs the original question of free speech exceptionalism.

It does not answer the question why Europe and Canada's approach to freedom speech is so different from that taken in the United States. Frederick Schauer points to many factors in his insightful essay, *The Exceptional First Amendment*.[3] He contends among other things that the United States protects speech more than other countries because of the text of the First Amendment, because of the country's general preference for liberty, and because of the general attitude of distrust for government.

Schauer first points to the text of the First Amendment: "Congress shall make no law abridging the freedom of speech."[4] He observes that the European Convention on Human Rights and the Canadian Charter of Rights and Freedoms have qualifying language suggesting circumstances in which speech might be abridged. For example, the European Convention provides that freedom of expression "carries with it duties and responsibilities, may be subject to such formalities, conditions, restrictions or penalties as are prescribed by law and are necessary in a democratic society, in the interests of national security, territorial integrity or public safety, for the prevention of disorder or crime, for the protection of health or morals, for the protection of the reputation or rights of others, for preventing the disclosure of information received in confidence, or for maintaining the authority and impartiality of the judiciary."[5]

So too, the Canadian Charter "guarantees the rights and freedoms set out in it subject only to such reasonable limits prescribed by law as can be demonstrably justified in a free and democratic society."[6] Schauer suggests that the seemingly stronger language of the First Amendment not accompanied by qualifications has played some role in forging the strong positions taken in favor of free speech. The language of the First Amendment, however, is not as strong as it sounds. It does not say Congress shall make no law abridging speech; it says Congress shall make no law abridging "the freedom" of speech. This requires a determination of what the freedom of speech might be. Indeed, as a historical matter, freedom of speech was distinguished from license or abuse.

Even if the language were more powerful than it is, there is another consideration. I can illustrate it by pointing to a casebook on constitutional law in which I have been responsible for the materials on speech, press, and association. The eleventh edition of the casebook contained more than seventeen hundred pages of cases.[7] About a third of those pages were devoted to freedom of speech, press, and association. At the end of the book, among other things, we included a copy of the Constitution. Mark Tushnet once put the point I want to make quite well, "Is the Constitution the front of the book or the back of the book?" Applied to the First Amendment, I think that the substantial body of precedent has considerably more force than the language of the First Amendment. Indeed, the overwhelming majority of cases do not rely on the language of the First Amendment. This is not to say that the language has had no influence; it does suggest that the language has little explanatory force.

I think the same applies to the claim that the country has a general preference for liberty. We, of course, have seen many contexts in which the preference for the liberty of free speech over other important values is manifest. But in other contexts liberty takes a backseat. The constitutional case law regarding search and seizure, interrogation, and the right to counsel reads more like a charter of police power than a part of the Bill of Rights affording protections for the liberty of the accused.

So we value liberty except when we don't. This leads back to the question of why free speech is special.

Related to the claim about liberty, Schauer suggests that US citizens trust governments less than Europeans do and that the culture is more individualistic and communitarian than the Europeans. These factors support the preference for liberty and play a strong role in explaining the resistance to government regulation of free speech. In reflecting on the cultural differences, Seymour Martin Lipset has a particularly interesting analysis that buttresses the position taken by Schauer in some respects, but also points in a different direction in another. Lipset points to the different religious demographics between Europe and the United States at the time of the founding and for a substantial period thereafter. Europe, he explains, has been dominated by hierarchical churches.[8] The United States was founded by those who protested against hierarchical churches.

Lipset believes this explains quite a bit. Europeans are more comfortable with authority and hierarchy. This has led them to accept strong government with powerful welfare states. At the same time, it would follow that they have been less leery of speech regulation by government for purposes of accommodating other interests.

By contrast, he contends, that the American distaste for authority has led to a form of market individualism that resists the welfare state. At the same time, the resistance to church, government, and elitist authority carries over to a commitment to free speech and conscience that resonates with the congregationally independent Protestant tradition. On its face, this analysis could provide a powerful explanation of free speech exceptionalism, and combined with the text of the First Amendment, and the notion of a country dedicated to liberty for all held in a country long marked by an open frontier, it becomes more powerful still.

But Lipset's analysis is broader than Schauer's, and his analysis reveals aspects of American culture that are consistent with strong limits on freedom of speech. Specifically, Lipset argues that the American tradition is resolutely moralistic: "Americans are utopian moralists who press hard to institutionalize virtue, to destroy evil people, and eliminate wicked institutions and practices."[9] We fight and oppose wars on moral grounds; we incarcerate criminals at high rates for their sins; we invoke the death penalty; and as will shortly become clear, we accepted the punishment of offensive speech for long periods in our history.

The problem with crediting Schauer's cultural explanations for our exceptionalism is that our exceptionalism is a relatively recent phenomenon. If the exceptionalism stemmed from broad cultural differences, we would not have had to wait until the twentieth century to see it emerging. To be sure, as I mentioned in Chapter 5, the Court in *United States v. Stevens,* the case involving depictions of animal cruelty, claimed that "From 1791 to the present ... the First Amendment has 'permitted restrictions in a few limited areas' and has never 'include[d] a freedom to disregard these traditional limitations.'"[10] These "historic and traditional categories long familiar to the bar"[11] were said to include obscenity, defamation, incitement, and speech integral to criminal conduct. Roberts concluded that the Court had no authority to add new categories of unprotected speech to those that were historically and traditionally unprotected.

If this were true, we could say that First Amendment exceptionalism got off to an early start and that the cultural factors mentioned by Schauer and Lipset were substantial. The problem is that US free speech protections in the eighteenth and nineteenth centuries were insubstantial by modern standards. To be sure, licensing of speech or press or injunctions against speech or press (both referred to as prior restraints) were generally impermissible. Leaving prior restraints aside that were rarely permitted, however, the state and federal constitutions provided "only limited protection for after-the-fact punishment for what they uttered or wrote."[12] As Joseph Story wrote in his 1833 treatise on the Constitution, quoting Blackstone, if a freeman "publishes what is improper, mischievous, or illegal, he must take the consequences of his own temerity,"[13] and also quoting Blackstone, he maintained that the state needed to be able to punish any "dangerous or offensive writings."[14] Under Blackstone's view, government could only criminally punish speech when it was a "public vice" – meaning that it posed some kind of threat to civil society.[15] Given Blackstone's understanding, private vices could not be criminally regulated, but the spreading of false news about any great man of the realm was a public vice.[16] Imagine how Fox News and MSNBC would fare under a regime in which the falsity of their news could give rise to a criminal prosecution. Although Story wrote in 1833, his description of First Amendment law was largely accurate through the end of the nineteenth century, and the federal law of freedom of speech was for the most part followed in the states.[17]

When speech could be punished for being improper, mischievous, dangerous, or offensive, it is obvious that the regulation of speech in the eighteenth and nineteenth centuries could not properly be described as a body of law in which restrictions were permitted only in a few limited areas. The language in *Chaplinsky* cited in *Stevens* to support the claim of restrictions in only a few limited areas (and repeated all too often) was false the day it was written. Once we understand the character of speech regulation in the eighteenth and nineteenth centuries, it becomes impossible to conclude that the United States was a bastion of free speech protection.

This is not to deny that the United States protected freedom of speech more than many other countries for substantial periods of time. European countries have been marred by dictatorships with deplorable records of censorship. No one would praise the free speech records of Hitler, Mussolini, Franco, Salazar, or Vichy France to take just a few examples. Indeed, the adoption of a Bill of Rights in European countries is a post–World War II phenomenon. But the free speech exceptionalism I am focusing on is the substantial privileging of speech over other important values, values that we have discussed throughout this book, and that privileging is for the most part a post-1950s phenomenon.[18]

In the 1950s, the Court followed the lead of the unanimous decision in *Chaplinsky v. New Hampshire*,[19] which held that a Jehovah's Witness could be criminally sanctioned for addressing abusive epithets at a police officer. The Court said that no constitutional problem was raised and that the epithets "are no essential part of any exposition of ideas, and are of such slight social value as a step to truth that any benefit that may be derived from them is clearly outweighed by the interest in order and morality."[20] The same language was employed in the 1952 case of *Beauharnais v. Illinois*[21] to uphold restrictions on group libel for racist hate speech and in the 1957 case of *Roth v. United States*[22] to uphold restrictions on obscenity. In short, in the 1950s, the Court adhered to a moderate view of freedom of speech – surely closer to the perspective of other Western countries than is the case today.

Indeed, Burt Neuborne observes, "The truth is that the First Amendment as we know it today didn't exist before Justice William Brennan and the rest of the Warren Court invented it in the 1960's."[23] But the protections for the First Amendment have escalated since Justice Brennan has left the Court. When the Court feels compelled to rule that violent video games, depictions of animal cruelty, and intentional infliction of emotional distress at funerals deserve protection under the First Amendment, it is fair to say that it is in the grip of an extreme interpretation of the meaning of free speech. If cultural factors do not explain the shift, the question is how the liberals and conservatives on the Court moved away from a moderate position on free speech to the extreme position they hold today.

In exploring this, it will become clear that the liberals and the conservatives arrived at a similar destination via quite different routes inspired by different political and judicial ideologies. Indeed, for most observers it is not surprising that liberals cling to extreme views of First Amendment protection. The surprise is that conservatives are on board the same ship. In exploring this, I want to discuss the broad ideological factors that have influenced liberals and conservatives, and I want to discuss individual justices. I discuss the latter because it is interesting to note that similar conclusions are consistent with important differences in judicial ideology. Also, in the conclusion, I want to sort out which decisions depend upon the particular justices on the Court and which are now more firmly embedded in the First Amendment culture writ large.

Turning first to the liberals, as is clear from *Chaplinsky*, liberals have not always been staunch defenders of First Amendment rights. In 1948, for example, the ACLU, a group that has been enormously influential among liberals, maintained that the First Amendment did not protect verbal and graphic expression that was indecent, obscene, or immoral if the charges were substantiated by objective proof.[24] Moreover, in *Dennis v. United States*,[25] when the federal government charged the leaders of the Communist Party with conspiring to advocate the overthrow of the government, the ACLU did not subscribe to an absolutist position, but settled for the argument that the government had not shown a clear and present danger.[26] Similarly, Justice Douglas's *Dennis* dissent argued that no clear and present danger to the nation had been shown, but he explicitly renounced an absolutist approach, "The freedom of speech is not absolute; the teaching of terror and other seditious conduct should be beyond the pale along with sedition and immorality."[27]

Nonetheless, Douglas and the ACLU moved toward an absolutist approach. By 1959, in the obscenity case of *Roth v. United States*, Justice Douglas maintained that, "I reject ... the implication that problems of freedom of speech and of the press are to be resolved by weighing against the values of free expression, the judgment of the Court that a particular form of that expression has 'no redeeming social importance.' The First Amendment, its prohibition in terms absolute, was designed to preclude courts as well as legislatures from weighing the values of speech against silence. The First Amendment puts free speech in the preferred position. Freedom of expression can be suppressed if, and to the extent that, it is so closely brigaded with illegal action as to be an inseparable part of it."[28]

The move from a moderate protective approach does not seem to have been the product of an abstract theoretical reconsideration. Rather it seems to have been a reaction to the insensitivity of conservatives to free speech values. *Dennis* was a particular affront to liberals. The Court purported to apply the clear and present danger test, but explicitly renounced the notion of applying it with any rigor. Accordingly, the leaders of the Communist Party went to jail for activities that in the eyes of liberals presented no substantial danger to the country. It was political censorship pure and simple. As Vicki Jackson observes, *Dennis* became a "negative precedent," a case presenting "cautionary notes of what not to repeat."[29]

Similarly, liberals were concerned about the censorial overreaching of governments in lashing out at sexually oriented materials. Although the courts ultimately protected Henry Miller's *Tropic of Cancer* and D. H. Lawrence's *Lady Chatterly's Lover*, liberals were concerned that books of merit were subject to litigation in the first place. Liberals wanted to make sure that the First Amendment was incompatible with political censorship and puritanical overreaching, and the safest course seemed to be absolutism even if it meant protection for the speech we hate. Freedom of speech was also associated with the civil rights movement, which also appealed to liberals in significant ways. Liberals wanted to assure broad latitude for civil rights demonstrators, and they were offended by the efforts of Southern states to compel disclosure of the membership lists of organizations like the NAACP. What united these strands together was a belief that the First Amendment was a bulwark against the suppression of political and cultural dissent.

Finally, the move toward absolute protection for free speech was compatible with a broader trend in liberal thought. Liberals faced a crisis in confronting the evils of Fascism, Communism, and Nazism. Prior to the outbreak of World War II, most liberals had primarily championed positivism and the scientific method. They had embraced the notion that values could not be demonstrated through scientific methods. If they clung to this notion, however, they had difficulty arguing that democracy was superior to totalitarian regimes.[30]

This, of course, was a political nonstarter. Against them stood conservatives and some liberals who maintained that a political regime had to promote virtue among its citizens for a culture to flourish. In response, the scientific liberals distinguished democracy from totalitarianism by its commitment to the open experimentalism of science. From this perspective, value absolutism was the predecessor of totalitarianism, and the imposition of values was the mark of a closed undemocratic society. Instead, the democratic society was marked by openness, experimentalism, and a refusal to impose a position on the nature of the good life.

This position was marred by its inability to explain without abandoning value relativism why openness and the like are better than the imposition of values. By the 1970s, liberal philosophers John Rawls and Ronald Dworkin had embraced moral grounding while continuing to insist that the government should not impose its conception of the good life on its citizens.[31] As Dworkin understood it, the commitment not to impose a conception of the good life on its citizens was a deduction from the moral principle that government owed equal concern and respect to each of its citizens. Also flowing from that commitment was absolute protection for freedom of speech, at least so long as it did not conflict with another right. In any event, the liberal move from moderation to extreme protection of First Amendment rights fit into broader intellectual currents in liberal thought.

Finally, the push toward freedom of speech by the liberals was animated by a pessimistic concern that the society was oppressive and unequal and an optimism that free speech would accelerate the process of needed reform.[32] Although the tendency of the liberal tradition is to lean toward absolutism, that tradition celebrates equality and self-government, so it is natural for liberals to endorse efforts in the campaign finance arena designed to level the playing field. Even more important, a comprehensive absolutism cannot serve as a general First Amendment methodology. There are too many exceptions to First Amendment protection to make that possible.[33] Nonetheless, whatever the explanations for the exceptions, the liberals have largely joined in the effort to keep the exceptions confined. Notably, Justices Stevens, Ginsburg, Breyer, and Sotomayor each signed the opinion of Chief Justice Roberts in *United States v. Stevens*, the case that struck down a federal law outlawing depictions of animal cruelty, an opinion designed to resist expansion of the categories of unprotected speech. Then Solicitor General Kagan argued to uphold the law, but it is not at all clear her argument matched her personal views.

Before she joined the Court replacing Justice Stevens, Justice Kagan argued that First Amendment doctrine could primarily be explained as an effort to prevent government from regulating speech out of illicit motives such as dislike for the speech or self-interest in regulating it.[34] So according to this reading of the doctrine, it made sense to treat content-based regulation more strictly than content-neutral regulation because the former by singling out particular content was more likely than the latter to be based on illicit motives. Kagan did not claim that ferreting our illicit motive was the exclusive purpose of First Amendment doctrine, and she did not even claim that she agreed with the thrust of First Amendment doctrine as she described it. Nonetheless, there were good reasons to believe she subscribed to the distinction between content-based regulation and content-neutral regulation as a normative matter, and that she thought her explanation was the best justification for the distinction. Kagan wrote her article as a member of the University of Chicago Law faculty, a law school whose First Amendment faculty was greatly attracted to the distinction.[35] Kagan's article was an independent contribution within that Chicago tradition,[36] a tradition that unfortunately has had substantial influence on the Court.

When she joined the Court, Justice Kagan quickly signed onto Justice Scalia's majority opinion in *Brown v. Entertainment Merchants Association*, the case that refused to set a new category of unprotected speech for violent video games. Nonetheless, Kagan did so despite a desire to vote the other way. She felt compelled to join the majority because of her theory of First Amendment interpretation. But the result was unsettling, and she has developed doubts about her theory of interpretation.[37] Her effort to tame absolutism was leading her down an unattractive path.

Shortly thereafter, in *United States v. Alvarez*, the Stolen Valor case, she joined an opinion by Justice Breyer, which flatly rejected the approach taken in the depictions of animal cruelty case and the violent video games case. Breyer stated that proportionality review best explained the approach taken by the Court in First Amendment cases. He said that the fit between means and ends was assessed by an examination of the seriousness of the speech-related harm the government regulation would likely cause, the nature of the government interest, the extent to which the regulation would advance the interest, and the possibility of less restrictive alternatives. This was not the first time Justice Breyer had embraced the proportionality perspective in the First Amendment context. He had mentioned it in cases going back to 2000,[38] and he had discussed it in his 2005 book on the Constitution.[39] Moreover, he had previously argued that American judges had much to learn from comparative law.[40]

His proportionality fit into a larger understanding of the Constitution and the First Amendment. Justice Breyer maintained that the Constitution was committed to democracy and that democracy entailed a commitment to self-government (or active liberty, the liberty of the ancients) and a commitment to many forms of liberty that called for freedom from government regulation (negative liberty or the liberty of the moderns, e.g., freedom of speech). Breyer believed that constitutional interpretation depended on a multiplicity of sources including the text, its history, tradition, precedent, its purpose, and the consequences in terms of the purpose in implementing an interpretation.

Breyer sees democracy as the primary lens through which to view the First Amendment. So political speech is centrally protected and commercial speech, though within the scope of the First Amendment, should receive substantially less protection. Even political speech is not absolutely protected. Breyer recognizes that campaign finance laws impact the negative liberty of free speech. But he also thinks that those laws protect self-government and believes in most such clashes that active liberty should take priority over negative liberty. Nonetheless, Breyer supported the free speech position in *Stevens* and *Alvarez* and when the government acted to suppress the speech of its employees, and he has been a strong supporter of the First Amendment in political speech cases including *Snyder v. Phelps* and *Holder v. Humanitarian Law Project*. If Breyer is the First Amendment moderate of the liberal wing, his votes in *Stevens* and *Snyder* still show that he is within the grip of an extreme view of the First Amendment.

The move by the conservatives to First Amendment extremism was more surprising and more complicated. After all, the conservatives were at the forefront of upholding the prosecution of the communists and fighting "smut" in public life. The lesson most of them drew from Communism, Fascism, and Nazism was that godless nations untethered from Christian moral law would deteriorate into totalitarianism. Accordingly, they saw little distance between relativistic liberals and totalitarians. For the conservative movement, a principled opposition to liberals in the universities, the media, and the government became a powerful uniting force. They regarded compromising with liberals as a form of political impurity that should not be tolerated. Indeed, if liberals had united around a concern that political and cultural dissent was being suppressed by the Establishment, so too conservatives came to see themselves as the victims of political correctness in the universities and of marginalization by the mass liberal media.[41]

Although liberals were always present on the Court as the modern First Amendment developed, the kinds of conservatives we see today were not. Indeed, the current conservatives could not possibly have been nominated or appointed in the 1960s. Indeed, it was a long hard trek for such conservatives to come to power and for that power to be translated in First Amendment decisions. The story is partly a general political story about the rise of conservatives in the

Republican Party, about the shift of the South from a Democratic stronghold to a Republican stronghold,[42] about the diminishing role of moderate Republicans in the party,[43] about the belief in the efficiency of the free market and the limits of government, about the perceived victimization of conservatives on college campuses for not being "politically correct," about a movement to cultivate conservative ideas among law students, faculty, and lawyers,[44] and importantly about the rise of a judicial philosophy that made absolutism attractive.

One could select a baseline earlier than the 1950s, but the conservative movement was certainly agitated by the compromising character of the Eisenhower administration. In 1955, William F. Buckley founded the *National Review* with the goal of making conservative ideas respectable and of offering a forum for an intellectual exchange among conservatives that would offer a less muddled view of appropriate policy than was perceived to be endorsed by moderate Republicans. The *Review* managed to maintain a coalition of libertarians, Catholic conservatives (and later Christian evangelicals), and Burkeans among others despite their disparate views. Of course, they were bound together by their opposition to communism. But an equally important bond among them was their opposition to liberals and liberalism, and their reluctance to compromise with liberals, and those themes persist as a rallying cry through the present day. Building on those themes, the *Review* strongly promoted the nomination and election of Barry Goldwater in 1964. Although Goldwater lost heavily, many millions of devoted citizens voted for him, and the building blocks of the movement were set in place for further organizing.

This was particularly important in the South. The battle to move the South from a Democratic region to a Republican region was initially based in linking racial messages whether in coded or more direct form to a hostility to the federal government, which was enforcing civil rights, to support states' rights and a market free of federal intervention. These themes were pressed by Dixiecrats creating divisions in the Democratic Party from the Roosevelt administration onward. Certainly, the decision of *Brown v. Board of Education* ignited a firestorm of racial emotions in the South, but it was difficult for Republicans to capitalize on it. After all, Republican Dwight

Eisenhower was responsible for enforcing *Brown*, and the Republican Party was the party of Lincoln.

Nonetheless, the nomination of Goldwater was a turning point for the Republican Party. Goldwater maintained that desegregation was a good idea, but he criticized *Brown* as usurping the power of the states. He maintained that the problem of race relations should be addressed by those people in the affected localities. This, of course, as applied, would mean that the South could continue to segregate. Accordingly, his message of states' rights and free markets (albeit compromised by prior support for Voting Rights legislation) resonated with the South. Nonetheless, his candidacy was burdened with various unpalatable positions, including his claim that he would sell off the Tennessee Valley Authority, would consider using nuclear weapons, and his suggestion that social security should be confined to an option. Despite these positions, he carried Alabama, Georgia, Louisiana, Mississippi, and South Carolina.

It would be too much to say that Goldwater's candidacy doomed the Democrats in the South, but it certainly set the seeds for a transformation.[45] That transformation was greatly assisted when Lyndon Johnson, who defeated Goldwater, pressed for the passage of the 1964 Civil Rights Act prohibiting, among other things, racial discrimination in places of public accommodation and for the Voting Rights Act in 1967, which enabled millions of African American citizens to vote for the first time. Despite the Civil Rights Act and a sympathetic presidency, riots exploded in the central cities in 1964 and 1965 in part because of alleged police racism and because of perceived economic exploitation. Coupled with this breakdown in law and order was the existence of the widely publicized counterculture of mainly white youth rejecting conventional mores involving sex and drugs.

Capitalizing on this, Richard Nixon ran for the presidency on a silent majority Southern strategy that appealed to law and order, opposed busing, and castigated the liberal media, the intellectuals, and the bureaucrats. The specifics of the strategy have varied, but the political landscape of the South profoundly changed in the decades after the passage of the 1964 Civil Rights Act. Essentially, what happened was this: black voters were added to the Southern Democratic Parties, thus liberalizing those parties, particularly on matters involving race. It took almost a generation for the process to complete, but white voters died, and transferred or joined the Republican Party in sufficient numbers that the solid Democratic South became the Republican South.[46] This transformation moved the Republican Party to the right. Similarly, the Democratic Party moved to the left in large part because it was no longer compromised by the Southern Democrats.[47]

Another significant factor moving the parties further away from the middle was the continuing rise of the primary system particularly after 1968. The structure of the primaries can make a difference,[48] but generally speaking the voting in party primaries has been dominated by party activists rather than the generally moderate average member of the electorate. Accordingly, politicians have to appeal to the activist core of their party in order to be nominated, and that pushed both parties further left in the case of the Democrats[49] and further right in the case of the Republicans.[50]

These transformations had an especially substantial effect on moderate Republicans outside the South.[51] First, many were repulsed by the racist appeals of the Republican Party and left as a result. But even more important, the new Republicans were more principled in their conservatism. After *Roe v. Wade* and a decision removing tax exempt status from Bob Jones University, evangelical Christians became politically active in the Republican Party. On many issues those Christians avoided compromise as part of their adhering to religious principle. The large bank bailouts passed in the second Bush administration ignited a populist Tea Party movement that resisted compromise in adhering to political principles. From both perspectives, moderate Republicans were anathema. The party was willing to run principled conservatives against the moderates even if the conservative victors were likely to lose in the general election. We have lived the results of this process: principles demand the filibuster at the drop of the hat; principles demand gerrymandering; principles demand doing whatever it takes to win from destroying reputations, lying to win elections, and disenfranchising those who deserve to vote. Above all, war against the other side takes precedence over what is good for the country. Of course, it is more than a little odd that many of these "principled" conservatives claim to be "principled" Christians. In fairness, however, I do not suggest that the Democrats are innocent. Not by any means.

I do mean to suggest that it should no longer come as a surprise that Republicans might be attracted to extremes.

This is part of the story of the Republican Party's move to the right. One other strand of the story was an outgrowth of improvements in technology in many fields, including transportation, digital technology, and a host of other areas where production costs were substantially reduced.[52] These improvements led to further globalization of markets, increased and destabilizing competition, to better deals for consumers, and to increased power of institutional investors who could move their money in a second.

At the same time, this fiercer form of competition put companies under pressure to cut jobs and wages; it put consumers and individual investors in a compromised position. They could get lower prices at Wal Mart, but in doing so they were supporting the exploitation of workers; they could invest in similar companies and do the same. For many millions, their interests as consumers and investors were at odds with their moral and political commitments.

These consumers and investors could expect little support from businesses. Capitalism has no moral soul; it seeks profits utterly without regard to morality. Businesses needed to make a profit to survive, and that led to a concerted effort by them to rid themselves of regulations that however important for worker safety or the environment were getting in the way of their efforts to compete and make profits to survive or even better to attract investors. What business wanted was a government that would respond to their needs for a better competitive environment for American business and its need for profits. To the extent business succeeded, it would diminish government's responsiveness to moral concerns and to the fact that the needs of businesses need to be considered as a part of the public interest, not as a substitute for it.[53]

Nonetheless, the technological revolution in the midst of increasing regulation of business made it plain that a business movement to place pressure on the American government and state governments was inevitable. Some trace the impetus for this movement to a 1971 memorandum by Lewis Powell, then president of the American Association, to the Chamber of Commerce in which he called for a broadly based public initiative by the Chamber and associated organizations to recognize that business and free enterprise was in deep trouble and to fight back in the media, the legislature, the courts, the schools, and in paid advertisements.[54]

In any event, there was a concerted and successful business movement in the 1970s. Among the key players was the Business Roundtable founded in 1972 by 200 chief executive officers of the nation's largest companies. Corporate political action committees multiplied exponentially. And so did lobbyists. By the end of the 1970s, employees hired to help represent the interests in Washington D.C. outnumbered all government employees put together. Equally important, the rhetoric employed by business in this period and since portrayed the corporation as an important part of democracy rather than a threat to democracy. Mobil Oil's editorials in the *New York Times* during that period presented the corporation as the good citizen contributor to the public dialogue that business sought to sell.[55]

Shortly after Powell's memorandum, President Nixon appointed him to the Supreme Court where he was a reliable vote for business including the commercial speech doctrine. Whatever the impact of the Powell manifesto, the movement he imagined took hold, and an important part of it was a concerted effort to make conservatism more respectable among lawyers, judges, law students, and law school faculty.[56] The effort was funded by various foundations though it was not without some failures; as a whole, it was extremely successful. Initially, businesses funded conservative public interest law firms. It turned out that the interests of principled conservatives and the funding businesses did not always coincide and the public interest law firms turned to foundations for more secure funding. The Olin Foundation funded law and economics seminars for law professors and judges.[57] The seminars were sold as providing education about what law would like from an economic perspective, but the underlying thought was that education from an economic perspective would have a free market tilt and could influence important figures in the law to respect conservative principles.

Most important in making conservatism respectable was the Federalist Society, an organization in which some forty-five thousand conservative students and lawyers participate.[58] After its founding in 1982, the Society faced the same kind of problem encountered by National Review: conservatives were deeply divided over important principles. Libertarians, religious conservatives, Burkean conservatives, and business conservatives are all part of a family, but it is a family full of squabbles that requires ingenuity to keep together. William F. Buckley kept his magazine together in large part through the force of personality and his power to exclude those who were too divisive or whose views were unpalatable.[59] The Federalist Society kept diverse conservatives together by committing itself not to take positions.

Instead, the Federalist Society was influential because it provided an intellectual network, indeed a support group, for marginalized conservatives, whether students, law professors, or lawyers. Moreover, it provided multiple fora for debates on issues important to conservatives. In a wise stroke, the Society adopted a policy of inviting faculty liberals to participate in these debates. The purpose and effect was to make conservative issues respectable and to force liberal professors to come to grips with arguments they might otherwise have ignored. Moreover, the debates between liberals and conservatives drew far larger audiences than would have attended if conservatives were merely talking among themselves.

Joining the Federalist Society was, of course, not like joining the chess club. It potentially could set up a person for employment discrimination in many circles. But membership has ended up becoming an important employment credential in important contexts. Indeed, as Michael Avery and Danielle McLaughlin report, "Throughout the administrations of all three Republican presidents since its founding, Federalist Society members occupied key positions in the White House, the Department of Justice, and as outside advisors with respect to the nomination of federal judges. Working together with other conservatives, they have moved the federal judiciary significantly to the right over the past thirty years. And as they predicted it would, the law has followed."[60] Indeed, every federal judge appointed in the Bush administrations (father and son) have been members of the Society or approved by members of the Society. That includes Chief Justice Roberts and Justices Thomas and Alito each of whom (along with the late Justice Antonin Scalia) have been members of the Society.

If it is understandable that the Republican Party moved to the right and that a rich supply of conservatives were available to become judges, the question remains why conservatism translated into the kind of extreme protection for speech afforded in the context of military funerals and depictions of animal cruelty. It is hard to believe it would have even occurred to the conservatives who upheld group libel laws to sign on to these extreme results. Initially, it deserves mention that not all conservatives would sign on to these results. Certainly, a Burkean conservative would not. And, in fact, in many respects, Samuel Alito is a Burkean conservative.[61] As such, he recognizes the need to balance free speech values against other values in a prudent way. Accordingly, he dissented in the military funeral case and in the depictions of animal cruelty case.

Justices Scalia, Thomas, Kennedy, and the Chief Justice adhered to extreme views, but their approaches have been different, thus exposing different brands in the Republican Party. For starters, however, none of them has been hostile to the government promoting values. Scalia, Thomas, and Kennedy each permitted government to promote majoritarian religious values, a permission that is quite congenial to a Burkean perspective. The votes of Scalia and Thomas are not likely to be explained by the belief that the market works (though they probably shared that belief) or by an enlivened commitment to free speech arising from a sense that conservatives have been discriminated against in an age of political correctness (though they surely have believed that conservatives have been victimized) or by an appreciation for depictions of animal cruelty or the intentional infliction of emotional distress at funerals. Presumably, they would recognize as Catholics that Catholic social thought would strongly condemn either form of conduct.

The votes of Justices Scalia and Thomas have been motored by an antipathy to judicial balancing. A strong theme of the Federalist Society and of these justices has been that judges too often have engaged in legislation rather than adjudication. To balance was regarded as perilously close to legislating by Scalia and Thomas. In opposition to balancing, many conservative scholars have argued that the judicial task is to determine the original meaning of the Constitution. An important pathbreaker in this line of thinking was the publication of Raoul Berger's *Government by Judiciary*.[62] Berger condemned the activism of the justices in amending the Fourteenth Amendment in the guise of interpretation. He maintained that the Constitution should be interpreted in line with its original meaning. The book had enormous influence within the conservative movement, and the originalism thesis ultimately was embraced in the Reagan Justice Department under Edwin Meese.[63] Meese's embrace of originalism in a series of forceful speeches substantially broadened the audience for the question of how to interpret the Constitution and made the phrase "original intent" a common term of political discourse. It was widely understood by conservatives that originalism was a mode of interpretation to be set against the liberal interpretations of the Warren and early Burger courts.[64]

Both Justice Scalia and Justice Thomas have subscribed to originalism, but in different forms.[65] Although Justice Scalia is deceased, his judicial philosophy remains influential and is conceptually important even though his absence from the Court will have implications for future cases, as I will discuss in the concluding chapter. Justice Scalia argued that the judicial task in interpreting the Constitution is to look to the original meaning of the text of the Constitution as it was understood at the time the text was passed. From this perspective, the writings of the Framers are relevant not to discern their intent, but rather to arrive at a reasonable interpretation of how the language was originally understood.[66] Justice Scalia once admitted that he might be a "faint hearted" originalist, meaning that his originalism might give way in the face of long-standing precedent or obviously unreasonable results.[67] Later he repudiated what he had previously said.[68]

Justice Thomas subscribes to a stronger form of originalism than that entertained by Justice Scalia. Justice Thomas joined Justice Scalia in trying to determine the original public meaning of a constitutional text. But he has been more likely to inquire into the general meaning of the text and more likely to combat those precedents that he believes are contrary to the original general meaning.[69]

More generally, Justice Thomas adheres to a broader, religiously centered form of originalism. He sees the Constitution as a flawed implementation of the Declaration of Independence, flawed because of its original compromise with slavery. He subscribes to that part of the conservative movement that sees the Declaration, the speeches of Abraham Lincoln, and the speeches of Martin Luther King as all of a piece in reading the Constitution as a religious and moral document whose purposes were not fully realized at the time of its adoption.[70]

Of course, many a liberal could accept an originalism rooted in the principles of the Declaration, Abraham Lincoln, and Martin Luther King, but Thomas's form of originalism ties religious morality to conventional morality. So he understands it to be an abuse of the Constitution to maintain that it embraces a right to abortion, or same sex relations, or gay marriage, or assisted suicide. Whether in the hands of Scalia or Thomas's brand of originalism, decisions have been likely to support old traditions and hierarchies that they have favored. It is unlikely that the political tilt of originalism is unrelated to the attractiveness of the interpretive strategy to conservatives.

These forms of originalism, of course, have been subject to serious criticism. One might recognize that Constitution adopts important principles that should be respected, but ask why the original understanding of how those principles should be applied should be privileged in those circumstances where the society matures to a different understanding of the principle.[71] So it may fairly be argued that the original understanding of equality did not recognize women to be equals, but the constitutional principle of equality should now be understood to apply to women in very different ways. One might ask why the original understanding should trump the law as it has been developed in more than two centuries of precedent. One might ask why originalism should be privileged as a constitutional theory of interpretation when it is not at all clear it was endorsed by the Framers.[72] One might ask why the original meaning attached to a text by eighteenth-century white male agrarian slave holders should be a strong source of interpretation in the twenty-first century.[73]

Leaving these questions aside, in explaining the votes of Scalia and Thomas as we have seen, it is not convincing to suppose that the original understanding of the Constitution was to freeze in categories of unprotected speech not to be added to in the judicial process. Nor is there any basis for the claim that a strict scrutiny test has anything to do with the original understanding of the First Amendment.[74] Instead, it seems clear that the desire to avoid balancing has been the principal reason for Justices Scalia and Thomas to adopt such rules. The attractiveness of creating a rule in which free speech is privileged subject only to being overridden by the nearly impossible showing demanded by strict scrutiny while grandfathering in the already established categories of nonprotection seems to be a solid resting place for a perspective that wants to minimize the possibility of balancing. This antipathy to balancing also helps explain Justice Scalia's approach in *Employment Division v. Smith*. By ruling that no freedom of religion issue of constitutional dimension is raised by a generally applicable statute burdening religion, the conservatives avoid the need to balance freedom of religion against the interest promoted by the statute.

Justice Kennedy, however, is not an originalist. He has accepted the responsibility to create new categories in the due process context, most notably the protection of gay rights. He has balanced values against each other in what he perceives to be a sensitive way in the abortion context. He has been willing to engage in a multifactor analysis in determining when demonstrators can get access to government property. Unlike Scalia or Thomas, it seems that Kennedy's view rests on a strong commitment to free speech. Indeed, although he has not uniformly supported freedom of speech, he is one of the strongest supporters of free speech on the Court.

Frank J. Colucci in his biography of Kennedy finds that his free speech views comport with his general constitutional philosophy.[75] As Colucci understands Kennedy (and there is much to support his view), the justice embraces a moral reading of the Constitution that emphasizes human liberty[76] and dignity.[77] Thus, Justice Kennedy would be responsible for the language in *Planned Parenthood v. Casey*, proclaiming that "the heart of liberty is the right to define one's own concept of existence, of meaning, and of the mystery of human life,"[78] and he would declare that "the heart of the First Amendment is the principle that each person should decide for himself the ideas and beliefs deserving of expression, consideration and allegiance."[79] Nonetheless, it is a stretch to connect these individualist principles of human dignity to embrace the protection of corporate speech, and Justice Kennedy is a strong proponent of free corporate speech in both the commercial and corporate spheres. This aspect of his thought, charitably explained, can be rendered in terms of equality for the listener and of a distaste for government setting the terms of speech in the public sphere particularly when it comes to democratic dialogue. Although it seems fair to say that libertarian principles held by one wing of the Republican Party play a strong role in Justice Kennedy's jurisprudence, there is reason to suppose that his support of freedom of speech is supported by a multiplicity of values.[80]

That leaves Chief Justice Roberts. The Chief scores high in votes in favor of the First Amendment side, but he does not have an overarching theory of interpretation, nor does he appear to have an overall theory of the First Amendment. On its face, he seems to believe that content regulation is particularly problematic, but he has no obvious agenda to revisit and overturn old categories. As the Chief, it is obvious that he has tried to write opinions that will draw as many justices as possible, so his opinions may not fully reflect his views. In the confirmation hearings, he attempted to convey the impression that he was a neutral umpire. That he is not. But his values thus far have been clothed in a pragmatic particularism.

Pragmatism cannot operate without an infusion of values, however. And you will recall from the introduction that this book with the exception of Chapters 8 and 9 has focused on cases in which speech has been outlawed across the board, not speech in special contexts or time, place, and manner regulations. Generally in the special contexts and in those cases involving time, place, and manner regulations (in the absence of clear cases), you can with a high degree of probability guess how justices including Roberts would vote based on their political party.

In campaign finance cases, when the conflict is between free speech and equality, it should come as no surprise that the Republicans defend corporate free speech rights, and the Democratic dissenters argue that the interests of democracy outweigh the concerns about free speech. So, too, when the issue involves a clash between the interest of unions in avoiding free riders and the free speech rights of nonunion members, the Democrats tend to side with the unions, and the Republicans defend the free speech rights of nonunion members. In special contexts, like schools, prisons, and workplaces, the Republicans defend those in authority, and the Democrats defend the dissenters. In time, place, and manner contexts, with the exception of cases involving pro-life dissenters, the Republicans uphold the government, and the Democrats defend the demonstrators. Note that in the corporate and union contexts, the Republicans defend the free speech position; in the special contexts and time, place, and manner contexts, the Democrats typically defend the free speech position. In these two groups of cases, with Justice Scalia on the Court, the Republican majority has typically prevailed. Viewed from a historical perspective, what is remarkable about so many of the other cases discussed in this book is that there is typically no obvious partisan tilt.

So to come back to Roberts, is there a Republican advantage to his methodology in *Stevens*? Perhaps, the commitment to absolutism in cases of free speech prohibition shores up protections for commercial and corporate speech more central to Republican interests than the depiction of animal cruelty. In any event, it should be clear that the absolutism of the Democrats and the Republicans arises from a different history and resonates with different values, and it should also be clear that the voting patterns of the justices stem more from ideology than general American cultural values.

11   WHAT NEXT?

I have argued that the US Supreme Court has wrongly privileged speech over important values including privacy, justice, racial and sexual equality, animal protection, public health, and democracy. I have also argued that it has given short shrift to the importance of protecting dissent and has displayed a conspicuous lack of vigilance in affording constitutional protection to religious minorities. My primary complaint has been the almost total absence of a sense of proportion in accommodating conflicting values. The sin has been speech worship in Part I and for the most part deference to authority and order in Part II.

With respect to speech worship, I should hasten to observe that I have not argued free speech should have no role to play in accommodating the values I have discussed. Even in the area of commercial speech, which I believe should receive no liberty protection under the First Amendment, I think it obvious that government could not restrict advertising employing Republican celebrities while permitting the employment of Democratic celebrities. The First Amendment houses an equality value limiting government regulation of otherwise unprotected speech. Leaving commercial speech aside, free speech can be unduly restricted in clashes with privacy, fair trial, racial and sexual equality, entertainment violence, and campaign finance. For example, regulation of speech involving racial and sexual equality risks censorship of speech merely because we think it is wrong-headed; we have a long history of censoring speech in new media for fear of its harmful effects; campaign finance legislation is too often designed as a form of incumbent protection.[1]

Nonetheless, there is no excuse for the mechanical privileging of free speech over other important values. It may be inappropriate to impose prior restraints on the press, but prosecutors and police should not generally be free to release incriminating information outside the trial process. Elementary considerations of privacy and dignity should preclude the successful invocation of the First Amendment to protect the intentional infliction of emotional distress at funerals or the publication of the names of rape victims without consent. Principles of equal citizenship and avoiding harm to the vulnerable counsel that the toleration of appropriately defined racist speech and pornography is unjustifiable. The notion that depictions of animal cruelty for entertainment purposes and gruesomely violent video games sold to children are so important that government may not act against them without a compelling state interest reveals that the First Amendment has stretched beyond any reasonable bounds. When the merchants of death and suffering can advertise the addictive drug of tobacco under a mantle of First Amendment protection, it is time again to question the sanity of the enterprise. And when millionaires and corporations can spend unlimited sums to influence election campaigns, it is time to say that the First Amendment has undermined our democracy. This is a sorry record.

To be sure, abandoning the mechanical privileging of free speech is not without risks. But it borders on the fantastic to claim, as did Judge Easterbrook, that outlawing pornography would put us on the totalitarian road to government "control of all of the institutions of culture, the great censor and director of which thoughts are good for us."[2] Or that it would be the "end of freedom of speech."[3] There is no reason to suppose American judges harbor a desire to lead us down a totalitarian path that would be unleashed if the mechanical privileging of free speech were abandoned.[4] Indeed, I would expect that if mechanical privileging were abandoned, American judges, as products of our culture, would produce more libertarian results than those in other Western countries. I do not claim that refusing to automatically place a thumb on the scales in favor of free speech will magically lead to optimal results. Sometimes speech will be underprotected; sometimes it will be overprotected, and we will disagree about which is which. My position is that the mechanical privileging of free speech has led us to plainly unacceptable results.

Putting aside the contexts in which free speech has been mechanically privileged, our record with respect to protecting dissent and the freedom of religious liberties also leaves much to be desired. In both cases, the Court has capitulated to government burdens on the freedom of speech and religion merely because the government did not discriminate against specific speech content or against specific religions. But when government tells people that they cannot demonstrate in a particular time or place, government is burdening important speech, speech that is surely as important as violent video games. Indeed, a system of justice requires that regardless of political ideology, those who speak out against existing customs, traditions, institutions, and authorities must be given broad scope to speak in the absence of a clear and convincing justification. Similarly, when government tells people they cannot ingest peyote, it burdens the religion of Native Americans, and that burden is important whether or not it was contemplated by those who passed the statute. Depriving individuals of the ability to act or not act upon the demands of their conscience (whether or not that conscience is the product of a religious upbringing in the traditional sense) is a fundamental invasion of human freedom. If burdens such as these are to be upheld, the government should also be required to provide a clear and convincing justification. Finally, despite narrow exceptions, government has no business pronouncing on matters of theology.

Note, I have not argued that dissent should be automatically protected. For example, there is no need to protect knowing falsehoods harming the reputations of innocent people; the government often needs to place some regulations on the time, place, and manner of speech; supervisors in workplaces and schools need some leeway in regulating speech to further the mission of the organizations; some speech should be limited in the interests of national security; the regulation of some forms of religious activity may be appropriate to advance substantial state goals, and, as I have suggested, some quite limited forms of governmental religious speech should in the prevailing culture pass constitutional muster.

But looking back over the terrain we have covered, there is a disturbing tendency to apply the First Amendment in ways that benefit the powerful. In a sense, this should not be surprising. An ideology committed to the notion that the truth always emerges in the marketplace of ideas and that government cannot regulate that marketplace will benefit those who dominate the marketplace. Recall Justice Kennedy in *Sorrell* and in *Citizens United* exuding confidence that the right drugs for the consumer will be selected by doctors (despite Vermont's evidence to the contrary) and his quixotic view that the citizenry will be mollified by the avalanche of spending by corporations and wealthy individuals because the public will be judging the political commercials they produce.

Whatever the cause, the First Amendment has unmistakably helped the powerful: business and wealthy individuals have become significant beneficiaries. So, as we have seen, the First Amendment shields tobacco companies as they cause pain and suffering; allows businesses in general to promote a hedonistic culture and possibly to undermine important health, safety, and environmental regulations; and imposes hands off deregulation on companies that sell depictions of animal cruelty or sell gruesomely violent video games to children, or pornographic materials that undermine equality. As John Coates concluded in a recent study, "[C]orporations have increasingly displaced individuals as direct beneficiaries of First Amendment rights."[5]

To be sure, the First Amendment protects the media, and that is a good thing, but it is not an unqualified good. The problem in some cases is that the very existence of truth in the marketplace may jeopardize important values, such as the disclosure to the public of inadmissible evidence before a jury is selected or the publication of the name of a rape victim invading her privacy. So, too, the First Amendment is a friend of the bureaucrats reinforcing the power of school authorities and employers over their subordinates even in circumstances where the exercise of that authority was not defensible. The First Amendment has lost its bite in protecting demonstrators who seek to challenge existing customs, habits, traditions, and authorities. And the First Amendment allows the state to impose burdens on religious minorities whose beliefs and ways of life are different without any resort to a challenge on constitutional grounds except in narrowly defined circumstances.

As is now obvious, I believe the gap between what should be and the status quo is quite large. I want to assess the possibilities for change in closing that gap. As I indicated in the Introduction, Charles Evans Hughes once said "We are under the Constitution, but the Constitution is what the Court says it is."[6] Accordingly, in many of the contexts I have considered, changes could take place without any broad change in the culture. The recent passing of Justice Scalia (at the time of this writing) could effect a change in the composition of the Court that could transform decisions in a number of important contexts.

Nonetheless, I believe that Charles Evans Hughes was not wholly correct. There is a meaning to the First Amendment apart from what the Court might say. At the same time I think it is a mistake to suppose that the Constitution is a perfect document[7] (although many Constitution worshipers would wince if that were said aloud). For example, a moral Constitution would recognize that human rights include a right to food, clothing, housing, and medical care. Our Constitution does not do that, and in that regard it is an immoral document. The First Amendment is also not perfect. The broad sweep of the results discussed in Part I though brought about by court decisions are now firmly embedded in the culture, or, at least, the legal culture. They are now the First Amendment – not merely what the Court says the First Amendment is.

In assessing the possibilities for change, I will begin with dissent and religious freedom. The decisions about protecting dissent tend to break along liberal and conservative lines. The liberals tend to support the protection of dissent. The conservatives tend to ratify bureaucratic decisions. For example, both the cases involving suppression of the dissident student in the school context and a dissident employee in the employment context broke along conservative/liberal lines. Since the composition of the Court has been divided between five conservatives and four liberals, the replacement for Justice Scalia could have significant implications for the protection of dissent.

The future of religious freedom is less clear cut. As was recounted in Chapter 9, *Employment Division v. Smith* held that government could impose significant burdens on religious freedom so long as its action was generally applicable and not discriminatory. Only one justice from the original majority remains on the Court, namely, Justice Kennedy. Among the remaining conservatives, Chief Justice Roberts and Justice Alito might be prepared to overrule *Smith*. Both are strong proponents of religious freedom, and neither of them is afraid to engage in judicial balancing of values.

It might be thought that a new majority of liberals and conservatives could combine to overturn the decision. After all, strong liberals like Brennan and Marshall dissented in *Smith*. Moreover, the decision has been widely criticized. As discussed in Chapter 9, shortly after the decision, Congress unanimously passed the Religious Freedom Restoration Act in an effort to overturn the case, and President Clinton signed the bill into law. Nonetheless, there are reasons to question whether the *Smith* decision is currently at risk of reversal.

Let us posit that the Chief Justice and Justice Alito would vote to reverse *Smith*. Presumably Justices Kennedy and Thomas would hold fast in upholding *Smith*. The reason is not that they are hostile to religion, but that they are uncomfortable with the kind of balancing that a different constitutional position would trigger. For Justice Thomas, the objection to balancing is central to his legal philosophy. For Justice Kennedy, the objection appears to be based on factors as they bear on this context.

Although liberals would have been quick to join Roberts and Alito many years ago (creating a six-justice majority to overturn *Smith*), there are some grounds to wonder whether any of the liberals would now vote to overturn *Smith*. In *Hobby Lobby*, Justice Ginsburg, joined by Breyer, Kagan, and Sotomayor, cited *Smith* as binding upon them without expressing the slightest hint that she was interested in reconsidering the case. Moreover, it is clear that ACLU liberals are generally concerned that protecting free exercise of religion means protecting those who would deny birth control to their employees or who would discriminate against gays and lesbians.[8] Nonetheless, it would be tempting for liberals to protect the freedom of religion interests of sympathetic plaintiffs, for example, Muslims, in circumstances where *Smith* would not provide protection. And, of course, a liberal could repudiate *Smith* and consistently find that the religious freedom interest is insufficiently strong for businesses to deny birth control in their insurance or to discriminate against gays or lesbians. Perhaps some of the liberals will do that,[9] but they have yet to make it clear that they intend to do so. In replacing Justice Scalia, a Republican President could appoint a justice with a fundamentalist aversion to balancing or a justice like Alito with a different jurisprudential style. A Democratic President could appoint a pro-*Smith* justice or one more sensitive to religious freedom. *Smith* could be reversed, and it could become more deeply entrenched. Its future is uncertain.

Different interpretations of the Establishment Clause fall more reliably along party lines. The Democrats with the occasional exception of Justice Breyer vote for the separation of church and state. The Republicans unquestionably with popular support on their side tend to permit government use of religious symbols without regard to the effect on religious minorities. It seems likely that if one of the Republicans were replaced in a Democratic administration, Establishment Clause jurisprudence would be turned upside down, and that is something for which to hope.

On the other hand, the possibilities for change with respect to the matters discussed in Part I are quite remote with two qualifications. The wildly unpopular *Citizens United* decision is vulnerable. If the Democrats achieve a Court majority, it is likely that *Citizens United* will be reversed. Indeed, a number of campaign finance cases could be changed. Since Roberts has become the Chief Justice, five Republicans have outvoted four Democrats in four campaign finance cases. Those outcomes could be changed with significant implications for the democratic process.

So too, if the commercial speech doctrine is extended beyond advertising, I would expect the liberals to dissent as three of them did in *Sorrell*. Unfortunately, I do not see them as prepared to overturn the doctrine altogether, but they are unlikely to extend it. Hopefully, someday liberals will come to recognize that a tradition fashioned to help the vulnerable against the abuses of the privileged is not assisted by a First Amendment that so routinely helps the powerful. Hopefully, they will come to see that an absolutist stance designed to combat the evils of Joseph McCarthy and those of sexual censorship is embedded in a different context and needs to be adapted. But that day has not yet come.

I do not expect that the general run of free speech cases involving fair trials, privacy, race, sex, violence, and commerce are likely to be changed given the widespread support for the results among the justices. It has become a part of the American identity to protect the speech we hate, and it would take a significant shift to turn the country from its individualist liberty-loving preference for free speech back to the recognition that other important values may outweigh free speech values. To be sure, history, even modern history, has involved significant change that few would have regarded as likely. The erosion of racial segregation, the franchise for women and the cultural changes wrought by the women's movement, the downfall of the Soviet Union, the rebellions in Eastern Europe, the rise of the religious right in American politics, the extreme craziness of the Republican primaries, and the profound cultural shift in attitudes toward gays and lesbians are just a few of the changes that few would have thought likely or even possible before they happened.

The most vulnerable cases in light of events like the ones just mentioned, I think, would be the campaign finance and corporate speech doctrines. The changes mentioned all involved rebellions of dissenters formed in social movements reacting to genuine or perceived injustice. There already is an existing social movement triggered by *Citizens United* and fueled by the banks' contribution to the financial crisis and the multi-billion dollar bailouts among other instances of corporate capture combined with the substantial inequality of wealth that has developed over the decades. It is not possible to predict with any semblance of accuracy just how far this movement will enjoy political or constitutional success.[10] In any of its manifestations, such movements will be confronted with issues and circumstances that divide supporters not only over tactics,[11] but also between those who would pursue the politics of principle, conviction, or purity and those who would pursue the politics of pragmatism, reform, and responsibility.[12] The former will accuse the latter of selling out; the latter will accuse the former of a narcissistic failure to appreciate the necessity of compromise to get something done. Movements often falter and fall apart when these moments arise. But they often accomplish a great deal before their energy dissipates. Those who out of hand dismiss the idea that a constitutional amendment could ever happen ought to read a page of history and while they are at it, they might read the amendments to the Constitution and reflect on how they happened.

In terms of social movements, in addition to the movement challenging the domination of wealth in election campaigns, there have been social movements opposing pornography and racist speech; they have each raised consciousness about inequality; but they have not overturned the prevailing orthodoxy.[13] I do not see a social movement near the horizon that would successfully limit the First Amendment to protect fair trials for defendants or even to protect privacy. Still less do I see a social movement rallying around the idea that the First Amendment has become an icon inspiring reckless extremism instead of wise constitutional policy. Certainly, I do not believe that this publication will trigger any such movement. At best, it might provoke second thoughts in those who would otherwise automatically turn to the First Amendment card. It might also help readers to understand that those who claim they favor free speech, Republicans and Democrats alike – in fact favor free speech – except when they don't.

Even if change is unlikely or impossible, I am reminded of Derrick Bell's argument that racism will never go away, but the moral responsibility to speak against it persists.[14] So, too, the First Amendment, as now interpreted, in many ways is profoundly unjust. Silence in the face of that injustice is out of place no matter how invisible that injustice might be to academics, journalists, and citizens who have been raised in a culture that worships the First Amendment.

NOTES

Introduction

1 The best presentation of such a theory in my view is C. Edwin Baker, *Human Liberty and Freedom of Speech* (New York: Oxford University Press, 1989). For a briefer version of the theory, see C. Edwin Baker, "Autonomy and Free Speech," 27 *Const. Comm.* 251 (2011). The concern with legitimacy is also a central focus of those committed to discourse theory or deliberative democracy. Those theories provide less justification for extreme libertarian interpretations of freedom of speech than does Baker. For a strong version of discourse theory as a means of legitimation, see Jurgen Habermas, *Between Facts and Norms* (Cambridge, MA: MIT Press, 1998).

2 See James Weinstein, *Hate Speech, Pornography, and the Radical Attack on Free Speech Doctrine* (Boulder, CO: Westview Press, 1999); Robert C. Post, "The Constitutional Concept of Public Discourse: Outrageous Opinion, Democratic Deliberation, and *Hustler Magazine v. Falwell*," 103 *Harv. L. Rev.* 603 (1990); Robert C. Post, "Participatory Democracy and Free Speech, 97 *Va. L. Rev.* 477 (2011). Weinstein is indebted to Post, but their theories are not carbon copies of each other. See James Weinstein, "Participatory Democracy as the Central Value of American Free Speech Doctrine," 97 *Va. L. Rev.* 491, 493 n.9 (2011).

3 Mari J. Matsuda, Charles R. Lawrence III, Richard Delgado, & Kimberle Williams Crenshaw, *Words That Wound: Critical Race Theory, Assaultive Speech, and the First Amendment* (Boulder, CO: Westview Press, 1993). Each of the authors of *Critical Race Theory* have published articulate and insightful work that has called into question the easy assumption that racist speech should be protected under the First Amendment. So too, with respect to pornography, Catharine MacKinnon has been the leading legal scholar to make the relationship between pornography and the First Amendment subject to public debate.

4 James Weinstein & Ivan Hare, "General Introduction," in *Extreme Speech and Democracy* 1, 5 (Ivan Hare & James Weinstein, eds., New York: Oxford University Press, 2009).

5 Indeed, speech within the meaning of freedom of speech cannot be defined without reference to its underlying values. See, e.g., Frederick Schauer, "The Boundaries of the First Amendment," 117 *Harv. L. Rev.* 1765 (2004); Frederick Schauer, "Out of Range: On Patently Uncovered Speech," 128 *Harv. L. Rev. Forum* 346 (2015).

6 I agree that culture influences law and politics. See Marc Howard Ross, "Culture in Comparative Politics," in *Comparative Politics* 134–162 (M. Lichbach & A. Zuckerman, eds., 2d ed., New York: Cambridge University Press, 2009). I maintain in Chapter 10, however, that the standard cultural factors tending toward protecting speech are confounded by others.

7 New York Times Co. v. Sullivan, 376 U.S. 254, 271 (1964).

8 Thomas W. Joo, The Worst Test of Truth: The "Marketplace of Ideas as Faulty Metaphor," 89 *Tulane L. Rev.* 383 (2014); Frederick Schauer, "Facts and the First Amendment," 57 *UCLA L. Rev.* 897, 909 (2010).

9 Charles Taylor, *Hegel* 381 (Cambridge: Cambridge University Press, 1975).

10 Isaiah Berlin, *The Crooked Timber of Humanity* 18 (Henry Hardy, ed., New York: Vintage Press, 2013).

11 *Id.*

12 *Id.* at 17.

13 *Id.* at 15. Berlin's work emphasizes the unlikelihood that problems can be solved by moral geometry or general theory and that important values invariably collide. In addition to Berlin, *supra* note 10, see Isaiah Berlin, *Against the Current* (Henry Hardy, ed., 2d ed., Princeton: Princeton University Press, 2013).

14 *Addresses and Papers of Charles Evans Hughes, Governor of New York, 1906–1908*, at 139 (New York: G.P. Putnam's Sons, 1908).

1 Privacy

1 See Andrei Marmor, "What Is Privacy?" 43 *Philos. Public Aff.* 3 (2015).

2 For a particularly good discussion, see Julie E. Cohen, "What Privacy Is For," 126 *Harv. L. Rev.* 1904 (2013). In the same vein, see Neil M. Richards, "The Dangers of Surveillance," 126 *Harv. L. Rev.* 1934 (2013). For a discussion of the evidence of conformity, see Margot E. Kaminski & Shane Witnov, "The Conforming Effect: First Amendment Implications of Surveillance, Beyond Chilling Speech," 49 *U. Rich. L. Rev.* 465 (2015).

3 Neil M. Richards, "Why Data Privacy Law Is (Mostly) Constitutional," 56 *Wm. & Mary L. Rev.* 1501 (2015). But see Eugene Volokh, "Freedom of Speech and Information Policy: The Troubling Implications of a Right to Stop People from Speaking about You," 52 *Stan. L. Rev.* 1049 (2000).

4 Scholars debate whether privacy is a unitary concept or a label covering many separate rights. For discussion of some of the important literature, see David Matheson, "A Distributive Reductionism about the Right to Privacy," 91 *Monist* 108 (2008). For a powerful case that privacy is rooted in a social

practice of respect that "recognizes – and communicates to an individual – that his existence is his own," see Jeffrey H. Reiman, "Privacy, Intimacy, and Personhood," 6 *Philos. Public Aff.* 26 (1976). General theories, however, do not offer sufficient guidance as to the appropriate boundaries of privacy whether it is unitary or not. For helpful discussions rooted in theory, see Anita L. Allen, *Unpopular Privacy: What Must We Hide* (New York: Oxford University Press, 2011); Daniel J. Solove, *Understanding Privacy* (Cambridge, MA: Harvard University Press, 2008).

5 For a careful development of this perspective, see Steven J. Heyman, *Free Speech and Human Dignity* (New Haven: Yale University Press, 2008).

6 131 S.Ct. 1207 (2011).

7 *Id.* at 1213.

8 Snyder, Petition for Writ of Certiorari 3 (December 23, 2009).

9 131 U.S. at 1226.

10 *Id.* at 1215, quoting New York Times Co. v. Sullivan, 376 U.S. 254, 270 (1964).

11 *Id.* at 1217.

12 *Id.*

13 *Id.* at 1219.

14 *Id.* For criticism of the Court's sleights of hand and overall perspective, see Steven J. Heyman, "To Drink the Cup of Fury: Funeral Picketing: Public Discourse, and the First Amendment," 45 *Conn. L. Rev.* 101 (2012).

15 Hustler Magazine v. Falwell, 485 U.S. 46 (1988).

16 It seems to me that a different result should obtain with respect to criticism of public figures away from the scene of the funeral. See Brief Amici Curiae of the Reporters Committee for Freedom of the Press and Twenty-One News Organizations, Snyder v. Phelps, 2010 WL 2811207, at 27 (2010) (describing the vicious attack on William Jennings Bryan by H. L. Mencken in the press in the wake of his death).

17 420 U.S. 469 (1975).

18 491 U.S. 524 (1989).

19 See Marmor, *supra* note 1.

20 [2004] UKHL 22.

21 See generally James Q. Whitman, "The Two Western Cultures of Privacy: Dignity Versus Liberty," 113 *Yale L. J.* 1151 (2004) (excellent discussion of the culture of privacy in Germany and France).

22 *Id.* ¶ 149.

23 Anita L. Allen, "Privacy Law: Positive Theory and Normative Practice," 126 *Harv. L. Rev. F.* 241, 246 (2013).

24 Sipple v. Chronicle Pub. Co., 154 Cal. App. 3d 1040 (1998).

25 People v. Bryant, 94 P.3d 624 (2004).

26 For cogent criticism of the analytic moves purportedly justifying this inter- pretation of the Fourth Amendment, see Sherry F. Colb, "What Is a Search?

Two Conceptual Flaws in Fourth Amendment Doctrine and Some Hints of a Remedy," 55 *Stan. L. Rev.* 119 (2002). As I indicated previously, this kind of surveillance threatens values treasured by the First Amendment as well.

2 Justice

1 Duncan v. Louisiana, 391 U.S. 145, 149 (1968).

2 See generally, Gavin Phillipson, "Trial by Media: The Betrayal of the First Amendment's Purpose," 79 *Law & Contemp. Probs.* 15 (Fall, 2008).

3 427 U.S. 539 (1976). The case is richly explored in Mark R. Sherer, *Rights in the Balance: Free Press, Fair Trial, and Rights in the Balance in Nebraska Press Association v. Stuart* (Lubbock: Texas Tech University Press, 2008). I have freely drawn from it in my discussion of the facts. For an outstanding set of articles exploring issues implicated by the decision, see "Symposium, Nebraska Press Association v. Stuart," 29 *Stan. L. Rev.* 383 (1977). Although I am quite critical of postarrest publicity or publicity following the filing of charges, I think there needs to be substantial room for the criticism of public officials when they have yet to prosecute or are not prosecuting individuals, especially powerful individuals, for actions that critics believe deserve to be pursued in the criminal justice system. If the criticism succeeds, I acknowledge that it could have unwelcome impacts on a jury pool. But criticism of this sort serves a valuable purpose not present in postarrest or postcharge publicity.

4 James Goodale, "The Press Ungagged: The Practical Effect on Gag Order Litigation of *Nebraska Press Association v. Stuart,*" 29 *Stan. L. Rev.* 497 (1977). For example, Burger criticized the lower court for finding a clear and present danger that pretrial publicity could impinge upon the defendant's right to a fair trial because that conclusion was speculative. On his analysis, however, any such conclusion would be speculative.

5 Robert D. Sack, "Principle and *Nebraska Press Association v. Stuart,*" 29 *Stan. L. Rev.* 411 (1977) accordingly argues that the Brennan opinion would be improved if it abandoned the emphasis on prior restraints and recognized that the role of the press in a democratic society should make it immune from sanctions in this area whatever the governmental source.

6 427 U.S. at 560.

7 Neil Vidmar & Valerie P. Hans, *American Juries: The Verdict* 111 (Amherst, NY: Prometheus Books, 2007); Joel D. Lieberman & Jamie Arndt, "Understanding the Limits of Limiting Instructions," 6 *Psychol. Pub. Pol'y & Law* 677, 680–681 (2000); Christina Studebaker & Stephen Penrod, "Pre-Trial Publicity, the Media, and Common Sense," 3 *Psychol. Pub. Pol'y & Law* 425 (1997).

8 *Id.* at 601. In some circumstances, the devices are adequate, but they are often not protective particularly when inadmissible evidence has been published.

Benno C. Schmidt, *"Nebraska Press Association:* An Expansion of Freedom and a Contraction of Theory," 29 *Stan. L. Rev.* 431, 445–452 (1977).

9 In fact, prosecutors and criminal defense attorneys cannot be disciplined by bar associations without a showing that their speech creates "a substantial likelihood of materially prejudicing an adjudicative proceeding." Gentile v State Bar of Nevada, 501 U.S. 1030, 1063, 1082 (1991). In the event that the same standard applies to court orders, a fair amount of wiggle room is presented, and, in any event, prosecutors notoriously play fast and loose without repercussions. The *Gentile* standard suffers further from its intimation that the same standard should be applied to prosecutors and defense attorneys despite their different roles. See generally Margaret Tarkington, "Lost in the Compromise: Free Speech, Criminal Justice, and Attorney Pretrial Publicity," 66 *Fla. L. Rev.* 1873 (2014); Monroe Freedman & Janet Starwood, "Prior Restraints on Freedom of Expression by Defendants and Defense Attorneys," 29 *Stan. L. Rev.* 607 (1977). For the claim that *Gentile* insufficiently protects lawyer speech generally, see Erwin Chemerinsky, "Silence Is not Golden: Protecting Lawyer Speech under the First Amendment," 47 *Emory L. J.* 859 (1998).

10 Schmidt, *supra* note 8, at 436.

11 An independent prosecutor should be routine when the defendant is associated with law enforcement.

12 Generally, the English approach is similar to that in other Commonwealth countries such as Australia and New Zealand. On the other hand, despite a powerful dissent by Justice Gonthier, Canada's position is closer to that of the United States. Canadian Broadcasting Corporation v. Dagenais [1994] 3 S.C.R. 835.

13 [1997] E.M.L.R. 76.

14 *Id.* at 79.

15 *Id.* at 83.

16 Influenced by the European Court of Human Rights' decision in Sunday Times v. United Kingdom, App. No. 6538/74, 2 Eur. H.R. 245 (1979), the British Contempt of Court Act of 1981 added a public interest defense, a defense that was not met in this case.

17 For excellent discussion of the approach on the Continent in theory and as applied as well as the United States and England, see Giorgio Resta, "Trying Cases in the Media: A Comparative Overview," 71 *Law & Contemp. Probs.* 31 (Fall, 2008).

18 Recommendation Rec (2003)13 of the Committee of Ministers to member states on the provision of information through the media in relation to criminal proceedings ¶ 26, at 6 *(Adopted by the Committee of Ministers on 10 July 2003 at the 848th meeting of the Ministers' Deputies).*

19 *Id.* at ¶ 9, at 2.

20 *Id.* ¶ 15, at 3.

21 Guideline 8.1, www.rjionline.org/MAS-Codes-Germany-Press-Council (last visited September 13, 2014).
22 German Press Code, *id.* at Section 13.
23 *Du Roy and Malaurie v. France*, Application 3400/96, ¶ 34 (2000).
24 [1998] 25 E.H.R.R. 454.
25 *Id.* ¶ 23, at 465.
26 (2010) 50 E.H.R.R. 2.
27 *Id.* ¶ 61, at 35.
28 *Id.*

3 Race

1 www.washingtonpost.com/blogs/answer-sheet/wp/2013/09/17/new-census-data-children-remain-americas-poorest-citizens/ (last visited February 25, 2015).
2 www.washingtonpost.com/blogs/the-fix/wp/2014/09/06/black-unemployment-is-always-much-worse-than-white-unemployment-but-the-gap-depends-on-where-you-live/ (last visited February 25, 2015).
3 www.pewresearch.org/fact-tank/2013/09/06/incarceration-gap-between-whites-and-blacks-widens/ (last visited February 25, 2015).
4 www.pbs.org/wgbh/pages/frontline/government-elections-politics/why-voter-id-laws-arent-really-about-fraud/ (last visited February 25, 2015).
5 It is widely held by whites that racism against them is greater than that experienced by blacks. http://ase.tufts.edu/psychology/sommerslab/documents/raceinternortonsommers2011.pdf (last visited February 25, 2015).
6 http://journalistsresource.org/studies/society/race-society/white-racial-attitudes-over-time-data-general-social-survey# (last visited February 25, 2015).
7 *Deeply Divided: Racial Politics and Social Movements in Postwar America* 281 (New York: Oxford University Press, 2014).
8 U.S. v. Schwimmer, 279 U.S. 644, 655 (1929).
9 For the intriguing argument that protecting speech in general and hate speech in particular has value in that it demonstrates and helps to develop a social capacity to control feelings incompatible with the virtue of tolerance (an attitude that he argues is not always appropriate), see Lee C. Bollinger, *The Tolerant Society* (New York: Oxford University Press, 1986). Even assuming that affording such protection does cultivate such restraint, my view is that Bollinger's position does not give sufficient weight to the considerations mentioned in the text. As to what the First Amendment should be taken to promote, I strongly prefer the views of Vincent Blasi expressed in his outstanding article, "Free Speech and Good Character," 46 *UCLA L. Rev.* 1567 (1999).
10 For criticism of the US position on hate speech, see Jeremy Waldron, *The Harm in Hate Speech* (Cambridge, MA: Harvard University Press: 2014);

Mari J. Matsuda, Charles R. Lawrence III, Richard Delgado, & Kimberle Williams Crenshaw, *Words That Wound: Critical Race Theory, Assaultive Speech, and the First Amendment* (Boulder, CO: Westview Press, 1993); Charles R. Lawrence III, "If He Hollers Let Him Go: Regulating Hate Speech on Campus," 1990 *Duke L. J.* 2320; Mari J. Matsuda, "Public Response to Racist Speech: Considering the Victim's Story," 97 *Mich. L. Rev.* 2320 (1989); Richard Delgado, "Words That Wound," 17 *Harv. C. R.-C. L. L. Rev.* 133 (1982). For defenses, see James Weinstein, *Hate Speech, Pornography, and the Radical Attack on Free Speech Doctrine* (Boulder, CO: Westview Press, 1999); Robert C. Post, "Racist Speech, Democracy, and the First Amendment," 32 *Wm. & Mary L. Rev.* 267 (1990). For an excellent collection presenting a variety of perspectives, see *Extreme Speech and Democracy* (Ivan Hare & James Weinstein, eds.; New York: Oxford University Press, 2009).

11 Quoted in Philippa Strum, *When the Nazis Came to Skokie: Freedom for Speech We Hate* 15 (Lawrence, KS: University of Kansas Press, 1999); Donald Alexander Downs, *Nazis in Skokie* 28 (Notre Dame, IN: University of Notre Dame Press, 1986). I have drawn from Downs and Strum in discussing the facts of the Skokie litigation.

12 Strum, *supra* note 11, at 17.

13 National Socialist Party of America v. Village of Skokie, 432 U.S. 43 (1977).

14 Village of Skokie v. National Socialist Party of America, 51 Ill.App.3d 279, 366 N.E.2d 347 (1977).

15 Village of Skokie v. National Socialist Party of America, 69 Ill.2d 605, 373 N.E.2d 21 (1978).

16 578 F.2d 1197 (7th Cir.), cert. denied, 439 U.S. 916 (1978).

17 Quoted in Strum, *supra* note 11, at 15 (1999).

18 578 F.2d at 1206.

19 Wendy Brown, *Regulating Aversion: Tolerance in an Age of Identity and Empire* 16 (Princeton: Princeton University Press, 2006).

20 This abstraction approach, which is rooted in a desire to avoid balancing the competing free speech and other interests, is generally favored by those who take the American approach, see Weinstein, *supra* note 10.

21 Mari Matsuda, *supra* note 10, at 2357.

22 This responds to James Weinstein's concern that permitting government to restrict racist speech based on the matter of its utterance risks sanctioning too much valuable speech. James Weinstein, "Extreme Speech, Public Order and Democracy," in Hare & Weinstein, *supra* 10, at 23, 57.

23 R.A.V. v. St. Paul, 505 U.S. 377 (1992). In a welcome partial retreat from *RAV*, Virginia v. Black, 538 U.S. 343 (2003) upheld a Virginia prohibition of cross burning with an intent to intimidate on the ground that it was a particularly virulent kind of threat.

24 §319 (2) of the Criminal Code, R.S.C., 1985, c. C-46.

25 [1990] 3 S.C.R. 697.

26 *Id.* at ¶ 3.
27 *Id.*
28 *Id.* at ¶¶ 83–84.
29 *Id.* at ¶ 92.
30 *Id.* at ¶ 93.
31 Beauharnais v. Illinois, 343 U.S. 250 (1952).

4 Sex

1 Catharine MacKinnon has been the most articulate advocate for pornography regulation. In particular, see "Not a Moral Issue," "Francis Biddle's
   Sister: Pornography, Civil Rights, and Speech," and the "Afterward," in
   Catharine A. MacKinnon, *Feminism Unmodified: Discourses on Life and Law*
   146, 163, 215 (Cambridge, MA: Harvard University Press, 1987). *Take Back
   the Night: Women on Pornography* (Laura Lederer, ed., New York: W. Morrow,
   1980) also contains an influential set of antipornography essays. An articulate, statement of the other side comes from former president of the ACLU,
   Nadine Strossen, *Defending Pornography: Free Speech, Sex, and the Fight for
   Women's Rights* (New York: New York University Press, 2000). Other significant work includes Andrew Koppelman, "Does Obscenity Cause Moral
   Harm," 105 *Colum. L. Rev.* 1635 (2005); C. Edwin Baker, "Of Course More
   than Words," 61 *U.Chi. L. Rev.* 1181 (1994); Nan Hunter & Sylvia Law, "Brief
   Amici Curiae of Feminist Anti-Censorship Taskforce," 21 *U. Mich. J. L. Ref.*
   69 (1987–1988); Lisa Duggan, Nan D. Hunter, & Carol S. Vance, "False
   Promises: Feminist Anti-Pornography Legislation," 38 *N.Y.L. Sch. L. Rev.* 133
   (1993).
2 For a copy of the ordinance as it was proposed in Los Angeles County, see *The
   First Amendment: Cases-Comments-Questions 151–54* (S. Shiffrin & J. Choper,
   eds., 5th ed.; St. Paul, MN: West/Thomson Reuters, 2011).
3 Paul Brest & Ann Vandenberg, "Politics, Feminism and the Constitution: The
   Anti-Pornography Movement in Minneapolis," 39 *Stan. L. Rev.* 607 (1987).
   The testimony is described in greater detail in that publication. For even more
   extensive coverage, see *In Harm's Way: The Pornography Civil Rights Hearings*
   (Catharine A. MacKinnon & Andrea Dworkin, eds.; Cambridge, MA: Harvard
   University Press, 1997).
4 *Id.* at 624.
5 *Id.*
6 *Id.*
7 *Id.* at 621–622.
8 Those who argue against this conclusion typically ignore the overall studies. Nadine Strossen, for example, does not even cite the important work of
   Neil Malamuth in her chapter on the empirical work. For an able discussion
   of the social science literature, see Drew A. Kingston, Neil Malamuth, Paul

Federoff, & William L. Marshall, "The Importance of Individual Difference in Pornography Use: Theoretical Perspectives and Implications for Treating Sex Offenders," 46 *J. Sex Res.* 216 (2009); Mark Huppin & Neil Malamuth, "The Obscenity Conundrum, Contingent Harms, and Constitutional Consistency," 23 *Stan. L. & Pol'y Rev.* 31 (2012). See generally Neil M. Malamuth, Tamara Addison, & Mary Koss, "Pornography and Sexual Aggression: Are There Reliable Effects and Can We Understand Them?," 11 *J. Sex Res.* 26 (2000).

9 It makes little sense to suggest that we should give up the fight to combat pornography because of its widespread availability on the Internet. We do not give up on combatting child pornography despite its ease of access.

10 Given the Internet, it is surprising to me that sexual aggression against women has not demonstrably increased though such aggression remains extensive; underreporting is common; what counts as aggression is contested; and psychotherapists continue to see a link in the lives of their patients. Even if there were no link, however, the negative impact on gender roles alone justifies regulation. Some might demand empirical studies despite the difficulty of controlling the variables, and despite the implausibility of the claim that a multibillion dollar industry that eroticizes twisted gender roles is producing communications without impact. Such a claim ranks with those who argue that advertisers are fools because their communications are bereft of impact.

11 www.alternet.org/story/146957/is_porn_bad_for_you?page=entire (emphasis in original) (last visited, January 2, 2016).

12 771 F.2d 323 (7th Cir. 1985), *aff'd*, 475 U.S. 1001 (1986).

13 *Id.* at 329.

14 *Id.* at 330.

15 *Id.*

16 *Id.* at 328.

17 *Id.*

18 *Id.*

19 *Id.* at 329.

20 *Id.*

21 Miller v. California, 413 U.S. 15 (1973).

22 354 U.S. 476. 485 (1957).

23 413 U.S. 49 (1973).

24 *Id.* at 69.

25 A compendium of official statements from religious bodies reveals that the overwhelming majority of the statements are conclusory and ill-considered. See *The Churches Speak On: Pornography* (J. Gordon Melton, ed.; Detroit: Gale Research, Inc., 1989). On the other hand, I find the statement of the Canadian Conference of Catholic Bishops to be quite thoughtful. *Id.* at 21–29.

26 (2006).

27 Brockett v. Spokane Arcades, Inc., 472 U.S. 491 (1985).

28 1992 CarswellMan 100 (1992).

29 *Id.* at ¶ 28.

30 For thoughtful critical commentary of the opinion, see Richard Moon, *The Constitutional Protection of Freedom of Expression* 105–125 (Toronto: University of Toronto Press, 2000).

31 1992 CarswellMan 100 (1992) at ¶ 78.

32 *Id.* at ¶ 118.

33 *Id.* at ¶ 50.

34 *Id.* at ¶ 101.

35 *Id.* at ¶ 82.

5 Violence

1 Immanuel Kant, *The Metaphysical Principles of Virtue* 105 (James Ellington trans., Indianapolis, IN: Bobbs-Merril Co., 1964). See also Immanuel Kant, *Lectures on Ethics* 239–241 (Louis Infield, trans., New York: Harper and Row, 1963). Many Kantians subscribe to this view on the ground that animals are not equal to humans stressing that they cannot participate in dialogue or assume duties, or have no sense of justice.

2 559 U.S. 460 (2010).

3 18 U.S.C. § 48.

4 I have relied on the government's brief for its description of the videos. Brief for the United States, United States v. Stevens (June 8, 2009). I should mention, however, that the nature of the videos is disputed and the Reporters Committee on Freedom of Press, for example, argues that the videos are not as bad as the government argues. Brief Amici Curiae, Reporters Committee on Freedom of Press and Thirteen News Media Organizations in Support of Respondent, United States v. Stevens (July 23, 2009). I need not resolve the dispute because even if the government's account is correct and the videos are as horrific as it maintains, the Court extends First Amendment protection to the videos.

5 Brief of Humane Society as Amicus Curiae at 3 (2009).

6 559 U.S. at 470.

7 *Id.* at 468.

8 *Id.*

9 For a thoughtful argument that *Stevens* and *Snyder* are united both by a desire to create a simple rule structure and by the failure to provide adequate reasons for doing so, see Mark Tushnet, "The First Amendment and Political Risk," 4 *J. Legal Anal.* 103 (2012).

10 559 U.S. at 470.

11 *Id.* at 472.

12 *Id.* at 470.

13 See Simon & Schuster, Inc. v. Members of the New York State Crime Victims Bd., 502 U.S. 105, 124–128 (1991) (Kennedy, J., concurring)(reviewing the cases).

14 Petitioner's Reply Brief at 9, Brown v. Entertainment Merchants Ass'n, 131 S.Ct. 2729 (2011).

15 Brief for Louisiana (and ten other states) at 1, Brown v. Entertainment Merchants Ass'n.

16 Petitioners Reply Brief at 46–47 (July 12, 2010)

17 Brown v. Entertainment Merchants Ass'n, 131 S.Ct. 2729, 2770 (Breyer, J., dissenting, 2011)

18 Cal. Civ. Code §§ 1746–1746.5 (West 2009).

19 131 S.Ct. 2729 (2011).

20 For the well argued claim that the First Amendment has been interpreted in ways that are damaging to children even before *Entertainment Merchants*, see Kevin W. Saunders, *Saving Our Children from the First Amendment* (New York: New York University Press, 2003). For a contrasting view, see Marjorie Heins, *Not in Front of the Children* (New York: Hill and Wang, 2001).

21 Ginsberg v. New York, 390 U.S. 629 (1968).

22 *Brown*, 131 S.Ct. at 2738, quoting United States v. Playboy Group Inc., 529 U.S. 803, 818 (2000).

23 *Id.* at 2769 (Breyer, J., dissenting).

24 *Id.* at 2669–2670. Some of the briefs richly detail a history of overreaction to new media. Those briefs are very well done, but changing the subject should not distract from the special characteristics of violent video games, nor should it be assumed that the problem of excessive violence is confined to video games. See Petitioner's Brief, at 44, Schwarzenegger v. Entertainment Merchants Ass'n, citing the Surgeon General and numerous professional associations (July 12, 2010). For an excellent changing of the subject brief, see Brief Amici Curiae of the Reporters Committee for Freedom of the Press and Thirteen News Media Organizations in Support of Respondent, Schwarzenegger v. Entertainment Merchants Ass'n (September 17, 2010).

25 There were competing professional amicus briefs, but the credentials of those who argued that violent video games are harmful to children vastly exceeded those on the other side. Seana Pollard Sacks, Brad J. Bushman, & Craig A. Anderson, "Do Violent Video Games Harm Children?, 106 *Nw. U.L.Rev. Colloquy* 1 (2011).

26 132 S.Ct. 2537 (2012). For regret that the Court did not adhere to a principled approach, see Rodney Smolla, "Categories, Tiers of Review, and the Roiling Sea of Free Speech Doctrine and Principles," 76 *Albany L. J.* 499 (2013).

27 132 S.Ct. at 2542.

28 *Id.* at 2543.

29 For an illuminating discussion of the issues raised by the case in a book that raises even broader issues, see Seana Valentine Shiffrin, *Speech Matters: On Lying, Morality, and the Law* Chs. 4 & 5 (Princeton: Princeton University Press, 2014).

30 *Proportionality and Constitutional Culture* (Cambridge: Cambridge University Press, 2013). Much of the discussion of proportionality that follows here is indebted to their work.

31 It would be a mistake to assume that special meaning attaches to terms like legitimate or rationally connected. Rather, these are interactive factors in which the courts look at the importance of the government purpose, the tightness of the connection between the means chosen and the purpose, and the possibility of less restrictive alternatives in achieving the purpose weighed against the impact on the protected right.

32 With respect to this last factor, it should be mentioned that implicit in the weighing is an assessment of the extent to which the regulation impacts on the values implicated by the right and the importance of those values in the particular context. Because of the flexibility of the proportionality test, I think readers could be misled by those who characterize proportionality as a form of strict scrutiny. Alec Stone Sweet & Jud Mathews, "Proportionality Balancing and Global Constitutionalism," 47 *Colum. J. Transnat'l L.* 72, 78 (2008); Jud Mathews & Alec Stone Sweet, "All Things in Proportion? American Rights Review and the Problem of Balancing," 60 *Emory L. J.* 797, 803 (2011). In fairness, Mathews and Stone Sweet ultimately describe strict scrutiny as not rigid, but a general balancing approach. It is certainly true that the US courts have called scrutiny strict on some occasions when its application has been anything but strict. One can call this an abandonment of strict scrutiny or one could say there are several kinds of strict scrutiny. See Richard H. Fallon, Jr., "Strict Judicial Scrutiny," 54 *UCLA L. Rev.* 1267 (2007).

33 *Proportionality and Constitutional Culture* at 2.

34 For an excellent discussion of the use of proportionality in American constitutional law combined with the recognition that other countries such as Canada have been more systematic in looking at the relevant factors, see Vicki C. Jackson, "Constitutional Law in an Age of Proportionality," 124 *Yale L. J.* 3094 (2015). I do not know, however, whether Professor Jackson would share my assessment of the degree to which American First Amendment law can be illuminated by an understanding that proportionality analysis has played a major role, but I am sure she would agree that the proportionality analysis I describe has not been systematic.

35 See Kevin W. Saunders, "A Comparative Look at Children and Free Expression," 22 *Transnational L.& Contemp. Probs.* 455 (2013) (discussing regulation in Canada, the United Kingdom, and Germany).

36 [2008] EWHC 203 (Admin).

6   Commerce

1 T. J. Jackson Lears, "From Salvation to Self-Realization: Advertising and the Therapeutic Roots of the Consumer Culture," in *The Culture of Consumption: Critical Essays in American History 1880–1980*, at 19 (Richard Wightman Fox & T. J. Jackson Lears, eds.; New York: Pantheon Books, 1983). For interesting discussion of the logic of desire promoted by advertising, see Jean Baudrillard, *The Consumer Society: Myths and Structures* (London: Sage Publications, 1998).

2 This phenomenon is detailed in C. Edwin Baker, *Advertising and a Democratic Press* (Princeton: Princeton University Press, 1993). I explore the issue in Steven Shiffrin, "The Politics of the Mass Media and the Free Speech Principle," 69 *Ind. L. J.* 689 (1994).

3 www.emarketer.com/Article/Total-US-Ad-Spending-See-Largest-Increase-Since-2004/1010982 (last visited April 8, 2015).

4 Advertisers have not been alone. At least since World War II, policymakers have promoted a pervasive consumer mentality. The story is well told in Lizabeth Cohen, *A Consumer's Republic: The Politics of Mass Consumption in Postwar America* (New York: Vintage Books, 2003).

5 John Dewey, *Individualism Old and New* 13 (New York: Capricorn Books, 1962).

6 *Sollicitudo Rei Socialis*, no 33 (1987).

7 *The Affluent Society* (Boston: Houghton Mifflin, 1958).

8 *The Cultural Contradictions of Capitalism* (New York: Basic Books, 1976).

9 *One-Dimensional Man* (Boston: Beacon Press, 1964). Bell, Marcuse, and Galbreath are put in historical context in Cohen, *supra* note 4.

10 Quoted in Charles McDaniel, *God and Money* 184 (Lanham, MD: Rowman & Littlefield, 2007).

11 The nature of Republicanism is disputed among historians, legal academics, and philosophers, and my rendition is contestable. Some important work on the subject includes Gordon S. Wood, *The Creation of the American Political Republic: 1776–1787* (Chapel Hill: University of North Carolina Press, 1969); J. G. A. Pocock, *The Machiavellian Moment: Florentine Political Thought and the Atlantic Republican Tradition* (Princeton: Princeton University Press, 1975); Quentin Skinner, *The Foundations of Modern Political Thought*, Vol. 1 (Cambridge: Cambridge University Press, 1977); Phillip Petit, *On the People's Terms: A Republican Theory and Model of Democracy* (Cambridge: Cambridge University Press, 2012); Frank Michelman, "Law's Republic," 97 *Yale L. J.* 1493 (1988); Cass R. Sunstein, "Beyond the Republican Revival," 97 *Yale L. J.* 1539 (1988).

12 Republicanism relied on systems of law, religion, and education to cultivate the needed civic virtue.

13 As James Madison observed, "A dependence on the people is no doubt the primary control on the government." James Madison, *Federalist* no. 51 (1788) in *The Federalist* 349 (Jacob Cooke, ed., Middletown, CT: Wesleyan University Press, 1961).

14 425 U.S. 748 (1976). For outstanding criticism of the commercial speech doctrine, see C. Edwin Baker, *Human Liberty and Freedom of Speech* Ch. 9 (New York: Oxford University Press, 1989); Tamara R. Piety, *Brandishing the First Amendment: Commercial Expression in America* (Ann Arbor: University of Michigan Press, 2012); Roger Shiner, *Freedom of Commercial Expression* (Oxford: Oxford University Press, 2003) (comparing and criticizing the positions taken in Canada, Europe, and United States).

15 372 U.S. 726 (1963).

16 The story is well told in Alan B. Morrison, "How We Got the Commercial Speech Doctrine: An Originalist's Recollections," 54 *Case Western Reserve L. Rev.* 1189 (2004).

17 Valentine v. Chrestensen, 316 U.S. 52 (1942).

18 Martin Redish, "The First Amendment in the Marketplace," 39 *Geo. Was. L. Rev.* 420 (1971).

19 425 U.S. at 763.

20 William Van Alstyne, "Remembering Melville Nimmer: Some Cautionary Notes on Commercial Speech," 43 *UCLA L. Rev.* 1635 (1996).

21 425 U.S. at 765.

22 *Id.*

23 *Id.*

24 *Id.* at 772 n. 24.

25 Ohralik v. State Bar Ass'n, 436 U.S. 447 (1978).

26 436 U.S. 412 (1978).

27 436 U.S. at 456.

28 447 U.S. 557 (1980).

29 *Id.* at 565.

30 David C. Vladeck, "The Difficult Case of Direct-to-Consumer Advertising," 41 *Loyola of L.A. L. Rev.* 259, 269 (2007)

31 Richard J. Bonnie, "The Impending Collision between First Amendment Protection for Commercial Speech and the Public Health: The Case of Tobacco Control," 29 *J. L. & Pol.* 599, 602 (2014) (excellent discussion of tobacco policy in the United States).

32 The extent to which advertisers target children in their alcohol and tobacco advertisements is discussed in Juliet B. Schor, *Born to Buy* 132–137 (New York: Scribner, 2004).

33 533 U.S. 525 (2001).

34 Alexander v. Cahill, 598 F.3d 79 (2d Cir. 2010).

35 *Id.* at 89.

36 Schor, *supra* note 32, at 12–13.

37 Seana Valentine Shiffrin, *Speech Matters: On Lying, Morality, and the Law* 188–191 (Princeton: Princeton University Press, 2014).

38 436 U.S. 447 (1978).

39 *Id.* at 456.

40 131 S.Ct. 2653 (2011).

41 Breyer, J., joined by Ginsburg & Kagan, J. J., dissented, contending that the Court's departure from prior law was indefensible. *Id.* at 2673.

42 *Id.* at 2659.

43 For trenchant criticism of *Sorrell*, see Tamara R. Piety, "'A Necessary Cost of Freedom'? The Incoherence of Sorrell v. IMS," 64 *Alabama L. Rev.* 1 (2012).

44 For another Supreme Court case in which the First Amendment is employed to disadvantage consumers, see Pacific Gas & Electric Co. v. Public Utilities Comm'n, 475 U.S. 1 (1986) (unconstitutional to compel a public utility company to include materials critical of some of its positions in its billing envelope). In the same vein, see Leslie Kendrick, "First Amendment Expansionism," 56 *Wm. & Mary L.Rev.* 1199 (2015) (D.C. Circuit strikes down N.L.R.B. regulation compelling employer to inform workers of their rights situated in the discussion of the general direction of cases). For lower court cases involving the First Amendment and the Securities laws, see Michael R. Siebecker, "Securities Laws, Social Responsibility, and a New Institutional First Amendment," 29 *J.L. & Pol.* (2014).

45 For an outstanding discussion of the social, political, historical, and legal aspects of these developments, see Amanda Shanor, "The New Lochner," link at http://papers.ssrn.com/sol3/cf_dev/AbsByAuth.cfm?per_id=756947 (last visited November 25, 2015).

46 For excellent discussion of the law in Canada and Europe up to 2003, see Shiner, *supra* note 14, at 70–110. A particularly significant Canadian case since Shiner's book is (2007) Canada (Attorney General) v. JTI-MacDonald Corp., 2 S.C.R. 610 (upholding restrictions on tobacco lifestyle advertising despite previous case striking down ban on tobacco advertising).

47 Directive 2003/33/EC of the European Parliament and of the Council of May 26, 2003, on the approximation of the laws, regulations, and administrative provisions of the member states relating to the advertising and sponsorship of tobacco products.

48 *Id.* at ¶ 3.

49 *Id.*

50 *Id.* ¶ ¶ 4, 6. Tobacco advertising on television was prohibited in another directive. *Id.* ¶ 14, referring to Council Directive 89/552/EEC of October 3, 1989. Owing to some quirks in US doctrine, a ban on tobacco advertising on television has been upheld against a constitutional attack, but the law here is old, and it is not clear it would withstand attack in the current Court.

51 Case C-380/03, Germany v. Parliament, 2006 E.C.R. I-11573.

52 Quoted in Shiner, *supra* note 14, at 102–103.

7 Democracy

1 Edmund Burke, "Reflections on the Revolution in France," in *The Classics of the French Revolution* (New York: Anchor Books, 1989). For trenchant analysis of the nuances of and tensions in Burke's position, see Hanna Fenichel Pitkin, *The Concept of Representation* 168–189 (Berkeley: University of California Press, 1967).

2 Walter Lippman, *Public Opinion* 311–312 (New York: Harcourt, Brace, & Co., 1922).

3 Joseph Schumpeter, *Capitalism, Socialism, and Democracy* (2nd ed., New York: Harper & Bros., 1947).

4 James Madison, *Federalist* no. 10 (1788) in *The Federalist* (Jacob Cooke, ed., Middletown, CT: Wesleyan University Press, 1961).

5 Robert A. Dahl, *A Preface to Democratic Theory* (Chicago: University of Chicago Press, 1956).

6 John Hart Ely, *Democracy and Distrust: A Theory of Judicial Review* (Cambridge, MA: Harvard University Press, 1980).

7 John Dewey, *The Public and Its Problems* 209 (New York: Henry Holt & Co., 1927).

8 Although Jurgen Habermas recognizes bargaining as an important part of politics, he has also emphasized the need for a deliberative public sphere. *Between Facts and Norms* 166–167, 283–286, 296–302 (William Regh, trans., Cambridge, MA: MIT Press, 1996). His work in this area was preceded by Jurgen Habermas, *The Structural Transformation of the Public Sphere* (Thomas Berger, trans., Cambridge, MA: MIT Press, 1989). Justice Brandeis expressed the hope that government would be a place where "the deliberative forces would prevail over the arbitrary." 274 U.S. 357, 375 (1927) (concurring opinion).

9 Conservative theorists are ordinarily associated with this position, but liberal politicians typically do not subscribe to the view that government should be neutral regarding the good life. John Stuart Mill certainly sponsored some forms of character and lives over others. See generally J. S. Mill, *Utilitarianism, with Critical Essays* (Samuel Gorovitz, ed.; Indianapolis, IN: Bobbs Merrill, 1971); J. S. Mill, *On Liberty* (David Bromwich & George Kateb, eds.; New Haven: Yale University Press, 2003); in particular, see J. S. Mill, "Principles of Political Economy" reprinted in 3 *Collected Works of John Stuart Mill* §1 at 936–937; §8 at 947–950; §15 at 968–970 (Toronto: University of Toronto Press, 1965).

10 John Rawls, *Political Liberalism* I §3, II §7, V §6 (New York: Columbia University Press, 1996).

11 John Dewey, *supra* note 7, at 327–328. See also Martin Schoolman & David Campbell, "An Interview with William Connolly," in *The New Pluralism: William Connolly and the Contemporary Global Condition* 304–336 (David

Campbell & Martin Schoolman, eds.; Durham, NC: Duke University Press, 2008) (Connolly agrees with Dewey, but also reflects upon the ways group identities are formed involving instrumental, deliberative, and visceral factors and the pervasive political effects of those formations).

12 *Democracy and Tradition* 22 (Princeton: Princeton University Press, 2004). There are many fine books about the power of the wealthy in our political system and the problems created by it. See, for example, Joseph Stiglitz, *The Price of Inequality* (New York: W.W. Norton & Co., 2012); Timothy Noah, *The Great Divergence: America's Growing Inequality Crisis and What We Can Do about It* (New York: Bloomsbury, 2012); Jacob S. Hatcher & Paul Pierson, *Winner-Take-All-Politics: How Washington Made the Rich Richer – And Turned Its Back on the Middle Class* (New York: Simon & Schuster, 2010).

13 See McCutcheon v. Federal Election Committee, pp. 6–7. For the permissible amounts after *McCutcheon*, www.fec.gov/ans/answers_general.shtml#How_much_can_I_contribute (last visited April 7, 2014).

14 For a strong defense of the First Amendment in the context of campaign finance, see Floyd Abrams, *Speaking Freely* 231–275 (New York: Penguin Books, 2005).

15 424 U.S. 1 (1976).

16 130 S.Ct. 876 (2010).

17 134 S.Ct. 1434 (2014).

18 For discussion of the case's background, reasoning, and importance, see Richard L. Hasen, "The Nine Lives of Buckley v. Valeo," *in First Amendment Stories* 345–373 (Richard W. Garnett & Andrew Koppelman, eds.; New York: Foundation Press, 2012).

19 This theme is well developed in Lawrence Lessig, *Republic, Lost: How Money Corrupts Congress – and a Plan to Stop It* (New York: Twelve, 2011).

20 Richard L. Hasen has been a persistent and articulate voice for the importance of equality in this arena. See *Plutocrats United: Campaign Money, the Supreme Court, and the Distortion of American Politics* (New Haven: Yale University Press, 2016); *The Supreme Court and Election Law: Judging Equality from Baker v. Carr to Bush v. Gore* (New York: New York University Press, 2003).

21 424 U.S. at 41.

22 Buckley v. Valeo, 519 F.2d 821, 841 (D.C. Cir. 1975).

23 Dan M. Kahan, "Neutral Principles, Motivated Cognition, and Some Problems for Constitutional Law," 125 *Harv. L. Rev.* 1, 59–66 (2011).

24 Frederick Schauer, "Facts and the First Amendment," 57 *UCLA L. Rev.* 897, 909 (2010).

25 424 U.S. at 45.

26 *Id.* at 46.

27 The Annenberg Public Policy Center of the University of Pennsylvania estimated that between $275 and $340 million dollars were spent on issue ads in the 1998 federal elections. Frank J. Sorouf, "What Buckley Wrought," *in*

If Buckley Fell 11, 20 (E. Joshua Rosenkranz, ed.; New York: The Century Foundation Press, 1999).

28 540 U.S. 93 (2003).

29 *Id.* at 686–689.

30 551 U.S. 449 (2007).

31 *Id.* at 522.

32 *Id.* at 526.

33 See Michael W. McConnell, "Reconsidering Citizens United as a Press Clause Case," 123 *Yale L. J.* 412 (2013).

34 For powerful criticism of the notion that corporations should have the same rights as human beings, see Jeffrey D. Clements, *Corporations Are Not People: Reclaiming Democracy from Big Money and Global Corporations* (2nd ed., San Francisco: Berrett-Koehler Publishers, 2014).

35 On the general problems associated with this, see Michael Walzer, *Spheres of Justice* (New York: Basic Books, 1984).

36 Charles E. Lindblom, *Politics and Markets* 356 (New York: Basic Books, 1977).

37 C. Edwin Baker, *Human Liberty and Freedom of Speech*, Ch. 10 (New York: Oxford University Press, 1989).

38 See Baker, *id.* Ch. 9. For emphasis on the notion that shareholders do not control corporations, see Leo E. Strine, Jr., & Nicholas Walter, "Conservative Collision Course: The Tension between Conservative Corporate Law Theory and Citizens United," 100 *Cornell L. Rev.* 335 (2015).

39 130 S.Ct. at 359.

40 For arguments that a campaign finance system should be structured to strengthen the role of political parties, see Richard H. Pildes, "Romanticizing Democracy, Political Fragmentation, and the Decline of American Government," 124 *Yale L. J.* 804 (2014) (Citizens United not the main villain); Heather Gerkin, "The Real Problem with Citizens United: Campaign Finance, Dark Money, and Shadow Parties," 97 *Marq. L. Rev.* 903 (2013).

41 See Zephyr Teachout, *Corruption in America* (Cambridge, MA: Harvard University Press, 2014). For an ever broader conception, see Laura S. Underkuffler, *Captured by Evil: The Idea of Corruption in Law* (New Haven: Yale University Press, 2013).

42 130 S.Ct. at 360.

43 On the importance of this to the legitimacy of government, see Robert C. Post, *Citizens Divided* (Cambridge, MA: Harvard University Press, 2014).

44 To get a sense (albeit dated) both of the diversity of approaches to regulating elections and the possibility of strict controls, see Fritz Plasser with Gunda Plasser, *Global Political Campaigning* 107–238 (Westport, CT: Prager Publishing, 2002).

45 Bowman v. United Kingdom, (1998) 26 EHHR 1, at ¶ 45.

46 Libman v. Quebec (Attorney General) 151 D.L.R. (4th) 385, ¶ 41 [1997].

47 See also Harper v. Canada, 239 D.L.R. (4th) 193 [2004] (upholding adver-
    tising restrictions). On some of the limitations associated with the Canadian
    approach, see Robert G. Boatright, *Interest Groups and Campaign Finance
    Reform in the United States and Canada* (Ann Arbor: University of Michigan
    Press, 2011).

8 Dissent

1 See generally Steven H. Shiffrin, *Dissent, Injustice, and the Meanings of
   America* (Princeton: Princeton University Press, 1999); Steven H. Shiffrin,
   The First Amendment, Democracy, and Romance (Cambridge, MA: Harvard
   University Press, 1990). For extended discussion of the meaning of dissent,
   see Ronald K. L. Collins & David Skover, *On Dissent: Its Meaning in America*
   (New York: Cambridge University Press, 2013). For economic and psycho-
   logical perspectives on the need for dissent, see Cass Sunstein, *Why Societies
   Need Dissent* (Cambridge, MA: Harvard University Press, 2005).

2 On the relationship between democracy, dissent, and hierarchy, see Ian
   Shapiro, *Democracy's Place* 224 (Ithaca, NY: Cornell University Press, 1996).

3 A fertile social science literature explores why social movements whether non-
   violent or violent do or do not emerge. For a cogent brief discussion, see Doug
   McAdam, Sidney Tarrow, & Charles Tully, "Comparative Perspectives on
   Contentious Politics," in *Comparative Politics* 260–290 (Mark Irving Lichbach
   & Alan S. Zuckerman, eds.; 2nd ed., New York: Cambridge University Press,
   2009).

4 Reinhold Niebuhr, "Why the Christian Church is Not Pacifist" 109 in *The
   Essential Reinhold Niebuhr: Selected Essays and Addresses* (Robert McAfee
   Brown, ed.; New Haven: Yale University Press, 1987).

5 468 U.S. 288 (1984).

6 *Id.* at 314.

7 Watt v. Community, 1983 U.S. S.Ct. Briefs LEXIS 969, Joint Appendix at 10.

8 Sarah Kunstler, "The Right to Occupy – Occupy Wall Street and the First
   Amendment," 39 *Fordham Urb. L. J.* 989 (2012).

9 For excellent discussion of the extent to which restrictions on public assem-
   bly have been unreasonably permitted, see Timothy Zick, *Speech Out of
   Doors: Preserving First Amendment Liberties in Public Places* (New York:
   Cambridge University Press, 2009). See also Marvin Ammori, "First
   Amendment Architecture," 2012 *Wis. L. Rev.* 1. (emphasizing the impor-
   tance of place).

10 376 U.S. 254 (1964).

11 *Id.* at 269.

12 Curtis Publishing Co. v. Butts, 388 U.S. 130, 163 (1967).

13 418 U.S. 323 (1974).

14 *Id.* at 354.

15 *Id.*

16 817 F.2d 762 (D.C. Cir. 1987).

17 Sheldon S. Wolin, *Politics and Vision* 418 (Boston: Little, Brown, 1960).

18 Fortunately, there are some statutory protections for employees. The National Labor Relations Act is a particularly important statute in this regard. See the series of reports by the Acting General Counsel of the National Labor Relations Board concerning Social Media Cases, OM 11–74 (August 18, 2011); OM 12–31 (January 24, 2012); OM 12–59 (May 30, 2012).

19 461 U.S. 138 (1983).

20 *Id.* at 141.

21 547 U.S. 410 (2006).

22 For discussion of the lower court cases, see Bridget R. Nugent & Julee T. Flood, "Rescuing Academic Freedom from Garcetti v. Ceballos," 40 *J. C. & U. L.* 115 (2014).

23 391 U.S. 563 (1968).

24 393 U.S. 503 (1969).

25 *Id.* at 511.

26 Jamin B. Raskin, "No Enclaves of Totalitarianism," 58 *Am. U. L. Rev.* 1193, 1196 (2009).

27 551 U.S. 393 (2007).

28 *Id.* at 409.

29 Raskin, *supra* note 26, at 1196. For excellent discussion of the government's repression of speech in the context of workplaces, schools, and jails, see Laurence Tribe & Joshua Matz, *Uncertain Justice: The Roberts Court and the Constitution* (New York: Henry Holt & Co., 2014).

30 563 U.S. 1 (2010). For criticism, see Martha A. Field, "Holder v. Humanitarian Law Project: Justice Breyer, Dissenting," 128 *Harv. L. Rev.* 434 (2014); Marjorie Heins, "The Supreme Court and Political Speech in the 21st Century: The Implications of Holder v. Humanitarian Law Project," 76 *Alb. L. Rev.* 561 (2013); David Cole, "The First Amendment's Borders," 6 *Harv. L. & Policy Rev.* 147 (2012).

31 18 U.S.C. § 2339B. See § 2339 A (b)(1)(defining support to include training).

32 561 U.S. at 47.

33 Lee C. Bollinger, *Uninhibited, Robust, and Wide-Open* 85–86 (Oxford: Oxford University Press, 2010); www.journalism.org/media-indicators/average-circulation-at-the-top-5-u-s-newspapers-reporting-monday-friday-averages/ (last visited December 31, 2015)(newspapers); www.nydailynews.com/life-style/average-american-watches-5-hours-tv-day-article-1.1711954 (last visited December 31, 2015)(television).

34 See, for example, Potter Stewart, "Or of the Press," 26 *Hastings L. Rev.* 631 (1975); Timothy B. Dyk, "Newsgathering, Press Access, and the First Amendment," 44 *Stan. L. Rev.* 927 (1992). But see Eugene Volokh, "Freedom of Press for the Press as an Industry or for the Press as a

Technology?,"160 *U Pa. L. Rev.*459 (2012). It may be desirable to create the same rule for both in some circumstances. For example, I do not believe that the rules in defamation should be different for media and non-media defendants.

35 First National Bank of Boston v. Bellotti, 435 U.S. 765, 795–802 (1978) (Burger, C.J., concurring); Austin v. Michigan Chamber of Commerce, 494 U.S. 652, 691 (1990) (Scalia, J., dissenting); Cf. Pell v. Procunier, 417 U.S. 817 (1974)(no special right of access to information held by government not otherwise available to public).

36 C. Edwin Baker, "The Independent Significance of the Press Clause under Existing Law," 35 *Hofstra L. Rev.* 955 (2007); Sonja R. West, "The Stealth Press Clause," 48 *Georgia L. Rev.* 729 (2014).

37 The denial of access is accompanied by the practice of opening prisoner's mail sent to the media as a "security measure" resulting all too often in retaliation against prisoners for complaining about treatment. Some courts hold that such letters should be considered privileged. For support of this position, see Dennis Temko, "Prisoners and the Press: The First Amendment Antidote to Civil Death After PLRA," 49 *Cal.W. L. Rev.* 195 (2013).

38 But cf. Pell v. Procunier, 417 U.S. 817 (1974) (denial of access to interview prisoners even on a limited basis does not violate freedom of press).

39 Zurcher v. Stanford Daily, 436 U.S. 547 (1978) (rejecting the argument that a search for evidence of unlawful acts possibly unearthed by a newspaper in its office should give rise to special First Amendment scrutiny).

40 Instead the privilege is a hit-or-miss patchwork leading to recent denials that the constitutional privilege exists at all. See Smolla & Nimmer on Freedom of Speech § 25.26 (Deerfield, IL: Clark Boardman Callaghan, 2015) (discussing recent cases including those of Judith Miller and James Risen).

41 Norman Soloman & Marcy Wheeler, "The Government War Against Reporter James Risen," www.thenation.com/article/government-war-against-reporter-james-risen/ (last visited December 24, 2015)

42 For a helpful discussion, see Sonja R. West, "Press Exceptionalism," 127 *Harv. L. Rev.* 2434 (2014).

43 Quoted in Charles A. Beard, *An Economic Interpretation of the Constitution of the United States* 155–156 (New York: Macmillan, 1935).

44 www.senate.gov/legislative/common/briefing/Senate_legislative_process.htm (last visited July 3, 2013).

45 Aziz Rana, *The Rise of the Constitution* (Chicago: University of Chicago Press, forthcoming in 2017).

46 Sheldon S. Wolin, *Democracy Incorporated.: Managed Democracy and the Specter of Inverted Totalitarianism* 64 (Princeton: Princeton University Press, 2008) (analyzing the ways in which the current system obscures its power and contributes to an uninvolved citizenry).

47 395 U.S. 444 (1969).

48 *Id.* at 447.

49 Eric Barendt, *Freedom of Speech* 166–170 (2nd ed.,New York: Oxford University Press, 2005). Barendt's book is one of the best comparative discussions of free speech issues.

50 376 U.S. 254 (1964).

51 Barendt's discussion here is also useful. See Barendt, *supra* note 49, at 198–226.

52 *Id.* at 268–311.

9 Religion

1 For constitutional purposes, I would define religion to include obligations of conscience whether or not they are based on traditional religious grounds. Alternatively, I would argue that under principles of equality, protecting religious conscience without protecting nonreligious conscience should not be permitted. For discussion, see "Symposium, Is Religion Outdated (as a Constitutional Category)?" 51 *San Diego L. Rev.* 971 (2014).

2 For discussion of this important point, see Andrew Koppelman, *Defending American Religious Neutrality* (Cambridge, MA: Harvard University Press, 2013). But cf. Christopher L. Sager & Lawrence G. Sager, *Religious Freedom and the Constitution* (Cambridge, MA: Harvard University Press, 2007) (powerful advocacy for affording religion equal liberty with criticism of separation metaphor).

3 For fuller discussion of the values underlying the two clauses, Steven H. Shiffrin, *The Religious Left and Church-State Relations* 20–23, 29–40 (Princeton: Princeton University Press, 2009).

4 My views on freedom of religion are more fully explored in *The Religious Left and Church-State Relations* though most of the cases I discuss here were decided after the book's publication.

5 494 U.S. 872 (1990). The story of the case is well told in Garrett Epps, *Peyote v. the State: Religious Freedom on Trial* (Norman: University of Oklahoma Press, 2009). In discussing the facts, I have drawn from Epps, the opinion, and the briefs.

6 People v. Woody, 394 P.2d 813, 818 (1964).

7 Epps, *supra* note 5, at 11.

8 374 U.S. 398 (1963).

9 480 U.S. 136 (1987).

10 450 U.S. 707 (1981).

11 494 U.S. at 890.

12 406 U.S. 205 (1972).

13 Murdoch v. Pennsylvania, 319 U.S. 105 (1943) and Follett v. McCormick, 321 U.S. 573 (1944) held that generally applicable license taxes violated freedom of religion as applied to the distribution of religious material, but also held that they violated freedoms of speech and press. On the other hand, the

taxes would not have violated the First Amendment if the door-to-door sales-
man had been peddling pots and pans.

14 494 U.S. at 890.

15 The federal government also passed the American Indian Religious Freedom
Act, 42 U.S.C. § 1996 (1978).

16 42 U.S.C. § 2000bb (1993).

17 Gonzales v. O Centro Espirita Beneficente Uniao do Vegetal, 546 U.S. 418
(2006).

18 Boerne v. Flores, 521 U.S. 507 (1997).

19 According to Douglas Laycock, twenty states have passed statutes and
eleven more have interpreted their state constitutions in ways that are contrary to *Smith*. www.weeklystandard.com/blogs/uva-law-prof-who-supports-
gay-marriage-explains-why-he-supports-indianas-religious-freedom-law_
902928.html (last visited April 30, 2015).

20 One important exception to this is Hosanna-Tabor Evangelical Lutheran
Church and School v. Equal Employment Opportunity Comm'n, 132 S.Ct.
694 (2012) in which the Court, relying on both the Free Exercise Clause and
the Establishment Clause, adopted the so-called ministerial exception, which
seemingly permits churches to hire ministers on any ground they choose
whether or not the ground is required by or even consistent with their religious doctrine. It seems to me that churches, like other nonprofit associations,
should be able to hire according to mission. Suppose, however, that a church
discriminates on the basis of race in hiring a minister when such discrimination is no part of the religious doctrine of the church. It seems to me that this
exercise of prejudice should not be immune from antidiscrimination laws and
should not be shielded by the ministerial exception.

21 134 S.Ct. 2751 (2014).

22 The members of the family run the company through a trust in which they are
the only trustees. *Id.* at 2766 n. 15.

23 The strictness of this test has led to unsettling results in the lower courts.
Elizabeth Sepper, "Free Exercise Lochnerism," 115 *Colum. L. Rev.* 1453
(2015).

24 I do not believe that mere inconvenience to third parties should justify overriding a constitutional right to religious liberty. Indeed, giving military exemptions to Quakers from the draft caused serious harm to third parties, and such
exemptions were long recognized as appropriate. A variety of factors need
to be taken into account in arriving at a decision. Here the harm to women
was substantial given the cost of contraceptives and forcing one to kill seems
different from forcing one to purchase even objectionable insurance, and it
should make a difference that the third parties harmed in the draft cases are
not identifiable. For a well-considered approach to religious accommodations,
see Andrew Koppelman, "Gay Rights, Religious Accommodations, and the
Purposes of Antidiscrimination Law," 88 *S. Cal. L. Rev.* 619 (2015).

25 Kent Greenfield, "In Defense of Corporate Persons," 30 *Const. Comm.* 309 (2015) (opposing the fusion of shareholders and corporations). See generally Caroline Mala Corbin, "Corporate Religious Liberty," 30 *Const. Comm.* 277 (2015).

26 I would have a quite different view if the owners were divided on the religious issue. I think the Court also supports this view. For commentary, see Jennifer Taub, "Is Hobby Lobby a Tool for Limiting Corporate Constitutional Rights," 30 *Const. Comm.* 403, 416–418 (2015).

27 For a fascinating discussion of the burden argument by a critic of the *Hobby Lobby* decision, see Nomi Maya Stolzenberg, "It's About Money: The Fundamental Contradiction of Hobby Lobby," 88 *S. Cal. L. Rev.* 727 (2015).

28 As I previously suggested, one way or another, the Court should have fashioned a remedy to assure that women were covered in the interim period.

29 Justice Kennedy may be opposed to abortion, but he has famously upheld the view that the Constitution places substantial limits on the power of government to criminalize abortions. I do not know his views on contraception. And to be precise, I am not sure of the theological views of the others.

30 The Hobby Lobby owners are evangelical Protestants, not Catholics, but they share many of the views on social issues held by conservative Catholics.

31 134 S.Ct. 1811 (2014).

32 Liberal theology in this area owes much to Jurgen Moltmann, *The Crucified God* (London: SCM Press, 1973). For a recent discussion of this position, see Tony Jones, *Did God Kill Jesus?* (New York: HarperOne, 2015).

33 Larson v. Valente, 456 U.S. 228, 244 (1982).

34 March v. Chambers, 463 U.S. 783 (1983).

35 *Id.*

36 134 S.Ct. 1821–22, citing *Marsh,* 463 U.S. at 794–795.

37 The Town Board has since apparently ruled that atheists are not welcome to give an opening invocation despite a representation made to the contrary in the case before the Court. www.slate.com/articles/news_and_politics/jurisprudence/2014/08/the_town_of_greece_s_new_prayer_policy_atheists_need_not_apply.html (last visited April 30, 2015).

38 134 S.Ct. at 1841.

39 *Remaking Europe: The Gospel in a Divided Continent* 59 (London: Society for Promoting Christian Knowledge, 1994).

40 93 BVerfGE 1 (1995).

41 Excerpted and quoted in Donald Kommers, *The Constitutional Jurisprudence of the Federal Republic of Germany* 475 (2nd ed., Durham, NC: Duke University Press, 1997)

42 *Id.* at 1184.

43 *Id.* at 1177.

44 *Id.*

45 Application # 30814/06 (2011).

46 *Id.* at ¶ 15.

47 *Id.*

48 *Id.*

49 Article 2, Protocol No. 1 of the European Convention on Human Rights.

50 Article 9 of the European Convention on Human Rights.

51 *Id.*

52 Application # 30814/06, at ¶ ¶ 70, 76. For a well argued defense of the result in Lautsi, see Marc DeGirolami, *The Tragedy of Religious Freedom* 124–129 (Cambridge, MA: Harvard University Press, 2013)

53 http://hudoc.echr.coe.int/sites/eng/pages/search.aspx?i=001-22643#{"itemid":["001-22643"]} (2001) (last visited August 6, 2014).

54 *Id.* at ¶ 4 (a).

55 *Id.* at The Law § 1.

56 http://hudoc.echr.coe.int/sites/eng/pages/search.aspx?i=001-90039#{"itemid":["001-90039"]} (2009) (last visited August 6, 2014).

10 How Did We Get Here?

1 Too much of it is triumphal in character celebrating a mythical democratic equality and downplaying slavery, the treatment of Native Americans, ethnic, racial, gender discrimination, and class inequalities, not to mention foreign imperialism. See Aziz Rana, *The Two Faces of American Freedom* 5–14 (Cambridge, MA: Harvard University Press, 2010).

2 Stephen Gardbaum, "The Myth and the Reality of Constitutional Exceptionalism," 107 *Mich. L. Rev.* 391 (2008). For a critical survey of a range of approaches to the exceptionalism issue, see Michael Kammen, "The Problem of American Exceptionalism," 45 *Am. Quart.* 1 (March, 1993).

3 Frederick Schauer, "The Exceptional First Amendment," in Michael Ignatieff, *American Exceptionalism and Human Rights* 29–56 (Princeton: Princeton University Press, 2005). Although I do not agree with the weight Schauer places on the factors I discuss in this chapter, I agree with his discussion of political factors that have particularly affected liberals.

4 *Id.* at 44.

5 European Convention on Human Rights, Article 10.

6 Canadian Charter of Rights and Freedoms, Article 1.

7 Jesse H. Choper, Richard H. Fallon, Yale Kamisar, & Steven H. Shiffrin, *Constitutional Law* (11th ed.; St. Paul, MN: Thomson/Reuters, 2011).

8 Seymour Martin Lipset, *American Exceptionalism: A Double-Edged Sword* 19 (New York: W.W. Norton & Co., 1996).

9 *Id.* at 63.

10 559 U.S. 460, 468 (2010), relying in part on Chaplinsky v. New Hampshire, 315 U.S. 568 (1942).

11 *Id.*

12 Genevieve Lakier, "The Invention of Low Value Speech," 128 *Harv. L. Rev.* 2166, 2179 (2015).

13 Joseph Story, III *Commentaries on the Constitution of the United States* § 1878, at 736 (1833).

14 *Id.*

15 William Blackstone, 2 *Commentaries on the Laws of England* 42 (George Sharswood, ed.; Philadelphia: J. D. Lippincott, 1893).

16 *Id.* at 148.

17 See Lakier, *supra* note 12.

18 On the suppression of dissent in the first half of the twentieth century, see C. Edwin Baker, "Autonomy and Hate Speech," in *Extreme Speech and Democracy* 139, 141 (Ivan Hare & James Weinstein, eds.; New York: Oxford University Press, 2009).

19 315 U.S. 568 (1942).

20 *Id.* at 572. I am not suggesting that the *Chaplinsky* test is an appropriate basis for interpreting the First Amendment, let alone that the case was rightly decided (though the decision was unanimous). Speech need not be an essential part of an exposition of an idea to be protected, and the value of the First Amendment is not fully captured by the value of truth. Nonetheless, the *Chaplinsky* test has the merit of recognizing that the value of speech needs to be weighed against other values of importance to the public interest in order to determine whether it deserves protection.

21 343 U.S. 250, 257 (1952).

22 354 U.S. 476, 485 (1957).

23 Burt Neuborne, *Madison's Music: On Reading the First Amendment* (New York· The Free Press, 2015). See also Floyd Abrams, *Speaking Freely* xvi (New York: Penguin Books, 2005)("By the time I began to practice First Amendment law in the late 1960's, the Supreme Court had decided only a few cases upon which a First Amendment legal defender could rely.")

24 Samuel Walker, *In Defense of American Liberties: A History of the ACLU* 228 (2nd ed., Carbondale: Southern Illinois University Press, 1999).

25 341 U.S. 494 (1951).

26 Walker, *supra* note 24, at 187. The ACLU wanted to file a brief at the Supreme Court level, but was blocked from doing so. *Id.*

27 341 U.S. at 581. See also Terminiello v. City of Chicago, 337 U.S. 1 (1949) (freedom of speech not absolute; endorsing clear and present danger test). In his autobiography, Douglas denies that he ever endorsed the clear and present danger test (William O. Douglas, *The Court Years: 1973–1975*, at 103 (New York: Random House, 1980). This claim is difficult to square with his opinions in *Dennis* and *Terminiello*.

28 354 U.S. at 513.

29 Vicki C. Jackson, "Constitutional Law in an Age of Proportionality," 124 *Yale L. J.* 3094, 3126 (2015).

30 This problem and some of the reactions to it are well explored by Edward Purcell, Jr., *The Crisis of Democratic Theory: Scientific Naturalism and the Problem of Value* (Lexington: University Press of Kentucky, 1973). For more recent work, see David Ciepley, *Liberalism in the Shadow of Totalitarianism* (Cambridge, MA: Harvard University Press, 2006). I think, however, that the positivist and naturalistic beliefs were largely embraced among liberal elites. It would be a rare politician who would declare that moral values are relative and that is not surprising given the religious saturation of the culture.

31 John Rawls, *A Theory of Justice* (Cambridge, MA: Belknap Press, 1971). Ronald Dworkin, *Taking Rights Seriously* (Cambridge, MA: Harvard University Press, 1978).

32 Burt Neuborne, *Madison's Music: On Reading the First Amendment* 110 (New York: The Free Press, 2015).

33 See Ronald K. L. Collins, "Exceptional Freedom – The Roberts Court, The First Amendment, and the New Absolutism," 76 *Albany L. Rev.* 409 (2013).

34 Elena Kagan, "Private Speech, Public Purpose: The Role of Governmental Motive in First Amendment Doctrine," 63 *U. Chi. L. Rev.* 413 (1996).

35 Although UCLA's Melville Nimmer and Harvard's John Hart Ely and Laurence H. Tribe had previously discussed the distinction, Geoffrey Stone, "Content Regulation and the First Amendment," 25 *Wm. & Mary L. Rev.* 189 (1983) was an important article in this vein. Cass Sunstein, *Democracy and the Problem of Free Speech* (New York: The Free Press, 1990) then at Chicago also made significant use of the distinction though his approach to the First Amendment was quite different from Stone's. Justice Scalia, formerly a faculty member at the University of Chicago, for the most part has treated content-based regulation as an unforgivable sin. For criticism of the Chicago approach, see Steven H. Shiffrin, *The First Amendment, Democracy, and Romance*, ch. 1 (Cambridge, MA: Harvard University Press, 1990).

36 She argued that government purpose was the primary factor in explaining the distinction while Stone had argued that the primary factor was the regulation's effect on the marketplace.

37 www.nytimes.com/2015/01/06/us/kagans-words-echo-at-the-supreme-court-19-years-later.html (last visited, June 7, 2015).

38 Nixon v. Shrink Missouri Government PAC, 528 US 357, 402–403 (2000) (concurring opinion). See also, Thompson v. Western States Medical Center, 535 U.S. 357, 388 (2002) (dissenting opinion).

39 Stephen Breyer, *Active Liberty: Interpreting Our Democratic Constitution* (New York: Alfred Knopf, 2005).

40 Justice Steven Breyer, "Changing Relationships among European Constitutional Courts," 21 *Cardoza L. Rev.* 1045, 1060–1061 (2000).

41 The political correctness concern became a strong basis for raising funds and initiating litigation by the conservative public interest law firm, the Center for

Individual Rights. Steven M. Teles, *The Rise of the Conservative Legal Movement* 232–235 (Princeton: Princeton University Press, 2008).

42 I have primarily relied on Joseph E. Lowndes, *From the New Deal to the New Right* (New Haven: Yale University Press, 2008) and Doug McAdam & Karina Kloos, *Deeply Divided, Racial Politics and Social Movements in Postwar America* (New York: Oxford University Press, 2014) on this topic.

43 I have primarily relied on Geoffrey Kabaserve, *Rule and Ruin: The Downfall of Moderation and the Destruction of the Republican Party, From Eisenhower to the Tea Party* (New York: Oxford University Press, 2012) and McAdam & Kloos, *supra* note 42 on this topic.

44 In this connection, I have primarily relied on Teles, *supra* note 41.

45 See Earle Black & Merle Black, *The Rise of Southern Republicans* 77 (Cambridge: Belknap Press, 2002).

46 For perceptive discussion of why it took so long, see *id.*

47 See Richard H. Pildes, "Why the Center Does Not Hold: The Causes of Hyperpolarized Democracy in America," 99 *Cal. L. Rev.* 273 (2011).

48 See Robert G. Boatright, *Congressional Primary Elections* (New York: Routledge, 2014).

49 The percentage of liberals in the Democratic Party has markedly increased. See www.washingtonpost.com/opinions/clinton-sanders-and-why-this-is-a-dangerous-moment-for-democrats/ (last visited February 6, 2016).

50 McAdam & Kloos, *supra* note 42, at 28. The Democrats' move to the left has been compromised by the need to raise funds from the wealthy and from businesses although the views of some quite wealthy individuals are decidedly on the left. The Republicans' need for money from the wealthy and from business ordinarily would not deter them from moving far to the right because the deregulatory aims of business are compatible with standard Republican ideology.

51 For further details, see Kabaserve, *supra* note 43.

52 For thorough and lively discussion, see Robert B. Reich, *Supercapitalism: The Transformation of Business, Democracy, and Everyday Life* (New York: Alfred A. Knopf, 2007).

53 In fact, business has succeeded to the point that human beings are increasingly being regarded exclusively as market actors in domains outside the market. This robs human beings of moral status (since as market actors they are as bereft of a moral soul as capitalism) and it undermines democracy since a body of market actors seeking their own individualized gratification cannot be a People. See interview with Wendy Brown, www.salon.com/2015/06/15/democracy_cannot_survive_why_the_neoliberal_revolution_has_freedom_on_the_ropes/ (last visited November 27, 2015). See generally Wendy Brown, *Undoing the Demos: Neo Liberalism's Stealth Revolution* (Cambridge, MA: MIT Press, 2015).

54 http://reclaimdemocracy.org/powell_memo_lewis/ (last visited June 11, 2015).

55 For discussion of the movement, see Robert L. Kerr, *The Corporate Free Speech Movement* (New York: L.F.B. Scholarly Publishing, 2008); Amanda Shanor, "The New Lochner," *Wisc. L. Rev.* (forthcoming in 2016).

56 For more detail on this, see Teles, *supra* note 41.

57 That work was primarily inspired by Richard Posner, *Economic Analysis of Law* (Boston: Little, Brown, 1972).

58 For excellent detailed discussion of the Federalist Society, see Michael Avery & Danielle McLaughlin, *The Federalist Society* (Nashville: Vanderbilt University Press, 2013).

59 Carl Bogus, *Buckley: William F. Buckley, Jr., and the Rise of American Conservatism* 9–13 (New York: Bloomsbury Press, 2011).

60 *Id.* at 21.

61 For discussion of the respects in which American conservatism is and is not Burkean, see John Micklethwait & Adrian Wooldridge, *The Right Nation: Conservative Power in America* 13–14 (New York: The Penguin Press, 2004).

62 Raoul Berger, *Government by Judiciary* (Indianapolis: Liberty Fund, 1977).

63 On the influence of Berger's work, see Ken I. Kersch, "Ecumenicalism through Constitutionalism," 25 *Stud. Am. Pol. Dev.* 86 (2011).

64 See generally Johnathan O'Neill, *Originalism in American Law and Politics* (Baltimore: Johns Hopkins University Press, 2005).

65 They at least subscribe in theory. In practice, they frequently ignore the history or twist it to avoid results incompatible with their conservative views.

66 For a brief explanation of Justice Scalia's approach, see Antonin Scalia, "Common Law Courts in a Civil-Law System," in *A Matter of Interpretation* 3–47 (Amy Guttman, ed.; Princeton: Princeton University Press, 1997). For more detailed analysis, see Ralph A. Rossum, *Antonin Scalia's Jurisprudence* (Lawrence: University of Kansas Press, 2006).

67 Antonin Scalia, "The Lesser Evil," 57 *U. Cin. L. Rev.* 849, 864 (1989).

68 http://nymag.com/news/features/antonin-scalia-2013-10/ (last visited May 28, 2015).

69 For detailed analysis of the approach taken by Justice Thomas, see Ralph A. Rossum, *Understanding Clarence Thomas: The Jurisprudence of Constitutional Restoration* (Lawrence: University of Kansas Press, 2014).

70 For discussion of this form of originalism, see Ken I. Kersch, "Beyond Originalism: Conservative Declarationism and Constitutional Redemption," 11 *Md. L. Rev.* 229 (2011). See also Clarence Thomas, "The Higher Law Background of the Privileges and Immunities Clause of the Fourteenth Amendment," 12 *Harv. J. L. & Pub. Pol'y* 63 (2011); Clarence Thomas, "Toward a 'Plain Reading' of the Constitution – The Declaration of Independence in Constitutional Interpretation," 30 *How. L. J.* 983 (1987).

71 Ronald Dworkin, "Comment," in *A Matter of Interpretation, supra* note 65, at 115–127. Justice Thomas would look at the general purpose of a clause, but

would not reject the original public understanding of an application of the clause.

72 H. Jefferson Powell, "The Original Understanding of Original Intent," 98 *Harv. L. Rev.* 885 (1985).

73 For a variety of perspectives on originalism, see *Originalism: A Quarter-Century of Debate* (Steven G. Calabresi, ed.; Washington, DC: Regnery Publishing, 2007).

74 Justices Scalia and Thomas abandon their purportedly favored methodology in a variety of important contexts. See Eric J. Segall, "The Constitution According to Justices Scalia and Thomas," 91 *U.Was. L. Rev.* 1663 (2014).

75 Frank J. Colucci, *Justice Kennedy's Jurisprudence: The Full and Necessary Meaning of Liberty* (Lawrence: University Press of Kansas, 2009)

76 See generally Helen J. Knowles, *The Tie Goes to Freedom: Justice Anthony M. Kennedy on Liberty* (Lanham, MD: Rowman and Littlefield, 2009).

77 *Id.* at 3–4. For the argument that Justice Kennedy's views comport with those of the Catholic Church, see Anne Jelliff, "Catholic Values, Human Dignity, and the Moral Law in the United States Supreme Court: Justice Anthony Kennedy's Approach to the Constitution," 76 *Alb. L. Rev.* 335 (2013).

78 505 U.S. 833, 851 (1992).

79 512 U.S. 622, 641 (1994). Both quotations appear in Colucci, *supra* note 75, at 100. For Colucci's general discussion of Kennedy's free speech jurisprudence, see *id.* at 75–101.

80 See Anthony D. Bartl, *The Constitutional Principles of Justice Kennedy: A Jurisprudence of Liberty and Equality* 55–72 (El Paso, TX: L.F.B. Scholarly Publishing, 2014).

11   What Next?

1 Laurence Tribe recognizes the importance of forging a middle ground here permitting the Court to uphold schemes designed to combat corruption and to strike down those that are simply forms of incumbent protection. "Dividing Citizens United: The Case v. the Controversy," 30 *Const. Comm.* 463, 484–486 (2015).

2 *Id.* at 330.

3 *Id.*

4 It is worth noting that justices who put a heavy thumb on the scales in favor of free speech in the cases involving depictions of animal cruelty and violent video games abandoned free speech favoritism, rolled over, and deferred to dubious claims of national security in *Holder v. Humanitarian Law Society*. The point is that commitments to free speech favoritism are selective. No scheme of interpretation binds judges who do not wish to be bound.

5 John C. Coates IV, "Corporate Speech & the First Amendment: History, Data, and Implications," 30 *Const. Comm.*, 223, 223 (2015).

6 *Addresses and Papers of Charles Evans Hughes, Governor of New York, 1906–1908*, at 139 (New York: G.P. Putnam's Sons, 1908).

7 For outstanding efforts to resuscitate the history of those who were highly critical of the Constitution, see Aziz Rana, *The Rise of the Constitution* (Chicago: University of Chicago Press, forthcoming in 2017); Louis Michael Seidman, "The Secret History of American Constitutional Skepticism," 17 *U. Pa. J. Const. L* 1 (2014).

8 For exploration of this, see Paul Horwitz, "The Hobby Lobby Moment," 128 *Harv. L. Rev.* 154 (2014).

9 I would note that former national ACLU legal director Burt Neuborne has recently criticized *Smith* in *Madison's Music: On Reading the First Amendment* 134–135 (New York: The Free Press, 2015).

10 For an indispensable discussion of the factors giving rise to social movements, their structure, which is often diffuse, their staying power, their shifting strategies, methods, and tactics, their relationship to conventional political forces, and their success or lack of it together with a discussion of the literature, see Sidney G. Tarrow, *Power in Movement: Social Movements and Contentious Politics* (3rd. ed.; New York: Cambridge University Press, 2011).

11 For an intellectual history of debates about the morality of various tactics among radicals, see Marc Stears, *Demanding Democracy* (Princeton: Princeton University Press, 2010).

12 *Id.* at 206–208 discussing basically the same tension as factors that often press movements in one direction or another.

13 For a brilliant discussion of antipornography feminism, critical race theory, and the opposition to protecting the relatively unlimited spending of money in election campaigns, see J. M. Balkin, "Some Realism About Pluralism: Legal Realist Approaches to the First Amendment," 1990 *Duke L. J.* 375 (the three movements employ legal realist arguments).

14 Derrick Bell, *Faces at the Bottom of the Well: The Permanence of Racism* 198–200 (New York: Basic Books, 1992); *Cf.* Myra Marx Ferree, "Political Context of Rationality," in *Frontiers of Social Movement Theory* 33 (Aldon D. Morris and Carol McClurg Mueller, eds. New Haven: Yale University Press, 1992) ("Many social movements are committed to … moral principles and attempt to realize them in the process of collective mobilization itself as much as in the stated outcome of such endeavors").

INDEX

Absolutism, 167, 168, 169, 170, 183
Abstraction, as a way to avoid hard
    questions, 18, 21, 22, 40, 43, 45
Access, denials of, 126–27
Alexander v. Cahill, 90–91
Alito, S., 18, 71, 72, 73, 75, 76, 104, 177,
    178, 188, 189, 190
Allen, A., 23
Alvarez, United States v., 74–75, 170, 171
American Booksellers Association v.
    Hudnut, 51–52
Animal cruelty, 62–67
Antipornography ordinance, 47–48, 51, 53
Attorney General v. British Broadcasting
    Corporation, 30
Audience interest, and commercial
    advertisement, 89–90
Austria
    fair trial and freedom of press, 31–32
Austrian Media Act, 32
Autonomy, right of, 41
Avery, M., 177

Baker, C.E., 193n1
Balancing, 5, 65–68, 75, 78, 142, 178, 180,
    181, 189–90
    and proportionality, 76–78
Barendt, E., 131
Beauharnais v. Illinois, 165
Bell, D., 80, 192
Berger, R., 178
Berlin, I., 7
Bipartisan Campaign Reform Act,
    103–04, 105
B.J.F. v. Florida Star, 19, 20–21
Black, H., 5

Blackmun, H., 138
Blackstone, 164
Bonner, R., 83
Brandenburg v. Ohio, 131
Brennan, W., 26, 27, 28–29, 57, 166
Brest, P., 48
Breyer, S., 5, 75, 76, 125, 169, 170–71, 189,
    190, 207n41, 219n39, 219n40
Bribery, 109, 111
British Video Recording Act, 78
Brown v. Board of Education, 172
Brown v. Entertainment Merchants
    Association, 71–73, 76, 170
Buckley v. Valeo, 97, 98–104
Buckley, W.F., 172, 177
Burger, W.E., 26, 196n4
Burke, E., 95
Burwell v. Hobby Lobby Stores, Inc.,
    138–40

Calabresi, G., 90
Campaign finance, 97, 98, 100, 103, 106,
    107, 110, 111, 171, 182, 184, 190, 191
    contributions limitation, 102
Campbell v. MGN LTD, 21–23
Canada, 9
    election spending, restriction on, 112
    obscenity and pornography, prohibition
    of, 52, 58–61
Canadian Charter of Rights and
    Freedoms, 161
Capitalism, 160, 175
Case of Lautsi and Others v. Italy, 152, 154
Central Hudson Gas and Electric Company v.
    Public Service Commission, 88–91
Chaplinsky v. New Hampshire, 165, 218n20

Citizens United v. Federal Election Commission, 98, 106–10, 128
Civic Republicanism, 81, 96
Civil Rights Act, 173
Clark v. Community for Creative Non-Violence, 116–19
Coates, J., 187
Collin v. Smith, 38
Colucci, F.J., 181
Commercial advertising, 79–80, 81, 84, 85, 86, 93
Commercial speech, 79
    and non-commercial speech, 92
    and political speech, distinguishing between, 86
    as political speech, 84, 85
    test, 88–89
Conflict of values, 7
Connick v. Myers, 122–23
Conscience, freedom of, 133, 140
Conservatism, 4–6, 112, 171, 174, 176
Conservative justices, 142
Consumer culture, 80–81
Corporations, 2, 9, 85, 91, 95, 97, 102–03, 107, 139–40
Cox Broadcasting Corporation v. Cohn, 19
Culture and attitudes toward free speech, 3–4, 6–7, 163–66

Dahl, R., 95, 96
Dahlab v. Switzerland, 155
Defamation, 36, 57, 66, 72, 75, 76, 119–22
    group defamation, 36
Deliberative Democracy, 96
Democracy, 19, 20, 97, 171, *See also* Dissent; Political speech
    and defamation law, 119
    and corruption, 109–10
Democratic legitimacy
    and autonomy, 3
    different theories of legitimacy, 95–97
    and racist speech or pornography, 2–3, 47
Demonstrations/demonstrators, 118
Dennis v. United States, 166, 167
Dewey, J., 80, 96
Dickson, R.G.B., 44, 45–46
Dissent, 1, 115, 116, *See also* Democracy
    defamation, 119–22
    and governmental structure, 128–31
    and national security, 125–26

Press Clause, 126–27
    by students, 122–23
    time, place, and manner regulation, 116–19
    values of, 8
    by workers, 122–23
Dogru v. France, 155
Donnerstein, E., 48
Douglas, W.O., 167
Dworkin, A., 47, 48, 49, 168, 200n3, 219n31
Dworkin, R., 168

Easterbrook, F.H., 51–52, 56, 185
Eisenhower, D., 172, 173
Eliya, M.C., 77
Ely, J.H., 96
Employment Division v. Smith, 134–39, 143, 181, 188
England
    free trial and freedom of press, 30–34
    privacy protection, 22
Europe, 9
    demonstration regulations, 131
    election campaign finance, 111
    religious freedom in, 148, 152
European Convention on Human Rights, 21, 152, 161
European Court of Human Rights, 155, 156
    commercial advertising, 93–94
    dissent by workers, 132
    free election rights, 111
    on pretrial publicity, 31–32
    regulation on violent video games sold to children, 78
Exceptionalism, 164–65

Fair trial, 25–26, 27, 29, 31–32, 33, 192
False ideas, insistence that there is no such thing, 3–4, 148
False speech, 41
False statements, 74, 75–76
Farley, M.A., 56
FEC v. Wisconsin Right to Life, Inc., 104–06, 107
Federal Election Campaign Act, 98, 103
Federal Trade Commission, 86
Federalism, 177
Feingold, R., 104
Ferguson v. Skrupa, 81–82

France
  privacy protections, 22
Fraud, 75, 76
Free flow of information, 84
Free market capitalism, 160
Free speech
  cultural influences, 4
  generally, 2–4
  idolatry, 10
  regulation, 148
Frozen categories approach to First
  Amendment interpretation, 71, 74–76

Galbraith, J.K., 80, 85
Garcetti v. Ceballos, 123
Gardbaum, S., 159
Gentile standard, 197n9
German Classroom Crucifix Case II,
  150, 152
Germany
  Press Code, 31
  privacy protection, 22
  proportionality in law, 77
  public denominational school, 150
  religious liberty violation and
    establishment prohibition issue, 151
  religious rights, 149
  violence regulation, 77
Gerrymandering, 128
Gertz v. Robert Welch, Inc., 120
Ginsburg, R.B., 169, 189, 207n41
Goldwater, B., 172, 173
Government speech, 10, 133, 148
Group defamation, 36

Habermas, J., 208n8
Hamilton, A., 128
Hanseld v. Norway, 32–33
Hate propaganda, 45
*Hobbie v. Unemployment Appeals
  Commission*, 136
Holder v. Humanitarian Law Project,
  125–26, 171
Hughes, C.E., 9, 188
Human dignity, 14, 19, 55, 181
  and privacy, 14
Human flourishing, 2, 13, 45
Hume, B., 149

Ideology and the development of attitudes
  toward free speech
  conservative ideology, 4, 174–83

liberal ideology, 4, 166–71
Idolatry, 8, 10, 71
Independent expenditures provision, 102
Individualism, 163
Intentional infliction of emotional distress,
  17, 18, 67, 185
  outrageousness standard, 17–18
Issue ads, 103
Italy
  religious liberty, 152

Jackson Lears, T.J., 79
Jackson, V., 167
Johnson, L., 173

Kagan, E., 5, 75, 76, 147, 169–70, 189,
  207n41
Kant, I., 63
Kantianism, 55, 57
Kennedy, A., 5, 74, 109, 110, 111, 142,
  146, 147, 178, 181, 182, 187, 188, 189,
  216n29, 222n77
Kloos, K., 35

Lawrence, D.H., 167
Laycock, D., 215n19
Legitimacy of government, and
  autonomy, 3
Liberalism, 4–6, 115, 166–71
Lindblom, C., 108
Lippman, W., 95
Lipset, S.M., 163–64
Lorillard Tobacco Company v. Reilly,
  89–91

MacKinnon, C., 47, 48, 49, 50, 57, 193n3,
  200n1
Madison, J., 95, 109, 145, 149, 206n13
Maltz, W., 50
Manipulative advertising, 91
Marcuse, H., 80
Market individualism, 163
Marketplace of speech and truth, problems
  with, 6–7, 14, 41, 187
Marsh v. Chambers, 146
Marshall, M.H., 26
Marshall, T., 116
Matsuda, M., 42
McAdam, D., 35
McCarthy, J., 5
*McConnell v. Federal Election
  Commission*, 104

McCutcheon v. Federal Election Commission, 98, 110–11
McLaughlin, D., 177
Mechanical privileging, of free speech over, 185, 186
Media corporations, free speech rights, 108
Meese, E., 179
Mill, J.S., 41, 208n9
Miller, H., 167
Morrison, A., 82
Morse v. Frederick, 124

National Labor Relations Act, 212n18
National Review, 172
National Socialist Party of America, 36–42
Nebraska Press Association v. Stuart, 26–28
Neibuhr, R., 80, 116
Neuborne, B., 166
New York Times Co. v. Sullivan, 119–20, 131
Nixon, R., 173
Nonprofit corporations, free speech rights, 107
Non-US approaches to free speech
    Canada, 43–46, 58–61, 76–78, 112, 131
    Council of Europe, 31
    England, 22, 30–34, 78, 131
    European Court of Human Rights, 31–34, 78, 93, 111, 131–32
    European Court of Justice, 94
    European Parliament and Council, 93–94
    France, 22
    Germany, 22, 31, 76–78
    Ireland, 78
    Israel, 76–78
    Italy, 78
    Norway, 32–34
    South Africa, 76–78
    Turkey, 131
Non-US approaches to religious freedom
    European Court of Human Rights, 152–56
    France, 152, 155–56
    Germany, 149–52
    Italy, 152–54
    Poland, 152
    Switzerland, 152, 155
Norway
    free trial and freedom of press, 32–33

O'Connor, S.D., 147
Obscenity, 53, 72, *See also* Pornography

morality, 55–56
O'Connor, J.P., 104
Ohralik v. State Bar Association, 87, 88, 92
Originalism, 180

Parents, right of, 154
Participatory democracy, 3
Pickering v. Board of Education, 123
Planned Parenthood v. Casey, 181
Pluralism, 95, 96
Point-of-view discrimination, 52, 56
Political campaigns, fundings for, 130
Political speech, 3, 9, 45, 83, 85, 86, 148, 171
    commercial speech as, 84, 85
Porat, I., 77
Pornography, harm of, 47, 48–50
    defined, 47–48
    Internet, 49
Positivism, 168
Powell, L., 175, 176
Pragmatism, 182
Prescription drug advertising, 82
Press Clause, 126–27
Press, freedom of, 22, 99, 106, 128
    and fair trial, impact on, 25–26
    and privacy, 23
Pretrial publicity, 25–26, 27, 33, 34, *See also* Fair trial
Primus, E.S., 87
Privacy
    concept of, 13–14
    dignity, relationship to, 14
    rape victims, 19–21
Privileging of free speech, problems with, 2–3, 7, 63–65
Proportionality analysis, 76–78, 204n34
Protecting the powerful, and free speech's contribution, 95–97, 187
Public figures, 121
    criticism of, 19
    kinds of, 120–21
Public opinion, 3, 20, 84
Puffery doctrine, 91

Questioning of prospective jurors, 28

Racist speech, nature of the harm, 35–36
    defined, 42
    prevalence of racism, 35–36
Rana, A., 130
Raskin, J., 124

Rawls, J., 168
Regina v. Butler, 58–61
Regina v. Keegstra, 44
Regina v. Video Appeals Committee, 78
Religion protections
  Establishment Clause values, 133–34
  Free Exercise values, 133
Religious Freedom Restoration Act, 134,
    138, 189
Religious minorities, 1, 10, 138, 143, 148,
    149, 184, 187, 190
Religious symbols, display of, 153
  in state schools, 152
Republicanism, 177, 205n12
Roberts, J., 5, 17, 18, 65–66, 67, 69, 71,
    104, 105, 107, 124, 169, 177, 182, 188,
    189, 190
Roe v. Wade, 174
Roth v. United States, 54–55, 165, 167

Scalia, A., 5, 71, 73, 75, 76, 136, 137,
    138, 143, 170, 177, 178, 179, 180,
    181, 188, 189, 219n35, 221n66,
    222n74
Schauer, F., 161–62, 163
Schumpeter, J., 95
Science, 168
Sexual speech. *See* Obscenity;
  Pornography
Shareholders, limited liability of, 140
Sherbert v. Verner, 136
Snyder v. Phelps, 14–19, 67, 171
Social Democracy, 96
Socialization, 161
Sopinka, J., 59, 60, 61
Sorrell v. IMS Health Inc., 92–93
Sotomayor, S., 169
Spending
  equality concern, 100
Sporting Dog Journal, 65
Stevens, S.D., 104, 169
Stevens, United States v., 63–66, 76, 164,
    165, 169, 171
Stewart, J.H., 26
Stolen Valor Act, 74, 76
Story, J., 164
Stout, J., 96, 97
Strict scrutiny test, 69, 71, 73

Strossen, N., 200n8
Switzerland
  religious freedom, 155

Taft Hartley Law, 103
Tavoulareas v. Piro, 121
Taxpayers with religious objections, 140
Taylor, C., 6
Thomas v. Review Board, 136
Thomas, C., 5, 75, 76, 177, 178, 179, 180,
    181, 189, 208n8, 221n69, 221n71,
    222n74
Tillman Act, 102
Tinker v. Des Moines School District,
    123–24
Tobacco advertising, prohibition of, 94
Toleration, 35–36, 40, 59
Town of Greece v. Galloway, 143–48
Tushnet, M., 162

Undue exploitation of sex, 59
Unprotected speech, 65, 66–67

Vagueness, in First Amendment law, 57, 61,
    72, 104
Value of free speech, refusal to judge,
    3–4, 148
Value of speech, 3, 8
Van Alstyne, W., 84
Vandenberg, A., 48
Violence, 62
  animal cruelty, 62–67
  video games, 69–76, 78, 125
Violent video games sold to children,
    69–76, 125
*Virginia State Board of Pharmacy v. Virginia
    Citizens Council*, 81–87, 90, 91
Vladeck, D., 88
Voting Rights Act, 173

Warren, E., 120
Wealthy people, free speech rights,
    108, 130
Weinstein, J., 199n22
White, B., 118
Wisconsin v. Yoder, 137–38
Wolin, S., 121
Worm v. Austria, 31–32